Echoism

This book introduces the importance of echoism as a clinical entity and a theoretical concept. In Ovid's version of the myth of Echo and Narcissus, the character Echo receives equal attention to her counterpart, Narcissus, yet she has been completely marginalised in the pervasive literatures on narcissism.

The author draws upon her work with patients who have experienced relationships with narcissistic partners or parents, and have developed a particular configuration of object relations and ways of relating to which she gives the term echoism. She uses psychoanalytic theory and existential philosophical ideas to underpin her formulations and inform her clinical thinking.

Donna Christina Savery is a psychotherapist and group therapist in private practice in Buckinghamshire and Harley Street, London.

"This book refocuses the Narcissus myth in a compelling way that illuminates and extends our views of narcissism as a personality trait and as a clinical disorder. Donna Christina Savery brings to Ovid's story a theatrical director's eye and a psychologically informed imagination that draws on existential and psychoanalytic writings to explore the complementary female partnership of male narcissism. It splendidly combines literary intuition and a clinical sense of personal development and inter-personal relationships. For anyone with a professional interest in psychodynamic marital work and couple relationships her concept of 'Echoism' is invaluable; for anyone who finds life interesting and art illuminating it is fascinating and stimulating; for those with a psychotherapeutic, clinical, practice it is eye opening."

– **Ronald Britton**,
Fellow of the Royal Society of Psychiatrists and Distinguished
Fellow of the British Psychoanalytic Society

"The idea of Echoism, with its potential to tell the other side of such a powerful story (and human dynamic) seems at first so blatantly obvious that I am incredulous that it has been so neglected. This book illuminates a truth about human relationships (therapeutic and otherwise) that has, until now, been hidden in plain sight. Practitioners of all theoretical persuasions should be encouraged to engage with Echo, and all that she has to tell us about ourselves, our clients and our society."

– **Susan Iacovou**,
Chartered Counselling Psychologist and
author of *Existential Therapy: 100 Key Points*

"In her original re-visitation of the Greek myth of Narcissus, psychotherapist Donna Christina Savery offers us here a convincing shift of emphasis to the 'other' dramatis persona, the nymph Echo. Left by most conventional readings, psychoanalytic ones included, in the shadow of the beautiful man she is in love with, Echo finds here her due voice, supported by literary and existential-philosophical considerations, in analytic theory and in its therapeutic applications. Described in detail by Savery, and illustrated by relevant clinical vignettes, the phenomenology of the resulting condition of 'Echoism', whose prominent feature is 'an absence of a self . . . most apparent in the absence of a voice', deserves our serious consideration."

– **Andrea Sabbadini**,
Fellow of the British Psychoanalytical Society, Director of the
European Psychoanalytic Film Festival; author of *Moving Images* (2014)
and *Boundaries and Bridges* (2014)

Echoism

The Silenced Response to Narcissism

Donna Christina Savery

Routledge
Taylor & Francis Group

LONDON AND NEW YORK

First published 2018
by Routledge
2 Park Square, Milton Park, Abingdon, Oxon OX14 4RN

and by Routledge
711 Third Avenue, New York, NY 10017

Routledge is an imprint of the Taylor & Francis Group, an informa business

British Library Cataloguing-in-Publication Data
A catalogue record for this book is available from the British Library

Library of Congress Cataloging-in-Publication Data
A catalog record has been requested for this book

ISBN: 978-1-78220-483-1 (pbk)

Typeset in Times New Roman
by Apex CoVantage, LLC

MIX
Paper from
responsible sources
FSC   FSC® C013056
www.fsc.org

Printed and bound in Great Britain by
TJ International Ltd, Padstow, Cornwall

For Christina, my mother (1941–1987)

Contents

Clinical vignettes

Acknowledgements

I would like to thank Oliver Rathbone of Karnac Books for offering me a publishing contract, giving me an opportunity to present my ideas and findings, when I am a largely unknown author. His team, and in particular, Rod Tweedy, have provided help and guidance along the way, and delivered the manuscript into the hands of Taylor & Francis, who kindly honoured all the agreements made between myself and Karnac. I am delighted that Klara King agreed at short notice to provide the index for my book, and would like to thank all those involved in the technicalities of taking a manuscript to publication, for which I am very grateful.

I am indebted to the patients with whom I have worked individually, in couples and in groups, who have allowed my observations and our shared experiences, to be reproduced in the many vignettes in this book. Their trust in me and openness to sharing the findings of this research with the wider community is at the heart of this book.

My use of literary and theatrical references has been an invaluable way of expressing some of the key ideas in the book, and I am grateful to have obtained permissions from Faber & Faber Ltd in the UK, and Houghton-Mifflin-Harcourt in the USA, to reproduce lines from *East Coker* by T. S. Eliot. I would also like to acknowledge with gratitude the permission of Faber & Faber Ltd to reproduce lines from Samuel Beckett's *Texts for Nothing and Other Shorter Prose* (1950–1976), and also to Grove Press for these works in the USA. I am also grateful to Penguin/Random House publishers for their permission to reproduce lines from *Metamorphosis*, by Ovid.

I am very grateful to the Bion Estate for permission to quote from the published works of W. R. Bion, whose ideas have been an invaluable catalyst to me in the conception of echoism. I acknowledge with gratitude the permission of the editor of the *Bulletin of the British Psychoanalytical Society*, Kannan Navaratnem, to reproduce a passage from a paper by Herbert Rosenfeld.

I would like to thank the Musée du Louvre, Paris, for their permission to reproduce on the cover of the book the image of the sculpture "La Nymphe Echo" (Photo (C) Musée du Louvre, Dist. RMN-Grand Palais/Pierre Philibert).

I would like to thank Rupert King, Faye Austen-Young, and Emmy van Deuzen, who saw something in me as a newly qualified therapist which they nurtured and developed.

I have been helped especially in the writing of this book by a number of supportive colleagues who have read parts of it, providing feedback, sharing their own experiences and offering their tireless support. These include Deborah Aita, Maria Turri, my IGA training group and Group Analyst Michael Parker, George MacDonald and Jonathan Lloyd, Tom Sykes, Holger Peters, Susanne Brandt and other colleagues who have offered their thoughts and feedback on parts of the manuscript or who have been receptive to my particular concept of echoism. I would also like to thank Arlo McCloskey from The Echo Society, with whom I have worked to share ideas and to promote opportunities for help for sufferers.

I am privileged to have had the opportunity to work with Alice Holzhey-Kunz, whose foreword lends a generous endorsement to the book, and to other inspirational figures including Ronald Britton, Susan Iacovou, and Andrea Sabbadini, who have kindly endorsed this book with their recommendations.

Many people in my life have, unknowingly, played a part in the genesis of this book, and in my confidence to write it. These include Susan Painter, Peter Thompson, Diana Hales, Jo and Hywel Hurn, my friends Louise Burgess, Katie Prout, Julie Barlow, Melissa Lake, Catherine Kelly, Julia Shanu-Wilson and Janet Lacey, to name but a few. I would like to thank Edward James for believing in my ability, in the book, and for his generous support and acceptance of me, and to Marianne James for being an inspiration, a sounding board in all my projects and a loving and generous daughter.

Finally, I owe a debt of gratitude to Chris Mawson, without whom this book would not be what it is. His wisdom, knowledge, experience, and unwavering support of my ideas and concepts along with his editor's eye and attention to detail have made this project a reality, and I cannot thank him enough.

About the author

Donna Christina Savery is a psychotherapist and group therapist in private practice in Buckinghamshire and Harley Street, London. At Exeter University she carried out research for her MA, which involved working with schizophrenic patients using drama and myth, an experience that sparked a lifelong interest in psychotherapy and psychoanalysis. Following a career as a theatre director and academic, she retrained in 2010 as an existential therapist, beginning her career at MIND.

She is a group work practitioner, having studied at the Institute of Group Analysis, and is currently undergoing training in Daseinsanalysis, an integrated form of psychoanalysis and existentialism.

Her clinical work combines different aspects of these trainings and she is never far away from her drama roots in her understanding and approach to working with her patients.

Publications

Savery D. C. (2013). The challenges of meaninglessness and absurdity addressed through myth and role play. In: E. Van Deurzen & S. Iacovou (Eds.), *Existential Perspectives in Relationship Therapy.* Basingstoke: Palgrave Macmillan.

Savery, D. C. (2015). Echoism and the container. *Hermeneutic Circular*, Society of Existential Analysis. London. April 2015.

Savery, D. C. (2015). Echoism: Is there a place for Echoism in existential analysis? *Journal of Existential Analysis, 26*: 243–255.

Savery, D. C. (2015). Revealment in theatre and therapy. *Hermeneutic Circular*, Society of Existential Analysis. October 2015.

Savery, D. C. (2016). Book review: *Boundaries and Bridges*, Sabbadini, A. *Journal of Existential Analysis, 27.*

Savery, D. C. (2018). Book review: *Daseinsanalysis*, Holzhey-Kunz, A. *Journal of Existential Analysis, 29.1.*

Foreword

This book breaks new ground, not only in terms of its content, but also in its method. Donna Savery writes about a new phenomenon: *Echoism*, which, of course, existed previously but, until now, has gone unnoticed.

She explores echoism through working with echoistic patients in a new way, combining insights about the human condition from existential philosophy with psychoanalytic theory and practice, mainly of the Kleinian school.

Let me dwell a little on these two points that make this book so special. When Donna Savery writes in this book about echoism she writes about a phenomenon that had no name before and therefore could not be identified as a psychological condition worthy of attention in psychoanalysis. This is regrettable, but by no means uncommon, because, for the most part, we give attention only to phenomena that are already named and conceptualised and therefore easy to recognise. This may sound pessimistic, and it certainly runs counter to an idealisation of the phenomenological method in the form valued by many existential therapists. Following the work of Gadamer (1960), in his *Truth and Method*, we know that we cannot easily rid ourselves unconditionally from assumptions, expectations and preconceptions, so as to become completely and directly open to phenomena, to be able to perceive the "things themselves" (Husserl). Every "thing" needs words to become something of which we can speak and discuss. Furthermore, we usually take up common words and phrases to name a certain phenomenon, in order to feel sure we are on safe ground when we speak about it.

Donna Savery had the courage to stay with a phenomenon that she encountered in therapy even though it made no sense for her as long as she only referred to the *current* psychopathological concepts. But instead of giving up, as we usually do in such circumstances, she puzzled over it with all of her thoughts and feelings, and she finally looked for help in the myth of Echo and Narcissus. This allowed her to trace an arc between the enigmatic kind of being of certain patients and the mythical figure of Echo, and to discover how much these patients had in common with the latter. This astounding affinity made it possible to give this "new" phenomenon its appropriate name: echoism.

Sceptics may question whether it is simply a new label for a long-established and already widely discussed phenomenon. By studying this book I came to the conclusion that the opposite is true: that it is a phenomenon constantly overlooked until now, which comes to light for the first time thanks to its being named. Therefore, it seems fitting, to me, to speak of a discovery, made by Donna Savery, in the field of psychopathology. The reader will soon gain a sympathetic understanding that this author is not claiming to have the final word on this newly discovered phenomenon, but that her intention is to open up a field for further investigation and discussion. What we find in this book, however, is already enough to enhance not only our theoretical understanding but also our therapeutic competence.

Let me say a word about what I have learned from this book about the important distinction between echoism and ordinary forms of what we call depression. Although in the echoist there are some features – or, psychoanalytically speaking, forms of defences – shared with depressed individuals, there is an important difference that the term "echoism" itself indicates, namely its intrinsic relationship to narcissism. It is essential for the echoist to be attracted by narcissistic people, to look for shelter in submitting to them, to play the silent – or, better– the *silenced* role in an imbalanced relationship with them.

This leads to the second point, which concerns the unique way Donna Savery has chosen to approach her topic. Her decision to combine existential philosophy with psychoanalysis is very courageous. In continental Europe this endeavour is represented in the Daseinsanalytic movement – psychoanalysis under an existential perspective, as Binswanger described it. Because, in the UK, many practitioners of existential therapy believe that this integration is neither necessary nor desirable, it may appear to some that in using this approach the author risks falling between two separate stools. Fortunately, Donna Savery takes this risk, and the reader will realise that it is highly suited to her subject, because it is only by using these two seemingly different perspectives, and by so skilfully combining them, that the complexity and richness of the phenomenon that is echoism can come into view.

But what is true for the phenomenon of echoism, is true for other psychopathological phenomena as well. The reader of this book therefore becomes acquainted with a new approach that is fruitful in the whole field of psychopathology and, indeed, psychotherapy. This means that this book has a pioneering role quite independent of its specialist topic. The psychoanalyst will hopefully realise that integrating philosophical ideas about the human condition does not go against psychoanalysis but deepens its insights. I hope too that existential therapy will realise that it is time to overcome its deep-rooted prejudice against the psychoanalytic discovery of the unconscious as being irreconcilable with a phenomenological stance. I am sure that the enormous value of existential therapy lies in its willingness to encounter clients not as people being afflicted by "mental disorders" but as individuals wrestling with existential problems. Yet, I consider it a weakness to dismiss the psychoanalytic perspective by holding on to the phantasy that existential philosophy can replace psychoanalysis. The psychoanalytic perspective is not only indispensable for understanding the childhood history of our clients or patients, but is even more important for reflecting on our dynamic interaction in the here and now of the therapeutic session. In this respect, the many vignettes in the book are very impressive!

Some of the psychoanalytic terminology is sometimes not easy to digest for a phenomenologist. But for me it is a rewarding task to become a translator of psychoanalytic terms by searching for their hidden existential meaning. We might look to Sartre who, in *Being and Nothingness*, rather than dismissing the unconscious, provides an existential concept of it, and in his phenomenological analysis of *bad-faith*, succeeds in demonstrating how the unconscious works in all of us.

So, in summary, this book by Donna Savery not only paves the way for a better mutual understanding by existential and psychoanalytic therapists, but also provides a broadening (widening) of the horizon of each of them. It requires readers therefore, with an open mind, who are ready to look over their own tea cup, so to speak. I am confident that it will find them.

Alice Holzhey-Kunz
President of the Society for
Hermeneutic Anthropology and Daseinsanalysis, Zürich.

Introduction

Introducing echoism

The narrative of Narcissus is a pervasive and well-known one, with a well-established history, language, and logic. This book reveals another story, one which, for reasons I seek to understand, has been both unsayable and unable to be heard. Mauriac (1958, p. 83) acknowledges the challenge that:

> [he] who speaks is carried along by the logic of language and its articulations. Thus the writer who pits himself against the unsayable must use all his cunning so as not to say what the words make him say against his will, but to express instead what by their very nature they are designed to cover up: the uncertain, the contradictory, the unthinkable.

This book presents the findings of an extensive, in-depth study of individuals who, because they resemble closely the character of Echo in the myth of Echo and Narcissus, I refer to as echoists. These individuals have in common a painful absence of Being, together with the lack of a voice that they can call their own. Almost invariably I have found a narcissistic parent or partner at the centre of their lives, and often there is a pattern of repeatedly seeking a dominant narcissist for a partner.

Until now, echoism as a distinct clinical phenomenon has gone largely unrecognised. It is the aim of this book to introduce echoism as a clinical entity and as a theoretical concept. Because patients to whom I apply this term lack what I call an *own-voice*, and are without a strong sense of self, echoists are often quiet, unable to take space, or are likely to adapt themselves to the perceived wishes of others. I do not begin with a sharply drawn definition of echoism as a syndrome, but instead I draw upon my own experiences to provide clinical vignettes throughout the book to help the reader recognise when they are in the presence of an echoist.

Echoism is the clinical counterpart to narcissism, and for every narcissistic individual there is usually an echoistic partner and any number of dependents. As the narcissist can often relate to himself as the only real subject, it raises interesting questions as to what happens to the children of such individuals, and as to who would choose a narcissist for a partner or friend and why this may be.

The group of patients on whom this book centres have been in relationships with narcissistic partners or parents, and have developed specific ways of relating, some of which go back to infancy.

I have spent the last six years working with this patient group in individual therapy, in couples where the echoist[1] usually presents with her narcissistic partner, and in groups. During this period, I have spent many hours trying to understand the echoist's particular ways of being, writing up case material, collating data from groups and feedback from courses I have led, the results of which are largely presented in this book.

The mainstay of my approach has been to listen to the stories of people who are not used to being heard, who find it difficult to use their voices, and who often feel themselves to be worth less than others. This work requires many hours of patience, tolerance, and faith. Although I have made many mistakes along the way, these have often proved helpful in revealing more of what the echoist does to the therapist, however unconsciously or unwittingly, in treatment.

The most common of these mistakes is to fill the space, and I go on to explain how seemingly naturally the therapist is pulled into such a position when working with echoistic patients, and why this is so counter-therapeutic. The empty space is where echoism most truthfully reveals itself – as a state that is uncomfortable to allow and in which it is most painful to bear witness.

I found very little guidance on how to work with patients who had come to me initially as part of a couple, and who presented in a very particular way with their narcissistic partners. I started to observe some interesting traits and patterns of behaviour in these co-dependent patients, that I have since come to identify as echoistic, once I began to see them alone for individual work. Eventually, after publishing some early research, I began to share my findings with trusted colleagues, and echoistic patients began to be referred to me by other clinicians, or to find their way to me themselves, after reading something I had written about the echoist that resonated with them and with which they could identify. This led to further enquiry into established methods of treating the patient group with whom I was working. As narcissism is one of the most widely discussed concepts, it seemed strange to me that there was not an equivalent body of literature regarding those who are found in relation to narcissists, either by choice or through birth. I returned to my reliable background in the arts, as a way of trying to address the lack, with something to which I could orient myself in trying to help and understand these patients.

The myth in Ovid

As a child I became interested in myth in its oral form and in theatrical representations, particularly those found in classical Greek drama. At the age of eleven

---

1 The gender of the character of Echo in the myth is female. Accordingly, in this book, the echoist will be referred to as "she". This concept is applicable equally to males, just as the term "narcissism" may be applied to females.

I persuaded my headmaster at junior school to allow me to stage a production of a play that I had devised with a small group of friends, and to invite parents as well as the school congregation to attend – a request to which he agreed, with some degree of apprehension. It was not until many years later, after I began directing plays as part of my degree and later professionally, that I began to regard this debut as a successful attempt to communicate something at a time when I had very little voice of my own, or hope that my deepest anxieties might be heard or understood. This was summarised beautifully by the playwright Eugène Ionesco in his astute observations of the functions of theatre as a tool of communication, in a response to an article about two of his plays by the critic Kenneth Tynan:

> To discover the fundamental problem common to all mankind, I must ask myself what *my* fundamental problem is, what *my* most ineradicable fear is. I am certain then to find the problems and fears of literally everyone. That is the true road into my own darkness, our darkness, which I try to bring to the light of day. … A work of art is the expression of an incommunicable reality that one tries to communicate – and which sometimes can be communicated. That is its paradox and its truth.
>
> (Ionesco, 1958)

As an adult I found myself drawn to classical Greek texts and existential Theatre of the Absurd plays, both of which offered to me, as a director, the opportunity to examine something of my own experience, as well as that of the human condition. These ancient and modern texts contain, in their very essence, characters with existential dilemmas who suffer the same fate, potential, and anxiety as I and all other human beings, no matter how mythically or absurdly they are represented – in fact, the more removed they were from my actual self and character, the more courageously I could imbue them with my own unresolved conflicts and deepest anxieties, under the guise of theatricality and metaphor. I came to trust these texts as containing human truths that could be relied upon for deep contemplation of myself and my relationship to others, and their connections to me through being human.

As a director and theatre academic, the classical works of Aristotle, Sophocles, Euripides, and the Roman poet Ovid, occupied much of my interest. The richness of these texts is polysemic in its potential to be represented, and for meanings to be both encoded and interpreted. The playwrights and practitioners Beckett, Brecht, Ionesco, Jarry, Artaud, and the theorist Martin Esslin influenced much of my understanding of the existential within theatre, and provided texts in which the human condition could be lived out within the safety of the theatrical container. I mention this because I found, in this period of my life and work, a reliable source of truth that often revealed to me, in the final stages of productions, my own unconscious or latent anxieties and fears and my unhealed wounds – which were, to some degree, offered the conditions for healing, within the world of the play.

When faced with the absence of theoretical material to guide me in my work with echoistic patients, I returned to this body of theory and art, which had served me so well in the past. As I was already very familiar with the work of Ovid, and with *Metamorphoses* in particular, I found a translation that most accurately corresponded, in its representation of Echo, to traits identified in many of the echoists I had encountered in my consulting room. In the myth, Echo is subjected to a curse by the goddess Hera: she must remain silent except for her right to repeat the last words of another. Because of this, she must, therefore, in order to have a voice, seek out another to echo back. She relies upon the beautiful youth Narcissus for her very existence, but when he rejects her she fades and ceases to exist except as a mere echo of him.

The value of having the Ovid text as a reliable source to consult whenever I am in doubt, combined with my particular experiences as a theatre person, and the undeniable reality of the dreadful plight of the patients I have worked with intensively for many years, has made it possible for me to continue to pursue this difficult area of research.

In Ovid's version of the myth of Echo and Narcissus, the character Echo receives equal attention to her counterpart, Narcissus, yet she has been completely marginalised in the pervasive psychoanalytic literature on narcissism – a fact noted by Levy et al. (2011) at the outset of their historical review of narcissism and narcissistic personality:

> The concept of narcissism has been the subject of so much attention and captured the public's mind [in a way that] would make Narcissus, the subject of the Greek myth from which the term is derived, very proud indeed.

Ironically, in the psychoanalytical literature too, Echo, and her clinical counterpart, the echoist, have become both the literal and symbolic embodiment of the completely marginalised or silenced female voice, even though we meet her in our consulting rooms on a regular basis. This book proposes to reinstate her as a subject in her own right in an attempt to restore her to existence and have her voice heard.

Psychoanalytic and other literatures

In 2011 I was invited to contribute a chapter to an existential therapeutic text on relationship therapy (van Deurzen et al., 2013, p. 88). My chapter applied various myths to a developing understanding of particular clients and the ways in which they related. I made an early speculation in this publication, that the potential to be both narcissistic and echoistic is possibly to be found in all of us. The in-depth study that I have carried out since has revealed some very different findings, which are described in detail in this book.

While there exists literature on "co-dependents" and narcissistic co-dependency, this lacks two important features: it does not identify or analyse the particular ways of being of the "co-dependent", neither does it name her as a subject in her own right. This failure reinforces the very state of non-existence found at the heart of the echoist, which I discuss at length in the book and to which I introduce the reader through vignettes.

In the first chapter I hypothesise as to why the phenomenon is virtually missing in the literature. Following a search made of relevant terms in the Psychoanalytic Electronic Publishing (PEP[2]) database of psychoanalytic papers going back to 1871, I found that while there are ubiquitous references to the term "narcissistic" (20,422 at time of writing) and to "narcissism" (12,573 at last count), there are just two references to "echoism" and one to "echoistic". There are some 3464 references made to "Echo", many of which are simply a use of the word as a noun or a verb in general discourse. Those that referred to "Echo" as a proper noun were almost always used to serve a further understanding of narcissism, with little or no interest in the echoistic figure as an entity in her own right. Those who have returned specifically to the character of Echo in the myth have theorised or speculated about the phenomenon of echolalia – a condition in which the individual literally echoes back the last words of the other's sentences, and which is often found in patients on the autistic spectrum.

The term "Echoism" has been used recently by Malkin (2015, Ch. 6) to mean an extreme negative presentation on the narcissistic spectrum. Pederson (2015) has written of the personality traits of two types of echoist, linking a typology of "conservative/liberal" to what he terms the "egoistic/narcissistic pole" or "altruistic/echoistic binary". In the comprehensive literature search, the first paper that engages with the phenomenon of echoism as a discrete psychoanalytic and clinical entity is by Davis (2005). In this paper, the echoistic patient herself is considered to suffer from a psychopathological condition. The paper describes the role of echoistic wives found in relationships with narcissistic husbands. Davis, in discussing a narcissistic-echoistic couple, acknowledges:

> … the [narcissist] husband is seen as the afflicted party, a victim of his own narcissistic introversion. The [echoist] wife is seen only as playing a foolishly passive neurotic witness. Oddly, social forces all seem to have conspired to generate an amnesia regarding the fundamental psychology of the wife.
>
> (Davis, 2005, p. 138)

Davis, who has made his own search of terms listed above, concludes:

> The only use of the term "echoism" was in an article from San Francisco in *Psychiatric Annals* that argues for the inclusion of co-addiction as a disease in the DSM III-R, but does not seem to elaborate on the concept in any theoretical depth.
>
> (Ibid.)

Davis' paper seems to set out to remedy this, and he makes some very interesting theoretical links between primary narcissism and echoism, as well as speculating

2 Archive 1 Version 10 (searched from 1871–2017)

upon the way in which Freud might have drawn more heavily upon the myth of Narcissus and Echo in what he describes as a "hasty generalization" in his theorisation of gender. Davis then veers away from the echoist as a subject worthy of interest in her own right, and the one whom we meet in the consulting room, to further theorise on emergent states of narcissism and echoism in the infant, and the speech patterns that result from these phases. The paper then enters into the territory of echolalia, and away from the dreadful state of Being to which the echoist is subjected.

Davis' application of Echo's story as the paradigm for gender, development, and cultural treatment, both in society and in psychoanalytic thinking, is interesting and valuable but again moves away from the plight of the suffering individual. He does, however, recognise a "vicious circle of echoism/narcissism", and he discusses the need for a comprehensive study of echoism.

He concludes:

> any therapeutic attempts to heal such a relationship must utilize techniques that address both the male's narcissism and the female's echoism. Indeed, what little literature that exists on this subject, which we have cited earlier in this article, seems to support this conclusion. We must observe, however, that echoism and narcissism are not the exclusive properties of gender. These are only the outcomes of external forces. Even though echoism is most commonly found in the woman and narcissism in the man, the converse and any variation therein does occur. We are confident that the psychoanalytic theory of echo-ism will prove most useful in developing a better understanding of these variations and any needed therapeutic techniques. It is probable as well that some therapeutic techniques that seem successful but need a stronger theoretical foundation may find some encouragement here. I can see so many directions where these observations can lead. But, these directions are probably better explored at length elsewhere.
>
> (Ibid., p. 149)

This book takes up that challenge, with a rich collection of clinical studies and a strong theoretical foundation, drawn from existential philosophy and psychoanalytic theories and models; it is further informed by my recent training in Daseinsanalysis and Group Analysis. I describe some key principles for treatment and an evolving approach based upon observations made from my in-depth analysis of this patient group and their responses to treatment.

Book sections and chapter outline

Part I comprises three chapters in which I provide the reader with descriptions and definitions drawn from a range of literary and theoretical material from different schools, which I use freely and in an integrated way thereafter. This may require readers from different backgrounds to do a little work in familiarising themselves with these quite different theories, to provide a vocabulary and an understanding of the concepts upon which the rest of the book depends.

While some of the theoretical conceptual models and framework in the book may be unfamiliar to some readers, I am sure that the vignettes contain experiences with patients that will recognisable to a great many therapists irrespective of their modality. For ease of finding the clinical examples in this book I have included in the contents section a listing of the vignettes used to illustrate and to clarify the main ideas and findings.

The particular translation of Ovid's *Metamorphoses* that I am using, that I have come to call the "source material", is where I begin the book in Chapter One, with a close reading of Echo's narrative. I introduce some literary theoretical concepts that help orient the reader towards particular ways of approaching and interpreting both the written text and the clinical situation.

I have found contemporary Kleinian psychoanalytic theories of narcissism invaluable as a body of thinking to help me in understanding the echoist, and I provide a detailed explanation of these in Chapter Two. I also give a historical account of how these theories have evolved from the first pre-psychoanalytic recognition of narcissism as a condition, which was, interestingly, based upon Ovid's version of the myth. I maintain that, at this stage, the whole of our current understanding of narcissism as a condition diverged from what we may have come to understand as a dynamic relationship between two characters who enable a particular form of functioning in the other. The absence of a consideration of the key role of Echo in relation to Narcissus has led instead to an unevenly weighted representation of just one character, upon whom the subsequent literature has become focused. This, as we can already see, is only half the story.

I use the term "Being" in an existential sense, as Being-in-the world, and of the individual's experience of Being. Chapter Three provides a very detailed explanation of Sartre's modes of Being and their specific application to a particular defence system operating in the echoist, to help the reader understand the existential ideas referred to in the rest of the book.

In Part II I define two primary types of echoism. Chapter four is dedicated to defensive echoism and Chapter Five to self-destructive echoism. I include, in both, examples of being with the different forms of echoism through clinical vignettes, to enable the reader to notice when they are in the presence of echoism and to be alert to echoistic traits and to the feelings evoked when relating to an echoist. I also describe and provide evidence to show how easily this phenomenon can be missed or misinterpreted.

Part III provides a critique of research and received ideas in both psychoanalytic and existential approaches. This begins in Chapter Six, with an in-depth exploration of the pioneering work on narcissism by Herbert Rosenfeld, upon which much of this book is based. I go on to explicate his ideas further and introduce a concept of a god-like object, basing my concept upon further work in the field by Wilfred Bion and Ronald Britton, and I provide a model for understanding the particular object relationships in the echoist's internal and external worlds.

Chapter Seven continues the theme of god-like objects, and focuses specifically on Kierkegaard's work in *Fear and Trembling*, on God's command to Abraham to sacrifice Isaac, and the Greek gods' requirement for Agamemnon to kill his daughter Iphigenia. The question of faith is central, and observations from Kierkegaard's text are used and applied to help us to further understand echoism. This section is completed by clinical work that provides real and lived examples of such phenomena, examples of how we may encounter them in the consulting room, and what we might learn from them.

In Part IV I argue for the acknowledgment of an echoistic-narcissistic complex, rather than echoistic traits being incorporated into the existing paradigm of narcissistic conditions. I look at the presentation of echoism in couples and groups in Chapter Eight, and in Chapter Nine I consider and discuss the possible consequences of echoistic traits in the therapist.

In the final part (Part V) I provide a detailed summary of the arguments extended in this book. Chapter Ten offers recommendations for an acknowledgment of the work, concepts, and treatment that I have begun in this area, and suggests areas for further development within the field of therapy and beyond.

I believe the particular combination of materials and theories explored in the writing of this book, and my experiences in the consulting room, have helped me to see something that is prone to being silenced and to which others have got so close, and – at the last minute – missed.

Part I

Important theories in understanding echoism

Chapter 1

The myth of Echo and Narcissus

Deconstructing dominant readings

Lost Echo sits amid the voiceless mountains
And feeds her grief
Percy Bysshe Shelley,
"Adonais", Stanza 15, 1821

This chapter argues for a repositioning of the marginalised narrative of the nymph Echo and her clinical counterpart. As Emslie (2012, p. 86) reminds us:

> In the end, one sees that the phallocentric narrative is paradoxically the most fruitful category open to the woman. It becomes the site of a feminine unpicking, a poststructuralist deconstruction that tackles the discourse on the levels of its deepest assumptions ... the dominant masculine narrative is always vulnerable to subversion.

Returning to the source material (Ovid, 2004), I apply a close reading to the myth of Echo and Narcissus, and critique dominant readings that focus primarily on the character of Narcissus. I highlight parts of the myth that are particularly relevant to the echoist as a basis for understanding her marginalisation and consider the consequences of this in the therapeutic situation and on her relationships in the world. I consider how Wilfred Bion's theory (1962, p. 6) of alpha-function, concerning the discharge of what he terms beta-elements into the mother in the container-contained process, might be applied to understanding myth as a container and a transformative process. I clarify how I apply this to inform my understanding of the echoist's particular needs in treatment. Finally, I draw attention to the need for acknowledgement concerning the very real experience of encountering the echoistic patient and the need for recognition and dialogue amongst analysts and therapists in order to further understanding.

The plethora of theories and clinical practices concerning narcissism purport to have their origins in the well-documented myth of Narcissus and Echo. In this chapter I draw attention to the ways in which the prevailing literatures have followed one dominant reading of the text, that which favours the narrative of Narcissus. I hope to reposition Echo as a subject equally worthy of our interest by returning to the myth itself, yet the task of doing so is made particularly difficult when such dominant ideas regarding narcissistic relating persist. To begin with Echo, when so much has been written of Narcissus, feels almost impossible, as the temptation is to use Narcissus as the touchstone, the subject, against which ideas, theories, and clinical observations of Echo must be bounced and tested. And yet to do so would be an act in its own right that reinforces the very essence of what we encounter in the narcissist – an important individual, entitled to special attention, over and above others. And so, in order to make her the subject of our enquiry, I begin with a detailed exploration of the character of Echo, through deconstructing and analysing her representation and manifestation in the myth. I then go on to compare this to more dominant readings in which Echo is viewed as secondary to Narcissus and in relation to him rather than as a subject in her own right.

There are many versions of the myth but, as Levy et al. (2011, Ch. 1) tell us, "Ovid's version [...] is undoubtedly the best known and most detailed, and contains elements that resonate with later developments on Narcissism."

The first clinical applications of narcissism, which appear as early as 1898 in the work of Havelock Ellis, and Paul Näcke (1899) [see Freud (1917, ftn1, p. 73], are based upon this version of the myth.[1] In their original contribution to the study of narcissism, the character of Narcissus becomes the symbol for a phenomenon, observed in certain individuals with difficulties relating to others, as "self-love". Psychoanalysis, psychiatry, and psychology have since amassed a vast quantity of literature, clinical diagnostic criteria, and clinical applications in which this phenomenon has become ubiquitous. While Echo is mentioned in various clinical papers, there are few references to Echo as a character of importance in her own right, and a complete absence of enquiry relating to echoism as a phenomenon in its own right.

For those unfamiliar with the myth itself I will provide a summary, after which I offer a close reading and analysis of the parts of the myth in Ovid's text specifically relevant to understanding and interpreting Echo's narrative.

The myth of Echo and Narcissus[2]

Echo, a young and talkative nymph, leaves a clearing where Zeus, the thunder god, ruler of the gods on Mount Olympus, is cavorting with other nymphs. Suddenly she encounters the goddess Hera, wife of Zeus. Known for her loquaciousness, Echo uses her verbal prowess to charm the unsuspecting Hera with words, distracting the goddess from sounds of laughter emanating from her husband's antics in the glade. On learning of this, the jealous goddess wreaks vengeance

---

1 Cited in Freud, S. (1905d, p. 218). *Three Essays on the Theory of Sexuality*, with the following ftn. added by Strachey, in 1920: "The term 'narcissism' was not introduced, as I erroneously stated in that paper ['On Narcissism: an Introduction'] by Naecke, but by Havelock Ellis." (Ellis himself subsequently discussed this point in detail and considered that the honours should be divided).

2 For the purposes of this book the Greek names will be used for the gods to replace Roman ones where they occur..

upon Echo, cursing her: "You shall no longer use your tongue to manipulate and deceive, from this moment you will be struck mute." As an afterthought she adds, "Since you are so fond of having the last word, I will grant you that. You may repeat the last words of another, and your echo shall be a reminder to all of the power of the gods." Echo is immediately struck dumb and loses the ability to communicate her original thoughts in words. Horrified at her loss of identity she hides away, unable to express her pain in words, with increasing resentment towards the goddess. Over time she begins to withdraw and fade from forest life. Without another with whom to converse, she begins to forget the sound of her own voice and she begins to lose the ability to make her thoughts manifest, and in so doing loses her connection to humanity. As she does so, her life force dwindles and she starts to fade away. One day there appears a youth, blessed with beauty and confidence, command and presence. He sees a movement in the trees and calls out, "Is anybody here?"

"Here," replies a voice. "Come out and let me see you," he calls, to which Echo appears with the words, "Let me see you." "Young beauty," calls Narcissus, to which Echo, suddenly filled with a voice, becomes enlivened, crying out enthusiastically as she runs towards the youth, "Young beauty!" But as she does so he notices the hollowness of her words, and sees the faded shell, asking her, "What do you want?" She is able only to repeat his last words and he becomes repulsed by this imitative creature in whom he sees no spirit, no challenge, with no life force of her own. "Go away," he says, "you repulse me", and as he pulls away Echo reaches out and clings all the more, knowing that without him she will again be reduced to a non-being. She is left to pine, and as she does, the life seeps out of her and her skin and bones meld into the rocks and shrubs where she lies, leaving her barely distinguishable from the insentient beings with whom she shares her existence. Narcissus, meanwhile, is cursed for his cruel treatment of Echo and others by Nemesis – so that he would love only himself and never another – following a prophecy made at his birth by Tiresias, the blind seer, that Narcissus would live a long life, "so long as he never knows himself." (Ovid, 2004, Book 3.347).

Following this, one day he returns from hunting and drinks from a pool, in which he sees the most beautiful image of a young man. Unable to recognise himself in the reflection, he tries to speak with it. Reaching out his arms to it, as his hands enter the water, the youth disappears from him, only to reappear as he pulls back. Tormented by love and the wish to possess this unavailable and beautiful creature, Narcissus becomes mesmerised. Unable to eat, and sleep, he focuses only on the youth. Eventually, he too begins to fade away and with each cry there is an echo from the woods, reminding him of his cruel treatment of the nymph. As he dies, Echo laments the loss of he who gave her an existence and a voice, and a deep howl of resentment is heard in the grove as she surveys the tragic state of their remains and joins him in his death cries. Eventually, Narcissus, too, ceases to retain his human form, leaving only a flower, a symbol of his fate, in his place.

Critical theory

Given the plethora of analyses and interpretations of Narcissus originating from Ovid's myth, we might question the need to subject it yet again to another close reading. I would argue, however, that the absence of engagement with Echo's experience in the myth, in the literature of psychoanalysis, needs to be investigated. The role of critical theory in literary practice has focused on considering how dominant readings reinforce a power structure where certain individuals' experiences are prioritised over all others. It argues that formerly unquestioned assumptions that maintain the idea that there is an absolute truth must be interrogated to challenge that which is presented as true when seen through a dominant cultural lens. Critical theory has helped draw attention to all the narratives and voices, and therefore unrepresented and unvoiced truths, that may have become marginalised through this hegemonic process. It helps to explain, in the first instance, why the experience of Narcissus may not only have been regarded as more *important* than that of Echo, but that those charged with the task of writing about the myth may well have identified more with the character of Narcissus, as it resonates much more strongly with their own identity and experiences. Interesting questions arise, therefore, regarding the degree to which the marginalisation of Echo's importance is culturally determined. For our purpose, I propose to offer an alternative close reading of the myth, which prioritises the experience of Echo over that of Narcissus and, in so doing, challenges many assumptions formerly made, and not questioned. This goes some way to understanding why Echo herself may have become marginalised, not just in analyses of the myth but in the psychoanalytic thinking that has prevailed.

Close reading of Ovid's version of the myth

The first description given of Echo is that she is manipulative and talkative. In Ovid's account she uses speech to hide truth, and prioritises the male god's hedonistic and self-serving behaviour over his wife's feelings:

> The goddess [Hera] would be all ready
> to catch her husband Zeus making love to some nymph, when crafty Echo
> would keep her engaged in a long conversation, until the nymph could scurry
>   to safety.
>
> (Ovid, 2004, Book 3. 362)

The words "scurry" and "safety" reveal how powerless and fearful the nymphs are in relation to the gods, belying representations of Echo as influential and manipulative of Hera. I suggest that where words and actions appear contradictory, there is a need for probing and exploration to understand exactly whose narrative is being represented and whose remains unheard, and why there is an experience of incongruity for the witness to the phenomenon. I will discuss in detail in Chapter Five the corresponding experience for the therapist as it is encountered in the clinical situation. It is important, however, to draw attention to its occurrence here in the myth, because the incongruence has largely been ignored, and is crucial to my understanding of echoism.

> When Saturn's daughter perceived what Echo was doing, she said to her,
> "I've been cheated enough by your prattling tongue.
> From now on your words will be short and sweet!" Her curse took effect at once.
> Echo could only repeat the words she heard at the end of a sentence and never
> reply for herself.
>
> (Ibid., Book 3. 366)

While this shows Echo's ability to dissemble, it is easy to see how Hera is locating her angry feelings towards her husband in Echo, whom she has some power to punish and damage. While Hera's punishment is perhaps a fitting one – the ability to speak her own truth is withheld from Echo – it seems unnecessarily harsh to curse her for protecting the most powerful god in existence. It demonstrates Echo's dilemma, and perhaps goes some way in justifying her choice to offend instead the god with the lesser power. The curse has the effect of rendering Echo to a mere fragment of her former self, and Ovid likens her to a parrot, one who mimics and imitates but has nothing original to contribute.

> Echo ... could only ... parrot the last few words of the many spoken by others.
>
> (Book 3. 359)

We might see this as the de-humanising effect of her punishment, leaving her with an inability to relate to another person as a human being in her own right. Whilst an objection may be raised on the basis that Echo is indeed a nymph, and not a human woman, I would argue she certainly fulfils the function of a woman in the myth, and has recognisably human emotions and feelings, and for our purposes we can therefore treat her as human. It is interesting to speculate that she has already been somehow 'transformed' before we meet her in the myth, but I leave this path of enquiry for further consideration elsewhere.

When Echo finally encounters the youth Narcissus, Ovid draws attention both to her lack of a voice and to her absence of Being:

> her nature imposed a block and would not allow her to make a start. She was
> merely permitted
> and ready to wait for the sounds which her voice could return to the speaker.
>
> (Ibid., Book 3. 376)

We can see in this extract how she requires the other in order not just to be able to speak, but to *be*. This is fundamentally important, as it points to the requirement of, and the dependence upon, another human being for Echo even to exist in a human form. It also leads us to some understanding of her active need to take in the other's words, and their Being, in order to experience a human life force running through her.

In the following passage, the poet describes Narcissus' reaction, which has poetic resonance with the actions of Zeus, who, in enjoying the bodies of the nymphs, neglects any feelings for a woman scorned and rejected by him.

> [Narcissus] yelled, "Hands off! May I die before
> You enjoy my body". [Echo's] only reply was "… enjoy my body."
>
> (Ibid., Book 3. 389)

I suggest that the idea of Echo enjoying Narcissus' body reinforces what he perceives to be a dependence on him not just as a source of words, but of Being. It also leads the reader to understand the Echo character as consuming of Narcissus in some way.

> Scorned and rejected, with burning cheeks she fled to the forest
> To hide her shame and live thenceforward in lonely caves.
>
> (Ibid., Book 3. 392)

The shame felt by Echo in the myth is strongly represented in the powerful image of the burning cheeks. In my experience of clinical work, it is feelings of shame that often provide the catalyst that brings the echoist into therapy in the first place. Alongside her own rejection there is shame at being party to, and unable to separate from, her partner's unacceptable behaviour. In the next line, we see a masochistic response to Narcissus' treatment of Echo, where the more he hurts her the more her love grows:

> But her love persisted and steadily grew with the pain of rejection.

Echo seems somehow to feed upon the pain, and Ovid understands this as love. If this is the case, then it is a love that knows no bounds in terms of its destructiveness. Indeed, he goes on to say of its effects on Echo:

> Wretched and sleepless with anguish she started to waste away.
> Her skin grew dry and shrivelled, the lovely bloom of her flesh
> Lost all its moisture.
>
> (Ibid., Book 3. 394)

The myth seems to suggest that the relationship persists even after they have parted. It is as if Echo has taken in a version of Narcissus that lives on inside her, and with which she continues to have a relationship in spite of the external physical object of her love having disappeared. The effect of such an internal relationship upon Echo is to eat away at her from the inside, and the voice of Narcissus not only fills the empty and unbearable void inside Echo, but actively depletes her, generating a loss of self that is made manifest not just psychically but in the most visceral sense, as described by Ovid below:

> … nothing remained but voice and bones;
> Then only voice, for her bones (so they say) were transformed to stone.
> Buried away in the forest, seen no more on the mountains,
> Heard all over the world she survives in the sound of the Echo.
>
> (Ibid., Book 3. 397)

In the final part of the myth, where Echo experiences Narcissus' destruction and eventual death as if living it herself, we learn how she resonates with his pitiful sighs:

> Echo had watched his decline, still filled with angry resentment
> But moved to pity. Whenever the poor unhappy youth
> uttered a pitiful sigh, her own voice uttered a pitiful
> sigh in return. When he beat with his hands on his shoulders, she also
> mimicked the sound of the blows.
>
> (Ibid., Book 3. 494)

It is interesting here to note that all the feelings expressed by Echo are those of Narcissus, with the exception of angry resentment. This is important, as it explains why Echo may find it difficult to take responsibility for her own words and actions, and why, in therapy, the echoistic patient may spend much of the time blaming the narcissist for all aspects of the relationship having reached such a destructive state, while being unable to take any responsibility for her own role in it. Indeed, the therapist, too, may experience angry resentment as one of the only genuine emotions felt to be coming from the echoist – resentment that the therapist cannot give her enough to sustain her – as well as shame at her dependency upon the narcissist, both areas on which I expand fully in Chapters Three and Five.

Analysis

If we consider the myth from the perspective of Hera, the punishment of Echo is poetically fitting. As well as the resounding echo of her words serving as a reminder to mortals of the power of the gods, and the nemesis that will ensue should an individual dare to believe that he can outwit them in their games, there is another more interesting interpretation for our purpose. Hera is the partner of a god who is omnipotent, vengeful, vain, and murderous. At the moment she encounters Echo, her husband is using his power as entitlement, seducing young females, leaving Hera bereft and full of resentment. In this moment he might be considered the archetypal model for the narcissist; indeed, so much so that the actual character Narcissus, whom Echo later encounters, is perhaps just a mortal version, who, without the actual power assumed by the immortal god, is subjected to a painful and tragic existence and death. Meanwhile Hera's curse places Echo in her own position, as if to say: "Now you will know how it feels being me, having no power, no voice, and being in a relationship with an entitled narcissist." If we take this one step further it could be argued that Echo, in betraying a fellow woman by deceiving her, has somehow been taken over or colonised by Zeus – uttering *his* words and thoughts, and avoiding or being unable to speak her own truth. This leads to interesting theorising regarding the role of projective identification in narcissistic relating (a concept that I define in Chapter Two, and to which I return in detail in Chapters Five and Six). However, for our purposes now it might be worth interpreting the feelings experienced by Zeus and Hera in their turbulent relationship as having been projected into two cursed mortals, to play out to its gritty conclusion, from a position of some distance and observation by the gods.

This, of course, deviates radically from dominant readings of the text and there are many considerations to be investigated as to why those interpretations have become so central and pervasive. Feminist critical theories are helpful in understanding why, to some degree, the character of Echo has become marginalised and silenced in the literatures. They reveal how processes, often unconscious, lead authors to express ideas that serve to reinforce patriarchal dominance. Feminist and post-feminist analyses of the writings demonstrate the ways in which the literatures conform to a linearity in thinking and a grammatical structure that is inherently masculine in its form. This has a hegemonic effect that dictates the need to respond through a repositioning of feminine narratives within the literary canon. While this may be considered to refer to writings relating to Narcissus in more contemporary literature, it seems unsatisfactory to me to classify the Ovid text amongst such writings. The poetic and eclectic nature of the myths in Ovid's *Metamorphoses* pay due attention to the matriarchal voice, and conform more to the oral tradition than dominant, and more patriarchal, styles of writing. It seems likely, therefore, that it is not simply this version of the myth itself that has caused such dominance, but something innate in the human psyche that seems to resist the character of Echo's very existence.

In attempting to understand what might be being resisted and why, it is useful to consider the functions of myth. In classical myth the plight of the mortal, subjected to the whims of the omnipotent gods, mirrors that of the infant to her parents. As Ferry (2014, p. 20) states:

> For the gods, time does not count … and this allows them both to endure and witness human passions with a superiority and from a vantage to which human mortals cannot aspire. In their sphere, everything is sorted out and settled sooner or later … Our principal characteristic as mere mortals is quite the reverse. Contrary to the gods and the beasts, we are the only sentient beings in this world to have full consciousness of what is irreversible: the fact that we are going to die.

Myths contain the most dreadful of all aspects of the human condition and experience, from matricide and incest, to eating one's own children to placate the gods. Such elements contained in myth might be considered as discharged and split-off parts of the self – parts which, without transformation into tolerable forms, cannot be symbolised or represented. In trying to understand the function of myth as a way of containing and transforming human dread and the impending awareness and fear of death, it is useful to consider myth as a *container* for anxiety, into which raw unprocessed feelings are projected.

It is useful also to link this aspect of the function of myths to the situation early in life when, as infants, we first meet with unbearable, dreadful experience, and the need for help with it. The psychoanalyst Wilfred Bion developed a theoretical model to explore this predicament. His model of the "Container-Contained" (1962, p. 90) considers the urgent need for another to bear what in the immediate situation is unbearable to the self, to take in the experience and to suffer it in such a way that it may eventually be returned in a more bearable form.

In 1959, in a paper titled "Attacks on linking", Bion wrote the following succinct description of his seminal idea:

> When the patient strove to rid himself of fears of death which were felt to be too powerful for his personality to contain, he split off his fears and put them into me, the idea apparently being that if they were allowed to repose there long enough they would undergo modification by my psyche and could then be safely re-introjected.
>
> (1959, p. 312; 1967, p. 103)

Bion wrote that a mother, faced with her baby in acute distress, is required to treat her infant's cry as more than a demand for her presence. From the infant's point of view, wrote Bion, "she should have taken into her, and thus experienced, the fear that the child was dying. It was this fear that the child could not contain. He strove to split it off together with the part of the personality in which it lay and project it into the mother" (1959, p. 313).

The transformations of anxiety made possible by the container were explored by Bion in terms of two types of "element", which he called "alpha" and "beta" – the former term referring to parts of experience made suitable for thinking, and the latter referring to those that were inimical to it. Bion's writing on the container-contained process, in which the infant's raw discharge of the parts of human existence that are unbearable to tolerate (beta elements), and which are transformed into what Bion termed alpha elements, which may be used for thinking, is helpful in shedding light on the human capacity to rid ourselves of nameless dread, and the fear of death, into a receptacle or container. Bion (1963, p. 31) wrote:

> I shall state the theory first in terms of a model, as follows: The infant suffering pangs of hunger and fear that it is dying, wracked by guilt and anxiety, and impelled by greed, messes itself and cries. The mother picks it up, feeds it and comforts it, and eventually the infant sleeps. Reforming the model

to represent the feelings of the infant we have the following version: the infant, filled with painful lumps of faeces, guilt, fears of impending death, chunks of greed, meanness and urine, evacuates these bad objects into the breast that is not there ...

If we consider myth as a container for such elements of the human condition as cannot be processed or tolerated, it goes some way to explaining the timeless-ness and universality of the ideas and truths contained within them. Freud's use of the myth of *Oedipus Rex* as a container within which preverbal and unconscious aspects of human relating can be transformed and thought about in the clinical sit-uation, is evidence of such a phenomenon. It is interesting, therefore, to consider which myths have *not* been taken up by psychoanalysis, and even more so to think about why only parts of a myth, or only some characters within it, have formed the objects of much psychoanalytic enquiry, while others have been largely ignored. Even Bion, who addressed this question directly in one of his notes (published posthumously in his *Cogitations*), still did not recognise the importance of Echo:

> But there is more of this story, the myth of Narcissus: there is a god who turns him into a flower. What is the patient saying that corresponds to this? There must be something because my myth tells me that these elements are con-stantly conjoined; or perhaps this is not the right myth. Either it is the right myth, and I have so far failed to see this aspect of it as it has appeared, or I am mistaken in thinking this is the myth to be employed. Perhaps I should seek for a more appropriate one – the Oedipus myth, for example.
>
> (Bion, 1992, p. 238)

If we consider the usefulness of the myth of Oedipus as a container within which to transform unconscious and painful feelings, it is evident that these aspects of the individual have become able to be symbolised in a way that enables them to be thought about consciously in the consulting room; the same might be said of narcissism. If, however, the very idea of echoism cannot, or has not been thought about, this suggests that this aspect of the myth has not undergone such a transformation. We might therefore wonder at the reason.

Bion (1962, p. 7) explains:

> Alpha-function transforms sense impressions into alpha-elements which resemble, and may in fact be identical with, the visual images with which we are familiar in dreams.

These are, he writes, "the elements that Freud regards as yielding their latent content when the analyst has interpreted them". We need to ask why Echo's par-ticular latency has not been able to have been transformed, through alpha-function, into thoughts and words with which we might be able to engage consciously. Her presence in the consulting room, and in the literature, provides ample evidence that such a person/character not only exists but is essential in narcissistic relating. I would suggest that there is something so dreadful about the state of the echoist that it has been avoided and resisted because of the anticipation of something unbearable for both therapist and patient – and that it is easier to deflect attention away from the echoist and towards the narcissist whose state is somehow more "known", bearable, and, therefore, amenable to being thought about. The impact of this is that the echoist's experience becomes split off, or repressed, from psychoanalysis, and as such remains latent and subject to a kind of acting-out that cannot be analysed and accounted for, as Bion (1962, p. 6) describes in his first use of the term "beta-elements":

> Beta-elements are not amenable to use in dream thoughts but are suited for use in projective identification. They are influential in producing acting out. They are objects that can be evacuated or used for a kind of thinking that depends on manipulation of what are felt to be things in themselves as if to substitute such manipulation for words or ideas ... Such an act is intended "to rid the psyche of accretions of stimuli".
>
> (Bion, 1962, p. 6)

While a discourse regarding echoism is noticeably absent from psychoanalytic literature, it is necessary to find a way that enables it to be addressed with the patient. It is incumbent upon the therapist to be able to provide a container that supports both therapist and patient to be with what we might consider to be unbearable, in order that some transformation might take place. It seems that myth and theatre have both served as containers within which transformations, in the form of catharsis[3] (a purging feeling that enables expression, thinking, and some degree of resolution), can and do take place.

In Aristotle's *Poetics*, catharsis, the act of purging, through both pity and fear for the state of a fellow human being, unites humankind. As a theatre director, I was engaged in processing, transforming, and making manifest, latent experiences and feelings, through animating them within the container of the performance. This generated some catharsis, in this specialised sense, which enabled a way to think about formerly unconscious feelings. It was my theatre background that alerted me initially to the phenomenon of the echoist and her plight, yet when working with patients presenting as echoistic in the consulting room, I found nothing in the literatures to help in understanding this particular phenomenon. I then returned to the myth itself, as I might when directing, to reveal less conscious aspects of the echoist's state, to try to understand the phenomena, and, further, to comprehend why they may have been neglected.

At this stage, it would be premature to list defining characteristics of the echoist. It is more important to try to communicate some of what is present in

---

3 In the specialised sense described by Aristotle in his *Poetics.*

encountering the echoist, in order that echoism can be thought about and acknowledged as a real phenomenon, with the experience of *being-with* taking precedence over *knowing*. A failure to do this leads, in the clinical situation, I would argue, not just to neglect but to potentially harmful interpretations and actions. Rather than simply missing the phenomenon, it can have the effect of further cementing and exacerbating it, rendering recovery not only unlikely but further reinforcing the echoist's need for a relationship with a narcissistic object.

The most prominent feature of the echoist, which perhaps goes some way to explaining the absence of her in the literature, is an absence of a self. This is made most apparent in the absence of a voice that is of the self and which can communicate its own thoughts. In this book I refer to this as an "Own-voice". Other features evident in a re-reading of the myth, such as we have undertaken in this chapter, indicate the following: the echoist's need for the other to speak first, thereby to animate her; an idealisation of the other, with a corresponding avoidance of the self as subject; and a resounding feeling of resentment, all of which are key to identifying the specific experience of being in the presence of the echoist, to whom the therapist can never give enough to sustain her.

This book explores much more fully the projective processes taking place in echoistic relating. However, for the purpose of this chapter it is important to acknowledge the feeling the therapist may experience of having the life sucked out of her by the echoistic patient. All these factors are indicative of a being who can only exist for or through others, with no life force of her own. It is this most terrible of states – of existing but not living – that, I would argue, has led to an avoidance of being with, and thinking about, echoism.

Chapter 2

Adam's rib

A psychoanalytic approach to understanding echoism

> So the Lord God caused the man to fall into a deep sleep; and while he was sleeping, he took one of the man's ribs and then closed up the place with flesh. Then the Lord God made a woman from the rib he had taken out of the man, and he brought her to the man.
> The man said,
> "This is now bone of my bones and flesh of my flesh;she shall be called 'woman', for she was taken out of man."
>
> Genesis 2: 21–23

In order to locate echoism in a psychoanalytical context, in this chapter I outline the theoretical developments that underpin my understanding of narcissism and its manifestations. I trace my understanding from the early writings of Paul Näcke, which precede a theory of psychoanalysis, charting a line through the ideas of Freud, Klein, and Segal, to the contributions of Herbert Rosenfeld and Ronald Britton. I focus on the importance of projective processes that take place in narcissistic relating and the clinical situation, the two main types of narcissistic presentation, and their counterpart in the echoistic patient, resulting in what I describe as the "defensive echoist" and the "self-destructive echoist".

In this chapter I also look at the contemporary Kleinian concept of projective identification as it appears in the literature, and I clarify a major distinction between narcissism and echoism in considering the *sequence* of introjection and projection. In order to do this I will define and clarify some current psychoanalytic concepts necessary to an understanding of the narcissist, the echoist, and the complex relationships between them, concepts that I use in this chapter and throughout the book.

In this chapter I am interested in the particular organisation of object relations found in narcissistic relating. I describe the projective mechanisms that take place, which can be experienced first-hand in the clinical situation through the therapist's countertransference, and I consider the correspondence of the internal object relations to the patient's relationships and behaviours in the external world.

I also discuss how I am guided by changes, and particular inflections, in the voice. I refer to such manifestations in the work, and the understanding that might be gained from paying close attention to them.

I will now define briefly the psychoanalytic terms to which I refer throughout this chapter. Later in the chapter I return to these and explain in detail how they have played a key role in helping me to distinguish between being in the presence of an echoist or a narcissist.

Psychoanalytic objects

In psychoanalysis the term "object" is used to refer to figures felt to be important in both the internal and the external worlds of the patient. It refers to an internal sense of the whole or a part of something felt to be psychologically linked to, and invested in by, the self.

Internal objects are internalised versions – constituting symbolic representations – of the individuals we have experienced. They are taken in, in either whole or part form in accordance with the infant's experience, and while they correspond to their external ancestors, they evolve and have lives of their own, acting and relating to one another and between each other in a specific configuration in the mind of each individual. This is known in psychoanalysis as unconscious phantasy.

In the work of Melanie Klein the concept is related to the notion of an inner world in which unconscious phantasy is a constant process, involving complex transactions of projection and introjection. The concept of an inner world is well expressed by the lines of Milton from *Paradise Lost*:

The mind is its own place, and in itself can make a heaven of hell, a hell of heaven.

Ronald Britton (1998, p. 3) describes object relations theory thus:

> Taking Melanie Klein's formulation that, "there is no instinctual urge, no anxiety situation, no mental process which does not involve objects, external or internal," I think it is better to say that we love things, hate things and want to know things than to speak of abstract drives. In view of the fact that we have an internal world of object relations in addition to a world of external objects, I envisage that love, hate and knowledge are also deployed in our relationship with ourselves. In both external and internal situations we have desires for and from our objects. We want to love, to hate and to know our objects, and we also need to be loved, fear being hated and want to be understood. Internally we are inclined to love ourselves, loathe ourselves, and want to understand ourselves.

Projective identification

In her work with children and adults, Melanie Klein (1946, p. 102), identified a particular form of splitting and projection, as a response to the fear of being overwhelmed by persecutory experiences, which, at first, she called simply a projective process, and – because it affects the sense of identity of self and others – it has become known by the term "projective identification".

According to this idea, primitive hatred and consequent rejection of parts of the self are directed by the infant against the mother and take residence inside her, a set of events that affect the actual relationship between mother and infant. Although they take place in phantasy, the effects and consequences are real. She theorised that the structure of the infant's self, or ego, was also altered:

> Much of the hatred against parts of the self is now directed towards the mother. This leads to a particular form of identification which establishes the prototype of an aggressive object-relation. I suggest for these processes the term 'projective identification'.
>
> (Klein, 1946, [1952 version, in Klein, 1975, p. 8])

Klein wrote that good parts of the self are also separated off and projected in this way – into an object. This also affects the normal development of object relations – irreversibly if the processes are carried out with excessive violence and excessive splintering of parts of the self.

Klein continued by spelling out the harm that can occur to the self if there is excessive projective loss of good parts:

> Another consequence is a fear that the capacity to love has been lost because the loved object is felt to be loved predominantly as a representative of the self.
>
> (Klein, 1946, p. 103)

Introjection is equally important to the formation of our object relations. Specifically, the strength of the developing ego depends, according to Klein, on the successful establishment internally of an undamaged version of the object.

Transference and countertransference

These two terms represent the patient's and the therapist's unconscious feelings encountered in the clinical situation, respectively.

Transference

According to Freud, the earliest relationships and experiences are, unconsciously, constantly seeking to be reproduced and relived in the present:

> the patient is frightened at finding that she is transferring on to the figure of the physician the distressing ideas which arise from the content of the analysis. This is a frequent, and indeed in some analyses a regular, occurrence.
>
> (Freud & Breuer, 1893d, p. 302)

Initially identified as a hazardous obstruction to psychoanalytic work, transference processes were later recognised by Freud as a major source of information about the unconscious of the patient, and considered by him to be the principal vehicle of the analytic process itself. Transference is a ubiquitous fact of all human relationships. Klein wrote (1952, p. 433):

> In some form or other transference operates throughout life and influences all human relations, but here I am only concerned with the manifestations of transference in psycho-analysis. It is characteristic of psycho-analytic procedure that, as it begins to open up roads into the patient's unconscious, his past (in its conscious and unconscious aspects) is gradually being revived. Thereby his urge to transfer his early experiences, object-relations and emotions, is reinforced and they come to focus on the psycho-analyst; this implies that the patient deals with the conflicts and anxieties which have been reactivated, by making use of the same mechanisms and defences as in earlier situations.

For Britton (2015), the current transference/countertransference relationship is itself a realisation of an earlier unconscious model of relating, and in its basic form it constitutes the latest version of that model.

Countertransference

While the idea of countertransference was initially understood in terms of impulses in the analyst that required further analysis, later developments in thinking began to recognise the analyst's countertransference as a useful tool through which the patient communicates his inner world, through projective processes such as those mentioned above. Paula Heimann made a valuable contribution to the debate in her influential 1950 paper, *On Countertransference*, presented at the 16th International Psycho-Analytical Congress in Zürich in 1949:

> Our basic assumption is that the analyst's unconscious understands that of his patient. This rapport on the deep level comes to the surface in the form of feelings which the analyst notices in response to his patient, in his 'counter-transference'. This is the most dynamic way in which his patient's voice reaches him. In the comparison of feelings roused in himself with his patient's associations and behaviour, the analyst possesses a most valuable means of checking whether he has understood or failed to understand his patient.
>
> (1950, p. 82)

Her contribution at the conference had been reported by Anna Freud in a bulletin of 1949 as follows:

> The thesis of this short note is that the analyst's counter-transference represents an instrument of research into the patient's Ucs.[1] In addition to an evenly hovering attention the analyst needs a freely roused emotional sensitivity.[2] This, however, needs to be extensive rather than intensive, differentiating and mobile. Freud's demand that the analyst must 'recognize and master his counter-transference' does not lead to the conclusion that the analyst should become unfeeling and detached, but that he must use his emotional response as a key for the patient's Ucs.
>
> (A. Freud, 1949, p. 199)

The therapist experiences pulls towards emotional experiences, and impulses to act, in relation to the powerful currents created by the dynamic forces of the patient's unconscious. The therapeutic relationship is affected by these ever-present forces of transference and countertransference, which provide valuable information as well as posing obstacles to understanding and treatment.

Ego-destructive objects

If the primary object (usually the mother) is felt, for whatever reason, to refuse to take in urgent projected distress, or to return it in an intensified form, it is likely, after continued failed attempts on the part of the infant, to be internalised as a profoundly destructive object. Bion wrote:

> Failure to introject makes the external object appear intrinsically hostile to curiosity and to the method, namely projective identification, by which the infant seeks to satisfy it ... The result is an object which, when installed in the patient, exercises the function of a severe and ego-destructive superego.
>
> (Bion, 1959, p. 107)

Unlike the formation of objects felt to be good when introjected from a symbiotic[3] container-contained relationship, the production of an ego-destructive object is not a healthy process; rather, it creates an object that prevents the ego from

---

1 Unconscious.
2 Heimann had used "sensibility", a term with a meaning that is distinct from "sensitivity".
3 See p. 33.

developing, and actively destroys growth. As we have seen above, the infant can, at first, manage its powerful emotions only by use of projective identification.

Bion goes on to say:

> The main conclusions of this paper relate to that state of mind in which the patient's psyche contains an internal object which is opposed to, and destructive of, all links … In this state of mind emotion is hated; it is felt to be too powerful to be contained by the immature psyche, it is felt to link objects and it gives reality to objects which are not self and therefore inimical to primary narcissism.
>
> (Ibid., p. 108)

Recognising the distinction between echoism and narcissism

In order to understand the echoist, we cannot separate her from her relationship to the narcissist. Indeed, it could be argued that the abundant literature on narcissism is somehow incomplete until the phenomenon of echoism has been explored fully and considered alongside the prevailing theories of narcissism. This raises the question of how we might turn the lens away from received wisdom towards our own experience, and prioritise a phenomenological approach over a theoretical one. I am reminded of Freud's recommendation, where he describes the psychoanalytic technique as, "a very simple one […]":

> It consists simply in not directing one's notice to anything in particular and in maintaining the same 'evenly-suspended attention' (as I have called it) in the face of all that one hears.
>
> (Freud, 1912e, p. 111)

It was a combination of applying this, and what Bion (1970, p. 125), following Keats, calls "Negative Capability" – holding back from premature and precocious "knowing" – which enabled me to remain with the experience in the room and not leap ahead to the body of theory that exists regarding the role of projective processes in narcissistic relating. In regard to this pull towards "reading ahead", Britton and Steiner (1994) have written about the difference between an overvalued idea and what Bion (borrowing from the mathematician Henri Poincaré) termed a selected fact.[4] Britton (2003, p. x) writes:

> In practice, until sufficient personal experience of the problem is garnered … it is the authority of teachers or teaching manuals that is relied upon.

---

4 Elements that "the thinking individual recognizes as unexpectedly harmonizing all scattered facts – it is one of them, but it allows the thinker to 'see' the meaning which had previously not been visible" (Bion Talamo, 1981).

The hope is that they based their authority on experience. With the best will in the world, however, they are likely to be contaminated by overvalued ideas.

He goes on to say:

> The patterns in analysis that eventually become familiar are those of the transference-countertransference relationship. It takes many years however, to see enough patients and hear about more for these patterns to become very familiar; in the meantime, the authority of the teacher/manual is relied on … As a consequence, the contamination of experience with overvalued ideas is a particular problem of psychoanalysis… We see that once such overvalued ideas have a foothold they are hard to shift …
>
> (Ibid.)

I have wondered whether perhaps I was helped in this regard by having come to my ideas on narcissism through a range of different channels – from literary to experiential. As I had not been schooled in the literature on narcissism from a purely psychoanalytic approach, I began with the minimum of preconceptions. This might have enabled me to acquire the very state of negative capability recommended by Bion, to avoid overvaluing particular theories over the clinical experience of *being with* the patient. For my own process, while I read extensively on the subject of narcissism, it was without much discretion, and from an eclectic range of sources. It was only later, in collating my experiences of clinical work with patients, that the body of contemporary Kleinian theory on object relations, and the application of the philosophies of Sartre and Heidegger on modes of Being (Chapter Three) seemed to correspond most accurately with the experiences encountered. I chose to use whatever felt true in helping me to describe the phenomena I was experiencing in order to help me understand and work with it.

In my clinical work over a period of years I came gradually to recognise, through examining my own affective and countertransference responses with a number of my patients, a recurrent pattern common to a group of them that, on the surface, resembled organisations of the personality described commonly in psychoanalytic literature as belonging to narcissists. They were, however, in my experience of them, distinct – showing in their essential features, and particularly in their impact on me, a greater correspondence with the character of Echo, as she appears in the original account of the myth, and with whom I was becoming increasingly familiar.

I will show later how manifestations in the clinical situation revealed distinct differences between characteristics to which I give the term "echoistic" and what have previously been gathered under the diagnostic category of narcissism, the latter having perhaps assumed the character of an overvalued idea.

I therefore propose to illustrate the developments in the concept of narcissism that have helped me to recognise when I am in the presence of the echoist.

Echoism and psychoanalytic theories of narcissism

I have asked myself frequently whether I may have missed something in the literatures, wondering whether this distinction between echoistic and narcissistic presentations might already have been made. Herbert Rosenfeld (1952, 1964, 1970, 1971, 1987), in his landmark papers on narcissism, describes strikingly similar experiences to those I have encountered in working with the echoist, and I have wondered if echoism may, in fact, simply be another *face* of narcissism, already covered in the psychoanalytic literature. Rosenfeld also classifies some of these patients – who at times present with psychotic as well as narcissistic characteristics – as borderline. Later in the book I will look in detail at some of the case studies where he describes a particular type of presentation that corresponds closely with my own experience of the echoistic patient, and which he interprets as a slightly different or unusual presentation of narcissism.

My clinical experiences with patients who, at the outset, strongly resemble narcissists reinforce for me the importance of sustaining doubt, avoiding defining and naming, and refraining particularly from reaching for preconceptions based upon pre-existing theories. If it is true that phenomena that are predominantly but silently echoistic can be mistaken for the louder and more vivid narcissistic features, it is important, in one's capacity to observe, to remain radically open to the experience, and to be prepared to remember the complexities of the myth.

In my individual work with echoists, in so called "co-dependent" couples and in homogeneous groups, the features to which I have been present bear a much stronger resemblance to the Echo of Ovid's myth, than the Narcissus with whom we are all so familiar.

First, it is important to understand the features of narcissism and how they may be experienced in the clinical situation. Britton comments on how the abundance of psychoanalytic ideas and literature on narcissism compounds the difficulty in defining it:

> There is probably no area of psychoanalytic literature more profuse than that on narcissism: it seemed endless as I worked my way through it. I have spared you most of it, quoting only that strictly relevant to my discussion but behind it is a hinterland of unquoted papers. Not only is the literature on narcissism large, it is very muddling. As well as there being different developmental models that complicate any discussion of narcissism, the confusion is further compounded because the word is used in different senses.

(Britton, 2004, p. 477)

I am going to draw upon Britton's meticulous work in the area to give a brief account of the psychoanalytic ideas from thinkers mentioned above that have been particularly useful in helping me to understand processes of narcissistic relating, and which have illuminated some of the observations made when working with echoistic patients. I also hope to take readers new to psychoanalysis through the specific contributions that have led to further developments of the concept of narcissism.

The concept of narcissism in psychoanalysis

Sin of self-love possesseth all mine eye
And all my soul, and all my every part;
And for this sin there is no remedy,
It is so grounded inward in my heart.
Methinks no face so gracious is as mine,
No shape so true, no truth of such account;
And for myself mine own worth do define,
As I all other in all worths surmount.
But when my glass shows me myself indeed
Beated and chopp'd with tanned antiquity,
Mine own self-love quite contrary I read;
Self so self-loving were iniquity.
'Tis thee, myself, that for myself I praise,
Painting my age with beauty of thy days.
                    (Shakespeare, Sonnet 62, 1609)

In this sonnet, Shakespeare draws attention to a phenomenon that is later to be taken up in thinking about the psychology of the individual, and eventually in psychoanalysis – that of self-love.

In 1899, Paul Näcke saw that the character of Narcissus provided a good illustration of excessive self-love with a corresponding withdrawal from external relations. He used the term "Narcissismus" to describe what was then referred to as sexual perversity, and later came to be thought of as self-love. Although Näcke's ideas did not spread widely at the time, his reference to narcissism caught the attention of Sigmund Freud, who made extensive use of the concept in his psychoanalytic discussions with colleagues in the early 1900s. Clinically, however, in analysis and psychotherapy, it has become apparent that the narcissism we meet is much more complex than self-love.

Anticipating the later work of Freud and the beginnings of object relations theory, Havelock Ellis described the person affected by *narcissismus* as one who regards his own body as though it were an external sexual figure, or a part of one. In 1910, Freud's work on Leonardo Da Vinci (1910c) was published, in which he extended the concept of narcissism beyond that simply of love of the self, to incorporate others whom the artist saw somehow as loved extensions of himself. As Steiner (2008, p. 44) has pointed out, Freud's account enables us to see how a narcissistic set of internal relations was formed by Leonardo in which his apprentices were treated as projected parts of the artist – parts of his own ego, which he then attended to as children located outside himself, "the mind's children" (Williams, 2007), as it were – where the narcissistic personality treats others as parts of himself. As Steiner (2008) has suggested, it contains perhaps the first foreshadowing description of the operation of what Melanie Klein and Herbert Rosenfeld were later to call projective identification – a clinical concept that Wilfred Bion expanded further between 1959 and 1962 – and which is described further in this chapter.

The Austrian psychoanalyst Robert Wälder (1925) was the first to coin the term "narcissistic personality", listing as its core features a lack of human empathy, condescension, feelings of inherent superiority, and a requirement for admiration from others. We can see how in Freud's account – because on the face of it Leonardo treated his apprentices well, and therefore projected good parts of the self and life-instinctual impulses into them – the narcissism involved seems, on the whole, benign. Freud then followed Wälder, and in 1931 linked narcissism with the self-preservative instincts, thereby emphasising initially its libidinal aspect. It has given rise to the concept of libidinal narcissism in the work of Herbert Rosenfeld and Ronald Britton.

Types of narcissism

Just as Rosenfeld and Britton have each described two broad forms of narcissism (primarily libidinal and primarily destructive), my clinical experience supports a similar but not identical distinction in echoism. There are, as far as one can provide a useful model to begin thinking about echoism as a psychoanalytic concept, two major types of echoist – the libidinal type whom I call the defensive echoist, and the self-destructive echoist. These correspond closely to the two prevailing types of narcissistic personality as described in contemporary Kleinian psychoanalytic theory.

In psychoanalytic theory, the term libidinal refers to a life instinct or force, which can be seen as standing in opposition to what Freud (1920g) called the destructive or death instinct.[5] It is appropriate for understanding the material in this book to make this distinction between the terms libidinal and destructive. The former relates to a part of the patient that, in spite of the needs for self-defence, can be reached by the therapist and contains an element that seeks growth, as opposed to the primarily destructive and triumphing part, or parts, of the patient that the therapist comes into contact with in the destructive narcissist and, indeed, the (self)-destructive echoist.

It is useful to return to Bion's theory of container-contained (as outlined in Chapter One) to help understand why some patients seem more predisposed to being reached in the consulting room than others. In the primarily libidinal patient there is some openness for communication with, and containment by, the therapist. Wilfred Bion attributed this predisposition to the container-contained

5 *Die Spekulation wandelt diesen Gegensatz in den von Lebenstrieben (Eros) und von Todestrieben um* (Freud 1920g, p. 60, fn1).

process, which he indicated by the symbols ($♀♂$). According to this model, there is a dynamic and formative process by which parts, and feelings, of the infant, experienced as unbearable, are discharged into the mother as raw and painful formless projections, which Bion termed "beta-elements" (see Chapter One). Through the container-contained process, which is one of normal, communicative projective identification, the mother is able to relieve the baby of such feelings by taking them into herself. This process, known as reverie and alpha-function, transforms them in the container of the mother, and returns them to the infant, as bearable parts of the self, separate from the mother, which enable the growth of an ego (self) and – by association – a mind, and, I would add, a voice of one's own.

It is worth noting that Bion delineated three general classes of the container-contained relationship, using the terms commensal, parasitic, and symbiotic. The third of these constitutes the one crucial for growth – the mutually beneficial relation between the container and contained. When this process has not been successful, and if the container-contained relationship stalls at what Bion describes as commensal,[6] or, at worst, becomes parasitic, the development of a healthy ego may be inhibited or become increasingly damaged. It should be added that the failure of the container-contained relationship means not only that the conditions for mental growth are lacking, but, in the worst case scenario, there may be the establishment of internal objects that are felt actively to attack the structures required for growth of an ego (self) and a voice of one's own. This can lead to what may be experienced in the room as the presence of an ego-destructive object, or in some cases a parasitic ego-destructive object (a subject to which I return in Chapter Five on self-destructive echoism).

Failure of the container-contained relationship can also lead to a completely idealised self, one unable to take in the therapist or receive anything nurturing from her. This is where the personality has developed in a particular way, recognisable within the literature of psychoanalysis, as narcissistic.

Britton draws attention to the term "ideal-ego", a state which he compares to "the idealized self of narcissistic infancy" (2003, p. 105). This is a state in which the infant is idealised in the parents' minds and regarded as an ideal child. He recommends differentiating this term from the term "ego-ideal", which in normal relating is an aspirational state of becoming, involving a wish to become someone, in which the self is therefore a subjective or fluid self (a point to which I return in Chapter Three). In a healthy organisation of the personality the individual recognises the ideal-ego as a would-be self, the loss of which must be mourned. But, in the case of the narcissist, Britton (ibid.) writes:

> the illusional perfect self, or ideal ego, is a result of identification of the subjective self with what should be the aspirational self.

---

6 etym: coexisting (literally, from the Latin, sitting at the same table).

In this situation there is a merging of the ego with its conception of an ideal ego in order to evade a catastrophic relationship with a deadly and terrifying internal object.

Herbert Rosenfeld referred to what he called narcissistic organisations of the personality. According to Britton, a predominantly libidinal defensive narcissistic organisation arises when maternal failure of the container-contained relationship is the main factor, and a predominantly destructive organisation tends to develop when the infant comes, through whatever route, to possess excessive, extraordinary hatred of his primary object (mother/parent).

Hanna Segal (1997, p. 79) has expressed some doubts about the significance given to the distinction made by Rosenfeld and (later) by Britton, stating that in both types of narcissism there is an inability to tolerate separateness between the self and objects, internal and external. Segal believed that narcissism always contained both envy and hostility to any life-giving relationships, and that even when apparently benign, some of these transactions may have harmful consequences. The difference between self and other tends to be obliterated by the nature and force of the projective process in narcissistic relating. Melanie Klein, following Abraham, drew attention to narcissism as a deep disturbance of the relationship between the self and its internalised objects, reflected in an equally disturbed relation to people in the outer world. Pathological splitting and projection[7] were held to be the underlying factors.

The psychoanalytic concepts defined at the beginning of this chapter have been used so far to show their application to understanding narcissism. I now take them further to describe how they have helped me to recognise and work with the particular set of characteristics in my particular conception of echoism.

Projective and introjective processes

Bion's description of the container-contained concept begins with the act of projecting, into the container, that which cannot be borne. Furthermore, projective identification can also be used to recruit the analyst into particular roles or to elicit certain behaviours, an aspect of analytic work which has been studied closely by Betty Joseph. As Spillius (1992) has stated:

> Building on Bion's ideas, Joseph further stresses the way patients attempt to induce feelings and thoughts in the analyst, and try, often very subtly and without being aware of it, to 'nudge' the analyst into acting in a manner consistent with the patient's projection (Joseph, 1989) … Joseph gives many detailed examples. A masochistic patient, having in unconscious phantasy projected into his analyst a sadistic aspect of himself or of an internal object, will act in a manner that unconsciously tries to induce the analyst to make slightly sadistic interpretations … An apparently passive patient will try to

---

7 This term is used here to refer to projective identification used in narcissistic relating to attack the relationship between patient and therapist, rather than serving the benign function of communication.

get the analyst to be active. An envious patient will describe situations of which the analyst might well be expected to be envious.

(Spillius, in Anderson, 1992, p. 63)

Joseph (1989) believes that the job of the analyst in such situations is to be prepared to be open to the projections of the patient and to experience them, and, as she says, "to respond internally to such pressures from the patient enough to become conscious of the pressure and of its content so that he can interpret it, but without being pushed into gross acting out". Spillius emphasises that "some degree of acting out by the analyst, however, is often inevitable in the early stages of becoming aware of what the patient is feeling".

In each of these examples there is a presupposition that the analyst is responding to a projection into herself, by the patient. This reinforces the conventional idea of the order, in the container-contained process, of projection into the container, transformation, and then re-introjection back into the infant/patient, as described by Bion. The analyst may experience such projections from the patient, split-off parts of the patient as described by Spillius above, or from an ego-destructive object that projects into both analyst and healthy parts of the patient. In my work with narcissists I have found myself subjected to such projection and have felt recruited into roles in response to the patient's phantasies.

In working with echoistic patients, from the outset of the work or the session I have been left with the feeling that I am being actively introjected *by them*. When this happens, it is as if the process of projection, transformation, and re-introjection is reversed. One might recognise this experience as introjective iden-tification, where the patient draws out of the therapist a life force to fill her and in so doing is unable to distinguish her own feelings from the therapist's. The intro-jected therapist is sometimes able to be received by a healthy part of the patient, but is frequently consumed by a destructive object within the patient. When this has happened in my work it often results in leaving the patient with feelings of resentment that she then projects into me, because she feels that she has not been able to receive anything good from me. It was this experience of feeling resented and unable to give enough to the patient that reminded me of the character of Echo in the myth, who, as we see in Chapter One, in experiencing Narcissus' rejection and subsequent death, is no longer able to receive the life force she requires to exist, and is filled with angry resentment towards him.

Bion draws the interesting conclusion that the patient who has used excessive projective identification in place of repression and introjection must work through this in treatment, to avoid further destructive attacks on the ego (Bion, 1957, p. 275).

I suggest that while this is the main challenge for the narcissistic patient in treatment, the echoistic patient does not use projective identification in this way; instead she retains the power of introjection. The consequence of this, however, is that she has a tendency to introject an external narcissistic bad object – to whom she is unfortunately and poetically drawn, due to the excess of projection avail-able in such individuals – to fill her.

For the purpose of this book the following definitions are helpful in thinking about what is meant by the transference relationship, in order that we might recognise what is taking place between patient and therapist. This requires the therapist to stay attuned to unconscious levels of communication, those which lie beneath the more conscious subjects under discussion. Where the therapist reflects on her own experiences and on the roles she has felt herself drawn into, this is known as paying attention to the countertransference. Because countertransference is, as Segal (1977) reminds us, unconscious, our awareness of how it operates on us is understood mostly in hindsight.

Countertransference and narcissism

Segal and Bell (2012) describe working with a narcissistic patient, Mr B, who lived almost exclusively through projective identification. They explained the relationship between the patient's envy and his inability to bear separation, and how he used "colonisation" to take over the analyst and consume him as part of himself:

> He felt separate from the analyst and was immediately faced with unbearable feelings of desire for an object that he did not possess. The wish to get inside the object through colonisation was a wish to wipe out the separation from the object and to possess it quickly and greedily.
>
> (Segal & Bell, 2012, p. 165)

The idea of consumption as a form of protection against the threat of the other goes back to the Greek myths of Hesiod's *Theogony* (700BC), in which parents consume their own children if they are perceived as a potential threat to the power of the parent. This phenomenon seems to have been part of an understanding of human relations as far as records go back, and even aspects of the Oedipus myth can, in some forms, be traced back to Hesiod.

Countertransference and echoism

In considering Segal and Bell's observations, I realised that the process that had taken place with some of my echoistic patients was different; it was as if they were existing through me, drawing my words, my thoughts, my life force out of me and into them, not through envy or a wish to possess me, but as a source to keep them alive, in much the same way as a baby relies upon a mother for its most basic survival. Once I understood this I was able to develop an increased ability to tolerate the echoistic patient's resentment when she felt that I was not giving her enough to sustain her.

The concepts of projective identification and countertransference relate to one another in relation to their function in mobilising role-related behaviour. Bion, in the following passage, is referring specifically to the group analyst in working with groups. This, however, can be assumed to apply equally to the dyad, as an example of the roles of projective identification and countertransference in the clinical situation:

> [I] state now a contention that I shall support throughout this paper. It is that … interpretations, and amongst them the most important, have to be made on the strength of the analyst's own emotional reactions. It is my belief that these reactions are dependent on the fact that the analyst is at the receiving end of what Melanie Klein (1946) has called projective identification … Now the experience of counter-transference appears to me to have quite a distinct quality that should enable the analyst to differentiate the occasion when he is the object of a projective identification from the occasion when he is not. The analyst feels he is being manipulated so as to be playing a part, no matter how difficult to recognise, in somebody else's phantasy – or he would do if it were not for what in recollection I can only call a temporary loss of insight, a sense of experiencing strong feelings and at the same time a belief that their existence is quite adequately justified by the objective situation without recourse to recondite explanation of their causation … I believe ability to shake oneself out of the numbing feeling of reality that is a concomitant of this state is the prime requisite of the analyst in the group.
>
> (Bion, 1961, p. 148)

This application of projective identification and the countertransference feelings evoked in groups is taken up more fully in Chapter Eight of this book.

Ego-destructive objects, alien objects, and echoism

Earlier in this chapter I introduced the concept of ego-destructive objects as described by Bion (1959). Referring to a clinical case, Ronald Britton (1998) gives an example of what he had described previously, in an unpublished paper (1986), as an "alien object". He describes the patient as having had a madly destructive father, whose actual destructiveness:

> provided an external location for her own conspicuous envious and nihilistic trends, as a result of which there was, by projective identification, a fusion between that hostile aspect of herself and her perception of her father's hostility. This introduced into her personality what I have called an, 'Alien Object'… which she experienced as both part of herself and not part of herself. In fact she used to say, 'It must be me but it doesn't feel like me'.
>
> (1998, p. 26)

In his work, *Sex Death, and The Superego*, Britton (2003, p. 74) expounds further on the role of such ego-alien objects, when they occupy a destructive role in the superego. He writes that in his opinion:

> All internal objects might operate as the superego and that there is a great deal of difference when they do if they are hostile or tyrannical. I see the position of superego as a place in the psyche to be occupied; indeed … therapeutic effect can follow from deposing a cruel internal object from the authoritative position of the superego, even if it remains substantially unmodified as an internal threat. Like terrorists, they are capable of causing damage, fear, and disruption, but that is not as bad a state of affairs as murderous figures ruling the country.

Britton seems to move beyond a model where the destructive object resides only in the superego and goes on to describe an object that colonises, and has an impact on, the ego. In an earlier work (1998, p. 55) he had referred to the creation myth of the "Chaos Monster", as a representation corresponding to Bion's notion of nameless dread (1962, p. 96), and noted that it resembled what Bion (1959, p. 314) called the ego-destructive superego. Britton revised in 2003 to suggest that the proper place for the Chaos Monster was the "deep unconscious" mentioned by Klein (1958), but that:

> in these disorders it has usurped the position of the superego. Second, *I am now suggesting that the third position of triangular space – that of self-observation – is within the ego*. It is, however, vulnerable to invasion by the superego, which substitutes its own language of self-reproach, self-depreciation, and self-admonition for self-appraisal; the language of achievement is replaced by the language of morality.
>
> (Britton, 2003, p. 74)

I have quoted Britton's research into this area because he discusses some key psychoanalytic ideas that I take up in relation to echoism. I am particularly interested in the notion of an object that resides in the mind and acts as if it has the authority of the superego. Such an object attacks the very life force, suppressing the ego through envious attacks, resulting in the patient being silenced, feeling guilt and shame, and experiencing a weakening libido. This is particularly destructive to the echoist, whose life force is already diminished. Britton sees creativity and independence as qualities that, if attained by the ego, provoke envious reactions in the object. When a patient makes advances in their treatment both she and the therapist might, therefore expect to experience not just hostility but envious attacks on each of them, and in particular on the progress of their work together. Melanie Klein (1957, p. 202) wrote that "creativeness becomes the deepest cause for envy", and Britton goes on to describe patients who are not identified with a murderous superego (those we might think of as the psychopathic or destructive narcissists) but who are:

internally menaced by a hostile superego, particularly when they show signs of independent personality, sexual maturity, or creativity. … In such cases, the stifling of their creativity is felt to protect them from the wrath of their internal furies or some representatives of them in the outside world.

(Britton, 2003, p.120)

This is particularly relevant in the echoistic disorders, where the patient is tormented by the types of envious ego-destructive objects described by Bion and Britton, and where an external source is also sought out to "protect" them from the anxiety that is produced by independence and separateness. It is not difficult to see how the echoist, who has become enslaved to a punishing internal object that masquerades as protective, is caught in the cycle of seeking an external version in the narcissistic partner.

Britton draws attention to a link between the production of such an object and the role of projection in the early situation between parent and infant. Indeed, he asks some of the most interesting questions, which I feel have a particular relevance for echoism: "How much does projection play a part in the production of this internal envious parental figure? How much and in what way does the nature of the original parental object play a part?" (Britton, 2003, p. 121).

While Britton's focus is not, of course, on the echoistic patient, if we apply to the echoist the link he draws between the creation of an ego-destructive object and the early situation, it seems to indicate the absence of a good internal object in the echoist, leaving her unable to guard against the force of the ego-destructive object. He concludes: "If we take Klein's view … we can see that it is necessary to mitigate the superego by the introjection of loving parental objects" (ibid., p. 128).

Vignette 1: Mrs A

A colleague came to me for supervision when he realised that his patient, Mrs A, a twenty-eight-year-old dental student, was quite clearly echoistic. She suffered from a critical internal voice and was severely hampered from expressing her own thoughts, emotions, and ideas. In her therapy she had gained some insight into this, recognising the malevolence and power of her object, and she had even gained a degree of freedom from it. In a session in which she felt demoralised, she grew tired of her therapist's repetitive interpretations about the dominance of her overbearing object, feeling also perhaps that he was "sitting back" a little too far. "Yes, I do know that it is my bloody object again!" she exclaimed. "You know that, I know that, but can't you just love me. Give me love!"

Analysis

It became clear that Mrs A had been experiencing her therapist as being content to notice and to name her persecuting object and to point it out to her, but he was felt to have been holding himself separate from her and not really bearing with her. She had felt that if only he would be closer to her in her suffering, she might be able to take in a feeling of being cared for, and thereby be strengthened from within against her oppressive object. The need for an experience of being-with was a more urgent requirement for this patient than interpretations in the realm of knowledge about what was happening, however accurate. Only upon receiving what she needed could she be expected to introject her helper and feel a measure of internal support against her oppressor.

The concept of introjection does not seem to have the same degree of importance in psychoanalytic writing as the concept of projection, perhaps because it is viewed as the healthy aspect of the container-contained process, whereby the infant who has introjected the good object is able to develop a functioning mind and ego. But with the echoist, and in particular the echoist who is the child of a narcissistic parent, Britton's questions are crucial. What happens if there is no loving parent to introject, but instead an envious narcissistic parent, who is not only unable to perform the work of a symbiotic container-contained relationship with the infant, but who actively discharges and projects *into* such an infant, creating a parasitic relationship? It suggests both the creation of a parasitic internal object and a propensity in the infant to introject, which overrides the infant's natural predisposition to project. If this is the case, we might expect to be in contact in the room with a very different type of patient than the narcissistic personality. The presence of such an object, however, and its attempts to sabotage any growth in the patient or the work, may well be experienced by the therapist as projection into her, which may lead her to mistake the patient as narcissistic. In fact, it is the narcissistic object who, as well as projecting into the therapist, is also projecting into healthy parts of the actively introjecting patient. We can see how this dynamic between narcissistic and echoistic dyads is open to misinterpretation, and may well lead the therapist to reach for an overvalued idea.

We do, however, as Britton concludes, need to rely upon our own internal good objects to sustain us when working with such complex and painful processes, to help us to bear the attacks from such objects, in order to begin to unravel the patient's particular internal dynamics.

> Undoing such pathological organizations in the course of analysis is somewhat like opening Pandora's box, and there are times when it feels like a foolhardy enterprise. At such times, the example of intrepid ancestors and the trust of respected colleagues is a source of inner strength. This, perhaps, is an example of how that complex organization – the superego – manifests itself in our professional lives in a benign way, and how very much we need good figures to have a place in that powerful internal moral position.
>
> (Britton, 2003, p. 128)

It is here that I have been helped by figures from existential philosophy, whose contributions I discuss in the next chapter.

Chapter 3

To be or not to be

An existential approach to understanding echoism

"Alone, I often fall down into nothingness. I must push my foot stealthily lest I should fall off the edge of the world into nothingness."

Virginia Woolf, *The Waves* (1931)

In the previous chapter I explained how I make use of psychoanalytic concepts to describe and make sense of the clinical experience of working with the echoistic patient. In this chapter I draw attention to an existential phenomenological approach to understanding Being, and I describe the discoveries I have made that have come from this particular method of working.

I relate the ideas described in the previous chapter to existential philosophical concepts, giving detailed attention to Sartre's ontological notions of Being (1943). For the reader less familiar with Sartre or with the methods employed in an existential therapeutic or Daseinsanalytic approach, I give a brief definition and explanation of his philosophical categories of Being, and his important concepts of "The Look" and "Shame".

I then describe the ways in which the ordinary individual[1] is impacted by, and defends against, being exposed to the painful ontological conditions of his existence. I go on to discuss my clinical findings showing how the narcissist defends in very specific ways against his ontological anxiety, providing a vignette to exemplify this. I then demonstrate how the two types of echoist use particular and distinct defences that differ from those of the narcissist and the ordinary individual.

In considering what Sartre describes as the ontological state of "Being-for-others", I show how the defensive echoist uses a defensive form of this to "be-for-others" as a way of fleeing from her responsibility to "be-for-herself". The self-destructive echoist defends against this state by taking an illusory refuge in what I refer to as "being-through-others". "Being-through-others" denotes an individual who, in order to avoid "being for-herself", becomes a channel through which others project themselves.

---

1 A term I use in the book for descriptive purposes to denote an individual not characterised by a particularly narcissistic or echoistic disposition.

I make a distinction between Sartre's use of these terms as ontological states of Being, and my own use of them as psychological defences. I draw attention to patterns of behaviour that I observe in my work with echoists and narcissists that demonstrate particular responses to the anxiety induced by one's ontological experience of being-in-the-world.

Applying Sartre's notion of *mauvaise-foi* (bad-faith) to understand her presentation in the clinical situation, I describe the echoist as being reduced to an almost constant state of bad-faith, unable to acknowledge her freedoms or responsibility, by living for or through another. And I discuss the shame resulting from this.

An existential phenomenological approach

Although a full account of the philosophical ideas is beyond the scope of this chapter, I will be describing the main concepts relevant to my work on echoism, and how using them has helped me to *be with* the phenomenon that is the echoist. It is useful to begin with what is meant by an existential, phenomenological approach and I refer specifically here to the practice and purpose of existential therapy.

Existential therapy is based on helping patients to understand their being-in-the-world. As van Deurzen (2010, p.1), one of the founders of existential therapy in the UK, explains:

> Existential thinking is a steadfast and loyal endeavour to reflect on everyday reality in order to make sense of it. As a practice it is probably as old as the human ability to reflect. Every now and then the human mind becomes so engrossed in itself that it replaces its humble search for truths that surpass and define us with the illusion of absolute knowledge and mastery over these same truths.

In applying philosophical thinking to our understanding of ourselves and what it means to be human, existential therapy seeks to cut through these illusions of certainty in order to acknowledge the fluidity of the human condition, and the self as a fluid being. Jean-Paul Sartre, who argued famously that "existence precedes essence", states that we are "condemned to freedom", and that clinging to the idea of a fixed self is what he refers to as "Bad-Faith". If we engage with this notion we can no longer blame our circumstances for all our problems, at least those that lie beyond the ontological conditions over which we have no control, because we are free to change many of them at any moment through making choices. If we see ourselves as fixed and therefore essential beings, we can take false comfort in such statements as "I am the kind of person who …"

Existential analysis emphasises the difficulty that arises from acknowledging our freedom, when we are forced to take responsibility for our choices, and for our attitudes and actions in the face of those conditions which we cannot alter.

For the patient in therapy who defines himself by his job or his role in a relationship, for example, existential thinking offers a challenge. In acknowledging the freedom to change his job, or do something different within the relationship, the patient is then forced to acknowledge that in *not* doing so he is choosing to stay in the same position, and that it is not imposed upon him from outside. This is liberating for the patient, who is then able to recognise the endless possibilities his freedom grants, while at the same time burdening him with responsibility for all the choices he makes, including those made unconsciously. In my work with echoists, the most striking presentation is that of a victim, oppressed by the wishes and actions of others. There are good reasons why the echoist does not recognise her freedoms, and I go on to explore these more fully in the clinical material in this book. It is important, however, to acknowledge that an awareness of these basic ideas of Sartre's is essential to understanding and working with echoistic phenomena.

In this section I will begin by outlining Sartre's ontological categories of Being and other concepts. This chapter considers the notion of *mauvaise-foi* (bad-faith) and how this relates to the aforementioned states of Being, as well as the concept of "The Look", and "Shame".

Existential concepts

The ontological

As I have used the term ontological many times in the introductory paragraphs of this chapter, it is necessary to give a working definition of the term. While in itself it is difficult to conceptualise, for the purpose of this book it is useful to think of the ontological as the universal state of being, or of what might be thought of as the human condition.

Swiss Daseinsanalyst, Alice Holzhey-Kunz, discusses Heidegger's use of the term ontological thus:

> From ancient times, 'ontology' was considered a basic philosophical discipline that enquired into the 'being of beings'; from this could be derived specialist ontologies that addressed, for example, the being of living nature in contrast to the being of the human subject. In this sense, Heidegger's daseinsanalysis is also an ontological undertaking to the extent that it enquires into the specific being of the human subject. What is radically innovative about the daseinsanalytic ontology is that it does not merely ascribe a specific being to the human subject but makes this 'being' the concern of every single human being. Heidegger in fact sees it as the crucial point about human being that the human subject does not simply (like all other beings) possess a specific constitution of being but *that he conducts himself towards it*.
>
> (Holzhey-Kunz, 2014, p. 43)

Existential therapy, therefore, is concerned with:

> The person's struggle with human existence and elucidat[ing] the parameters
> of the human condition that the person is trying to come to terms with.
>
> (van Deurzen, 2010, p. 236)

For this reason, the ontic, or more concrete aspects of the patient's life are always considered within the wider universal concept of Being, experienced by all human beings. Finally, it is impossible to consider Being in Sartrean terms outside the context of, and its relationship to, "nothingness".

Nothingness

In his most substantial work, *Being and Nothingness*, Sartre (1943) describes his theory of Being. He states famously that "existence precedes essence" and it is here that we can begin to understand the specific meaning of the term "nothingness" for Sartre. The individual is born without an essence, unaware that he is in the world. He projects himself into the world as pure intentionality, and exists through what he does, not who he is, because at this point he has no essence, he simply expresses his Being.

Sartre uses the term "intentionality" in a very specific way, following its introduction as a philosophical concept by Franz Brentano, later taken up by Edmund Husserl – the founder of phenomenology. For Brentano, intentionality is the psyche's capacity to direct itself towards objects. Husserl takes this further and sees consciousness of the world as intrinsically linked to the intended objects of which the mind then becomes conscious. For Sartre, intentionality is not "a conscious act of intention", it is the mind seeking objects on to which it will project itself, and – through reflection back – becoming conscious of a self that is seeking, and which is distinct from the object of which it has become conscious.

For Sartre, the becoming of a self is built upon what the individual receives back from others that allows her to know that she exists as separate from them, and from the world. This process is described by Barnes (see van Deurzen, 2010, p. 81) as "non-self-conscious" consciousness. Barnes has further described how the individual begins to notice that she is the one acting in the world, through her relationship with others, and from this an acknowledgment of an objective self, an ego, is born: "The acting of my *I* has created the *me*" (ibid.).

Existentially, because we are in the constant process of creating a self, unlike the irreducible objects that are beings-in-themselves, objects such as chairs and tables, for example, we are always at risk of being reduced back to our true state of nothingness.

As van Deurzen reminds us about Sartrean philosophy:

> Although we can fool ourselves into the belief that we are … something, we
> will keep on being confronted with the fact that we are nothing at all, as such

we are condemned to… hav[ing] to invent ourselves and make something of ourselves.

(van Deurzen, 2010, p. 81)

As we have seen, Sartre makes a distinction between two main orders of Being: the being-for-itself (*être-pour-soi*) and a being-in-itself (*être-en-soi*), which I will outline briefly here, as they are central to understanding the echoist.

Being-in-itself (être en-soi)

The Being-in-itself is a category of Being that describes those objects that are fixed and that are without consciousness. This state of being should not, however, be confused with the non-self-conscious consciousness of the being-for-itself described above. These beings include objects, such as a table or a tree, that exist in themselves with no wish or intentionality. They are fixed Beings and as such they are always something. They can only be reduced to "things-in-themselves" and never to nothing. Importantly, their existence does not depend upon anyone's consciousness of them, whereas the "being-for-itself" "logically depends upon something other than itself, and upon those things other than itself, of which it is conscious" (Danto, 1975, p. 42).

Being-for-itself (être pour-soi)

Beings-for-themselves are, as Danto describes: "conscious beings … whose nature is that they are aware of themselves and cannot exist as such without this awareness" (Danto, 1975, p. 42). Human beings fall into this category and are seen by Sartre as "condemned to freedom". By this statement he draws attention to the Being-for-itself as a Being without essence who is free to become whatever she chooses, within the ontological conditions of her existence. Because the *pour-soi* is not a fixed Being, it is subject to ontological *angst* regarding its own nothingness, and seeks to create a self to avoid the pain of this.

Danto also makes the point that for Sartre consciousness is always consciousness of something, "not … a pure state, and no one is merely conscious without there being something of which he is conscious" (ibid., p. 43).

For the being-for-itself, the consciousness of its own nothingness is a painful state through which, as well as being required to constantly invent itself, it also wishes to be a fixed being, as a way of avoiding its own nothingness, and as a means of avoiding responsibility for everything it does by behaving as if it is a being-in-itself. The being-for-itself can never simply be an entity in itself, it is always in relation to itself, and therein conscious of itself as a self.

For Sartre the reassurance to be found in the state called being-in-itself, with its fixed, known, and irreducible nature, makes it a real temptation for the being-for-itself, precipitating an act of self-deception in which the being-for-itself slips into the delusional belief that it is a being-in-itself. In so-doing, it acts against its becoming, which Sartre terms *mauvaise-foi* or bad-faith.

Bad-faith (mauvaise-foi)

For Sartre the term "Bad-faith" means primarily the act of self-deception. Referring to the ideas above, a being who is unwilling to acknowledge his freedoms in considering himself as a fixed self is in bad-faith. Because we all have roles and to some degree an identity based upon these (wife, teacher, friend, philanthropist, Labour voter, writer, etc.), Sartre understands that we are, and therefore cannot avoid being, in bad-faith for much of the time. He urges us constantly to reflect upon this and to consider what it is we are avoiding in deceiving ourselves that we have no choice but to have these roles.

Sartre alerts me to the awareness that the identity I have that I call "Me" is to some degree a me-for-others, which reinforces not just how I might like to be seen but also how others see me, fix me, and objectify me as a being-in-itself.

In his famous vignette of the waiter, Sartre describes an attitude that the waiter adopts of "waiterliness", whereby he holds the glass and greets the customer and flicks his napkin in just such a way as to create an image or idea he might have of how a waiter *is*. Sartre shows how the enacting of the notion of waiterliness is an act of self-deceit in which the individual (being-for-itself) gets lost and is subsumed by the role. When the existential therapist begins to notice that she is "acting as a therapist", saying things a therapist might say and behaving with a particular attitude that signifies "therapist" towards the patient, it is time for her to consider her own bad-faith, and to use her reflexivity to attempt to restore her to a being-for-itself in order to relate to the patient authentically, and with the freshness of a constantly becoming self and not a fixed one. In the example given above, the idea of waiterliness comes not simply from the waiter's own experience of being a waiter and falling into the bad-faith of a being-in-itself, but from his consciousness of what others may expect of a waiter – we might therefore say that he is observing his actions through the eyes or look of another and in this sense he is Being-for-others in a very particular way.

Being-for-others (Être-pour-autrui)

Danto (1975, p. 38) describes a third category of Being, which features importantly in the latter part of Sartre's *Being and Nothingness*, namely *Être-pour-autrui* (being-for-others). He tells us that the *pour-soi* does also, "as it happens to his torment, have this third sort of Being".

The first thing to acknowledge is that ontologically we are always beings-for-Others because we cannot not see ourselves externally to our relationship to others, as this is the process through which our consciousness has originally developed and it continues to evolve as relational. Sartre says:

> The other interests me only to the extent that he is another Me, a Me-object for Me, and conversely to the extent that he reflects my Me – i.e., is, in so far

as I am an object for him. Due to the fact that I must necessarily be an object for myself over there in the Other, I must obtain from the other the recognition of my being. But if another consciousness must mediate between my consciousness for itself and itself, the being-for-itself of my consciousness – and consequently its being in general – depends on the other. As I appear to the other, so am I.

(Sartre, 1943, p. 260–261)

This leads directly to Sartre's ontological concept of "The Look", which he describes using concrete examples, but to which we are all subjected ontologically, all the time, because we are visible to others and have an awareness of them even when we choose not to acknowledge them, and even when they are choosing not to look at us.[2]

The Look

Sartre uses two vignettes in *Being and Nothingness* that help to illustrate the effect of The Look on the individual's sense of being-in-the-world. In both cases the narrator of the vignette sees himself as the subject at the centre of his own universe – a universe existing only because he is the centre of it; it is his subjective universe.

In the first vignette, which takes place in a garden, he describes the presence of an Other in the centre of a green, around which the components of his immediate world organise themselves in a similar way to those of his own world. He notices that as this Other views and observes the green, in much the same way that he himself does, he emerges as having a similar form to the narrator and he is able to recognise that Other as distinct from himself. Here Sartre states:

The appearance of the Other in the world therefore corresponds to a fixed sliding of the whole universe, to a decentralization of the world which undermines the centralization which I am simultaneously effecting.

(1943, p. 279)

At this point the Other notices and looks at the narrator, who then understands that in being-seen by the other he is no longer simply *not* at the centre of his own universe, but at that moment he is an object in that of the Other. He describes how: "… through the revelation of my being-as-object for the other … I must be able to

---

2 This idea of always being watched is taken up in Bentham's concept of the Panopticon, an idea taken up by many thinkers including Foucault. As well as featuring in *Huis Clos* (1944), it can be seen how this idea was taken up in literature, perhaps most famously by Orwell in his *1984* (Orwell, 1949), and was a preoccupation of mid-twentieth-century thinkers.

apprehend the presence of his being-as-subject". At this point he experiences an Other as a subject, and not one of his objects, for the first time.

The above describes the impact of what Sartre calls "The Look" on what I am calling the ordinary individual, an individual not characterised by a particularly narcissistic or echoistic disposition. This leads to a feeling of ontological shame, which is further elaborated in Sartre's second vignette on The Look in *Being and Nothingness* (2003, p. 282).

Shame

In this vignette, where a jealous lover is drawn to look through a keyhole, Sartre goes on to describe how the look of another can be related to shame. The narrator in the vignette feels no self-consciousness as he bends to look through the keyhole to have his worst fears confirmed. He is led by feelings drawn out of him, and describes what he calls a state of pure consciousness, where he *is* his actions, and where his actions need no justification in a world in which he is the only subject. I perceive this as similar to the state of non-self-conscious consciousness referred to above.

He goes on to describe the powerful effect of hearing footsteps and becoming aware of a watcher observing him looking through the keyhole. In this moment he says, "I see myself because somebody sees me" – in other words, his state as subject, operating pure consciousness, becomes affected by being seen, and causes what he describes as an experience of "modifications appear[ing] in my structure – modifications which I can apprehend ... by means of the reflective *cogito*". This realisation is so destabilising that it modifies his whole sense-of-self-structure (reinforcing the idea that self is not a fixed state but a fluid one, which can be affected at any time, both by others and by choices of the individual).

A self has been revealed to him through the Other:

> a strange image ... present to me as a self which I *am* without *knowing* it; for I discover it in shame and, in other instances, in pride. It is shame or pride which reveals to me the Other's look and myself at the end of that look. It is the shame or pride which makes me *live,* not *know* the situation of being looked at.
>
> (Sartre, ibid., p. 284)

This final statement marks a distinction regarding a self that cannot be known, but can only be revealed through experience and being-with-others. Sartre writes extensively on the impact of The Look on the individual and the way in which it forces a confrontation for the subject between the self-for-others, which he sees reflected back to him, and his own notion of himself as a fixed self.

This conflict between his idea of himself as a being-in-itself with the shame (and indeed pride – if the look of the other is experienced as affirming or flattering) –

that comes from being seen-by-others, motivates him to take agency in his own becoming, and shakes him out of his bad-faith position into being-for-himself. Interestingly, in the keyhole vignette, there is no actual Other observing the narrator, but once he has heard the footsteps he can no longer see himself as before, but instead sees himself through the lens of the imagined other, and as a result he experiences the Other as everywhere, all the time, leading him to say, in *Huis Clos* (1944), "*L'enfer, c'est les autres*", "Hell is other people".

Defences against being-for-oneself

As we can see from Sartre's powerful vignettes, the state of exposure to one's ontological condition is a painful and anxiety-provoking experience. The individual is in constant conflict between acknowledging his subjectivity (freedom and responsibility) and his objectivity (a state of shame and impotence caused by the look of the other) and uses many defences against the pain of this state. For what I refer to as the ordinary individual, the most common defence is escaping into everydayness (*le quotidian*), as a way of avoiding the human ontological condition. Because all humans are subjected to this state, they suffer, but for those unable to exercise the defence of the everyday, other mechanisms are put in place, and these are particularly interesting in terms of the different ways they manifest in the narcissist and the echoist.

Sartre says of Hegel:

> Hegel's brilliant intuition is to make me depend on the Other *in my being*. I am, he said, a being-for-itself which is for-itself only through another.
>
> (Ibid., p. 261)

Quoting Hegel from his *Propädeutik* (Hegel, 1970, p. 20), Sartre adds:

> Self-consciousness is real only in so far as it recognises its echo (and its reflection) in another.

As we can see, Sartre refers here very specifically to the terms "echo", and "reflection", both key components of the myth of Echo and Narcissus. While he is referring to ordinary and necessary processes that take place to enable states of being-in-the-world, for which the individual must accept responsibility and the freedom that ensue from this, these two themes are particularly relevant in relation to both narcissistic and echoistic defences.

Being and the narcissist

While consciousness must always, as Sartre indicates, depend on recognition of self by the Other, the narcissistic patient is unable to acknowledge the Other as a subject in his own right, and instead shifts his thinking to objectification of the Other, even in the process of his own objectification by the Other.

This might be seen as the solipsistic argument for Being, whereby the individual must negate the Other who reflects him, in order to survive as a being-for-himself and not succumb to being the object of another being's consciousness.

In his case, the desire to annihilate the being of the Other presides to such an extent that relating to the Other as a subject, while holding one's own subjectivity in being-for-oneself, becomes impossible. Others are treated in the mind either as beings-in-themselves (things) by the narcissist, or, where possible, they will be colonised as beings-for-him. In psychoanalytic terms this is effected through projective identification (see Chapter Two).

In the case of the narcissistic individual, this is taken to an extreme and becomes a way of existing in the world, to avoid having to tolerate the being of others as real. In order to see how this might be observed in the clinical situation, I would like to provide an example of a narcissistic patient whose way of Being exemplifies the above.

Vignette 2: Mrs J

Mrs J came into therapy having lost her prestigious and lucrative position in the financial services sector, at a time of considerable change in her family circumstances. Her husband had been offered a temporary teaching post at a local university, having gained a degree by means of a correspondence course, which had allowed him to study part-time and to look after their young pre-school child. As she began therapy with me three times a week, her son was attending school and her husband was beginning his career, and he was earning the money for the family. Mrs J's awareness that the balance of the family had altered was the main source of conflict in the marriage. She felt that her husband was seeking a greater say in decisions affecting them both, and she resented this. She justified these feelings by discounting both the importance of his career and the financial contribution it provided.

Prior to the changes, her husband had willingly accepted her authority on financial matters and the way in which the money was spent and distributed, accepting her leading role, as she was the breadwinner who made their lifestyle possible. He had, in turn, enjoyed his role in the home. I could feel how strongly Mrs J had reacted to her husband's attempt to have a voice in their decisions. She told me that her career break was only temporary after all, and that his new position was so poorly paid that it certainly did not give him the right to tell her what to do.

During our sessions she spoke of his career and even his subject area (Art History) with mockery and contempt. She asserted that she needed to keep things just as they were, so she could regain a position "worthy of her". Tellingly, and very much implying the kind of "fixed identity" discussed earlier in this chapter, Mrs J did not want her husband "getting ideas above his station".

Prior to the changes, Mrs J had used her superior position to justify her extensive appetite for exotic holidays and fine dining. She clarified to me that she did not want to encourage him to become attached to a role that she considered very temporary, and that he might not want to leave once she regained a work position that allowed her to resume the dynamic that she had come to consider as fixed and right.

Analysis

My work with Mrs J revealed a powerful rage and hatred of anyone or anything felt to threaten her idea of herself as an absolute subject. She attacked her husband's developments and his newly discovered independence as foolish and ridiculous. She told me that the marriage was at risk of ending unless he accepted her authority. She told him things would return to how they were once she attained a new position, as she could earn "ten times his salary; his contribution is peanuts, and does not give him the right to have an equal say in the family's distribution of resources".

From her narcissistic perspective, if he failed to continue to validate and to support who she "knew" she was, he was of no use to her. In Sartrean terms, she felt that if her husband did not restrict himself to remaining a mere object for her, the relationship was neither satisfying nor sustainable. Following the loss of her job, her narcissism had driven her to use an even more omnipotent idea of herself to fight to retain the position in the family to which she felt entitled. Her husband's challenge to this seemed to be the threat to her fixed sense of self that had brought her into therapy, and once she began she soon attempted to recruit me unquestioningly into complete agreement with her, and, in so doing, becoming yet another object for-her.

In the conflict between being-for-others and being-for-ourselves, we can see that the narcissist negates the Other, in his mind, as a way of avoiding his own feelings of what Sartre calls "nihilation". In the latter part of *Being and Nothingness*, Sartre takes up a version of this idea and considers what he calls the "in-itself-for-itself":

> That is, the ideal of a consciousness which would be the foundation of its own being-in-itself by the pure consciousness that it would have of itself. It is this ideal which can be called God.
>
> (Sartre, 1943, p. 587)

For the destructive narcissist, this ideal, which enables him to consider himself god-like, is held as a central defence.

Being and the echoist

I find that in the echoist this attitude and position are reversed, and most strongly when she is in a relationship to or with a narcissist. Not only does she accept her objectification by another, and allow it to negate her, she avoids the anxiety of being-for-herself while existing for-others by denying her freedoms to be-for-herself and seeking out others for whom she can be. We can see here how the echoist is drawn naturally to the narcissist, whose illusion regarding his exist-ence depends upon his negation of others, through acquiring them as objectified beings-for-him. In other words, the echoist exists primarily as a being-for-others, and avoids the conflict involved in fighting for her own existence. She therefore seeks out the look of the other to reflect back acceptable modes of being-for-him and when this is met with approval adapts and conforms in order to have an exist-ence. While this existence may lack a sense of a self or any authentic being-in-the-world, it is at least a form of Being in which, through echoing back the other, she knows she exists because her echoes are met with acknowledgment, even if they are echoed back by a narcissist and taken to be a reflection of himself.

I am particularly interested in how modes of Being are used as psychic defences in the echoist, who functions primarily as a being-for-others, or – in extreme cases – a *being-through-others,* which is my own term for a category of Being found in the destructive echoist. I go on to discuss how these concepts are impor-tant in helping the therapist to recognise the echoistic patient, or echoistic traits in a patient, and the defences that may be in place to keep the therapist away from painful and unbearable feelings.

Sartre tells us:

> the [Being-]for-itself (*pour-soi*) is defined ontologically as a lack of being, and possibility belongs to the for-itself as that which it lacks ... Freedom is the concrete mode of being of the lack of being.
>
> (Ibid., p. 586)

The echoist, this self whom I have experienced in the room and described above, typically does not engage with the challenge of being-for-herself by taking her freedom as a potential for becoming. Rather, she seeks the other to provide the life force out of which Being is created.

"The Look" and shame in the clinical situation

It is necessary to explicate the other important Sartrean ideas that help to under-stand the plight of the echoistic patient, by referring to The Look and its further relationship to shame. As we have seen from the definitions above, Sartre's con-cept of The Look is closely related to the notion of being-for-others, as it also involves consciousness of one's self as reflected back through the eyes of another.

The vignettes describe the experience of what Sartre calls The Look on what I am calling the ordinary individual (an individual not characterised by a particularly narcissistic or echoistic disposition) were it not for her ability to employ the defence of what Heidegger calls "the everyday".[3] From the vignette we can observe the impact on such an individual's subjective existence as undermining her centralised position in the universe and her ideas of being a subject. For this individual, the system of defence in place, which stops her from becoming completely annihilated – is the defence against ontological reality, through accepting the everyday as real and concrete as a way of avoiding being subjected to their actual state of fragility in the world. Holzhey-Kunz (2014, p. 46, p. 48) writes of those whom she calls "reluctant philosophers" – those who are especially sensitive. Such individuals are unable to achieve the defensive shielding employed by the ordinary individual and so suffer more *angst* as a result of their exposure to the ontological facticity of their being. The narcissist and the echoist too, are especially sensitive and unable to use the everyday as an adequate way of protecting themselves from their psychic suffering. Instead they have developed very specific psychic defences against this, which have resulted in particular and recognisable defensive organisations of the mind, which I describe in detail below. In Chapter Ten I will consider possible difficulties for the echoist in relation to this special sensitivity, if she achieves some degree of her own subjectivity through therapy.

The Look is complex and particularly relevant to the clinical situation, where the patient is always with an Other (the therapist). We can understand the term to mean being seen by the other in a way that is experienced by the subject as having a penetrative impact. In psychotherapy, being understood is experienced as being "seen", and the way the therapist indicates this to the patient is through a verbal statement.

In the clinical situation the patient experiences the conflict between a fixed idea of herself and something not known but revealed to her through The Look/ interpretation of the therapist. The threat to an idea of a fixed self will cause great anxiety, and the defences against this will be aroused in the patient. The degree to which the therapist can bear the patient's anxiety can be seen to impact the degree to which the patient is able to reduce the natural defences and bear the uncertainty that leads to psychic growth.

Narcissism and The Look

I have observed a rather specific impact on the narcissistic individual resulting from the experience of being seen by the Other. Although he is, through his very existence, subject both to The Look and to verbal responses to his being, he is not destabilised

---

3 See Heidegger (1962, p. 163) and Holzhey-Kunz's (2014, p. 49) qualifying remarks.

by it in the same way, and does not experience the same conflict as the ordinary individual, as long as the narcissistic defence is maintained. This defence ensures that all others are reduced to the status of objects, as he is incapable of object-relating in a way that allows others to be considered subjects in their own right.

As I emphasised in Chapter Two, the colonising nature of the narcissist, even in more benign forms of narcissistic relating, reduces the other from subjectivity to being one of the narcissist's objects. As The Look is therefore perceived to come from an object that he considers a part of himself, it does not have the power to penetrate the narcissist and consequently cannot threaten his idea or feelings of being an omnipotent self. He is able to manipulate his interpretation of the look of the other to reinforce his superiority, to "enable the uninterrupted validation of the daydreamed self" (Mawson, 2004, p. 509). To some degree, through projective identification, he is actually able to manipulate the other to "look" and "see" what he wants her to see. In other words, he creates the ideal image for reflection by himself and others, much as he does in the myth, and while this reinforces his idea of himself as the only valid subject, it further isolates him from relating to others in a way that can promote growth. The echoist is especially vulnerable to becoming one of his objects and responds in a way that further reinforces his narcissism because of her very particular way of relating.

Echoism and The Look

As I stated in Chapter One, because narcissism has been written and thought about so exhaustively, it is possible to apply philosophical and theoretical ideas to an already extensive body of work with some confidence. In the case of the echoist, this proves much more difficult, and I am therefore required to extrapolate from the writings on narcissism the ideas that can be applied to the clinical experience of working with the echoistic patient. As we have seen, the echoist is a being-for-others in a way that avoids the conflict, and alleviates the responsibility, of taking up her freedom to be-for-herself. She therefore needs the look of the other to guide her. In addition, because her subjectivity is located outside her own self and in others, she might be considered less vulnerable to the look of the other, as destructive and annihilating to a self, than the ordinary individual. In this sense she might even be mistaken for a narcissist by the therapist.

This reduced vulnerability is reinforced when she is in a relationship with a narcissist, because to some degree the narcissist protects the echoist from the look of others by taking her place as the *subject* of their gaze. This becomes more complex, however, in the clinical situation, when the particular experience of shame has brought the echoist into therapy.

Shame in the clinical situation

As we have seen above, while the ontological shame of constantly being seen by the Other leads Sartre to say "Hell is other people", in the therapeutic encounter this is a necessary experience to suffer, in order to promote growth and improve relationships with others with whom one shares the world.

For the echoist it is the experience of shame that often brings her into therapy in the first place. While in relationship with a narcissist, she is, as we have said, to some degree protected by the narcissist's ownership of her and of her freedoms and responsibilities. Because the level of abuse that takes place in narcissistic relating can happen so gradually and seemingly naturally, the echoist may even fail to notice it herself. It is often only once the behaviour is noticed or seen by others that the echoist can experience such powerful feelings of shame, as her plight is reflected back to her in a way that challenges her willingness to see things from the narcissist's perspective. She is then faced with a dilemma – whether to confront her shame by acknowledging her role in an abusive relationship and the degree to which she has colluded in it as a way of avoiding taking agency, or to stay with the narcissist, closing others out and choosing to see things from his perspective. This dilemma, which takes place in external relationships, also takes place within the internal world, where the echoist has come to depend upon what she feels is the protection of the narcissistic object from the look of others – an area to which I return in detail in Chapter Six.

Two types of echoist

In the previous chapter I described how I have found the psychoanalytic ideas concerning narcissism, particularly those of Herbert Rosenfeld and Ronald Britton, resonant with my ideas on echoism, in a way that serves to further my understanding of echoism. Britton's (2004) paper focuses on two main types of narcissistic personality disorder, which can, loosely, be labelled defensive narcissism and destructive narcissism. These classifications are based upon the analyst's experience of being with the patient and an observation of the feelings stirred up in the analyst. This is a very similar process to the phenomenological approach in which being with the patient, offering "horizontalization"[4] (Spinelli, 2007), and openness to the experience, informs the existential analyst. In both modalities the helper attempts to understand the specific need in the patient in order to offer an authentic response aimed at promoting genuine relating.

I have experienced a corresponding distinction between two types of echoist: a defensive echoist, and a more extreme or self-destructive echoist. I have arrived at this distinction on the basis of my clinical experiences, and throughout this book these are the terms which I will be using to mark this distinction. They are underpinned by my understanding of some of Sartre's ideas outlined above.

---

4 Spinelli (2007, p. 116) refers to "horizontalization", the practice of paying attention to all aspects of the patient's communications without prejudice or the prioritising of any particular element over another based upon expectancy, prior assumption, or preference. In this respect it has great affinity with Freud's concept of evenly suspended attention (1912e, p. 111) and with Bion's recommendations on memory and desire (1965b) and his use of the concept of negative capability (1970, p. 125).

The defensive echoist

The defensive echoist uses the Other as a mirror in which The Look fixes her as an object, not only seen through the eyes of the other but one whose very existence is guided by what she reads into the other's gaze. In this sense, she echoes Narcissus' own fate in the myth, never knowing her true self, but in her case this self-conscious existence takes the form of a being-for-others, where responsibility for choice is replaced by bad-faith – an impersonation of whom the echoist imagines the other wants her to be. Interestingly, Britton (1998, p. 45) himself looks to Sartre on this very notion of The Look, stating: "The profound meaning of my being is outside of me", while noting Sartre's words: "I now exist as myself for my unreflective consciousness ... I see myself because somebody sees me".

Britton is relating this idea to the narcissistic patient's fear that an objective description of him will be destructive to his own sense of self as subject. This supports ideas that the thin-skinned or defensive narcissist must protect himself from relating to the other as a real being-for-itself. It further exemplifies how the echoist completes the dynamic nature of narcissistic relating through an avoidance of making choices and taking responsibility for her own existence in the world. In psychoanalytic terms, in therapy and in life the defensive echoist can often experience feeling like a passive or permeable membrane into which projections are pushed.

The self-destructive echoist

Just as the clinicians working with narcissistic patients have found it valuable to pay attention to their countertransference feelings, and to the associated pushes and pulls that they have experienced towards enactments of such impulses, I have found a corresponding set of experiences with my echoistic patients.

In my experience, the encounter with the self-destructive echoist can leave the therapist feeling inadequate, depleted, self-critical, and with a sense of having been unable to give the patient enough. I have often found myself extending a time boundary, feeling drained of energy after talking extensively, or trying to find solutions for the patient.

In psychoanalytic terms I have come to understand the self-destructive echoist's way of being as actively introjecting the other. In order to animate her own barely existent being, she draws the other into herself, becoming what I call a "being-through-others".

Being-through-others

In the clinical situation it can be observed time and again how the echoist becomes reliant upon the narcissist changing, in order that her experience can be changed *through* him. When invited to reflect on her own Being in the therapeutic situation, she is often unable to think of a single thing about herself that she considers worth saying, and deflects the focus back on to the narcissist. It is as though, confronted with her own nothingness, in that moment it is so unbearable that she clings to the only life force she can. This often manifests in the room as a constant fascination with her narcissistic counterpart. In this scenario the narcissist is in fact the subject through which she lives and upon whom she depends for her Being.

She needs him in order to exist, and she depends upon him utterly to avoid unbearable direct confrontation with her own absence of Being. Because the therapist often finds herself dealing with a narcissistic object presenting as a *subject* through the encounter with the echoist, the patient can, as we have said, be mistakenly identified as narcissistic herself, as she is acting at root from a similar motivation – to evade the ontological anxiety of being nothing. The echoist, however, is not functioning in the same way as a narcissist here. She is relating to objects in her internal world, and others in her external world, in a distinctly different way to that of a narcissistic patient. The narcissist is always the subject, but the echoist requires the narcissist so that she can introject him as a subject in her inner world, all of which is necessary in helping her to evade the terrible responsibility for Being, which she cannot withstand. The ego is not sufficiently strong in her, nor does it have enough good objects that she can draw upon to strengthen it. She is in touch with her own fragility in a way in which the narcissist is not. She therefore seeks out the Other introjectively, in ways that *appear* to protect her ego, but she becomes enormously dependent on them for survival.

Let us consider Sartre's fascinating passage on the individual who lives a life as a Not self:

> My consciousness is not restricted to *envisioning a négatité*. It constitutes itself in its own flesh as the nihilation of a possibility which another human reality projects as its possibility. For that reason it must arise in the world as a Not; it is as a Not that the slave first apprehends the master, or that the prisoner who is trying to escape sees the guard who is watching him. There are even men [….] who will live and die, having forever been only a Not upon the earth. Others so as to make the Not a part of their very subjectivity, establish their human personality as a perpetual negation. This is the meaning and function of what Scheler calls "the man of resentment" – in reality, the Not.
>
> (1943, p. 70)

In light of this we are helped to understand why resentment is the most prevalent emotion that we may experience as a therapist in the presence of an echoist, and the one to which Ovid draws our attention at the end of the myth of Echo and Narcissus.

Part II

Types of echoism

Chapter 4

Chimeras and chameleons
The defensive echoist

> We are all a sort of Camelions, that still take a Tincture from things near us.
> John Locke, *Some Thoughts Concerning Education*, 1693

Defensive echoism is, as I explain in this chapter, a trait that may be present in many individuals who are not necessarily echoists. The patient might be considered to be a defensive echoist, however, when such ways of being dominate the personality and relationships, and the patient adapts and modifies the self to meet the needs of others to the extent of not knowing who she really is.

When the patient presents in treatment as needing to know what the therapist thinks she should do, and adapts herself to an idea of who she thinks the therapist wants her to be, these may be signs of such a lack of self. Using clinical vignettes to illustrate this, I elaborate on the ideas in the previous chapter to show how this state is linked to Sartre's writings on a being-for-others. I go on to consider how similar presentations of this type have been classified in psychoanalytic literature in terms of as-if personalities, and how this is seen as part of a set of narcissistic conditions, which has been considered a contraindication for treatment. Describing my own countertransference experiences to explicate what might be elicited in the presence of such an individual, I discuss how I work with the free associations of the patient and am often made aware of what feels like an internal critical voice, preventing or hampering the echoist from developing a mind and voice of her own.

In the previous chapter we have identified two types of narcissism from psychoanalytic writing, which appear to correspond to the two types of echoism referred to in this book, defensive echoism and self-destructive echoism. In this chapter I will be focusing primarily on the defensive echoist whose characteristics can best be understood in relation to the defensive or libidinal narcissist, and to Sartre's category of being-for-others.

I think it is important to clarify that I am not using these terms as rigid categories or classifications. Like all presentations of pathology or behaviour, in life and in the consulting room, they are fluid and subject to change. I hope to communicate the observations I have made, and my learning through experiences in the consulting room, to enable the therapist to be aware of the range of presentations of echoism, to help realise when they may be in the presence of an echoist. It is in the patient's communications and the therapist's countertransference that these distinctions can appear, and the next two chapters focus on how these experiences might help the therapist to recognise the echoist, and to draw attention to how easily she might be mistaken or misinterpreted without some clinical examples for comparison. Later (Chapter Six) I give a whole chapter to this question of mistaken identity, when I consider how a set of traits and behaviours have been classified as narcissistic because echoism in its distinct and related forms had not been available as a concept.

Riccardo Steiner, writing on Rosenfeld's work on narcissistic disorders, has warned that we are faced with mental phenomena of great complexity and potential violence,

> which besides requiring certain specific capacities from the analyst, often were, and still are, quite new and obscure and need extremely careful observations and formulations and differentiations.
>
> (In: Steiner, J, 2008, p. 47)

I am stating the case in this book for careful differentiation between patients who embody clinical features that are much closer to the character of Echo in the myth than they are to those demonstrated by Narcissus.

In Chapters Eight and Ten, I argue for echoistic-narcissistic complexes to be considered as both intrapsychic and interpersonal dynamics. I think that this will make it less likely that echoistic patients will be considered as narcissistic, borderline or as-if personalities. For the purpose of this chapter I will go on to explore the propensity for confusion between the defensive echoist and the libidinal narcissist or the as-if personality. I think the nuanced differences will become clearer by engaging with the following clinical vignettes, with their very specific focus on, and analysis of, countertransference experiences.

Herbert Rosenfeld, whose contribution to theories of narcissism and narcissistic disorders has been a defining influence on contemporary Kleinian analysis, defined libidinal narcissism, the less destructive form of narcissism, thus:

> In considering narcissism from the libidinal aspect one can see that the overvaluation of the self plays a central role, based mainly on the idealization of the self. Self-idealization is maintained by omnipotent introjective and projective identifications with good objects and their qualities. In this way the narcissist feels that everything that is valuable relating to external objects and the outside world is part of him or is omnipotently controlled by him.
>
> (Rosenfeld, 1971, p. 173)

The vignettes that follow in this chapter contain examples of work with patients showing patterns similar to those described by Rosenfeld, but which reveal a very different meaning in terms of the patients' ideas of themselves. Specifically, while the libidinal narcissist attributes all progress and goodness in the therapy to be due to him, or under his own control, the defensive echoist avoids taking any owner-ship, or claiming any agency for these factors. In this sense, while both presenta-tions prevent meaningful relationships with the therapist, the echoist is quite the opposite of the narcissist in terms of how she sees herself in the world, for her *self* plays not only a peripheral or supporting role, but quite often an *absent* one in terms of its agency.

I have discussed the echoist both in relation to psychoanalytic ideas of projec-tion and to existential ideas relating to modes of Being. In Sartre's and Heidegger's philosophies the very notion of being-in-the-world refers to the individual as being in relation to others. We can observe a struggle at the heart of the individual where the desire to be a fixed being (leading to bad-faith), as a way of avoiding the *angst* of existential nothingness, is in conflict with acknowledging our freedoms and being-for-ourselves in the world.

This conflict inevitably includes the relation to others, and, as we have seen in the previous chapter, Sartre maintains that our conscious idea of ourselves is formed by what is reflected back from others. The existential philosophers warn us against powerful pressures, brought about by the inevitability of our nature as a being-for-others, to become what Heidegger (1962, p. 167) calls a "They-self" (*das Man-selbst*).

It is this feature that is perhaps most immediately evident in the defensive echoist who, from the moment of contact, attempts to draw the therapist into a position of agency and power. In my work with defensive echoists I have expe-rienced a wish communicated to the therapist by the echoistic patient to "tell her what to-do", from very early on in the process. The following vignette provides an example of encountering a defensive echoist.

Vignette 3: Jayne

Jayne, an executive in her early thirties, made an initial telephone call regarding a dilemma she was facing, and asked for an urgent appointment. In the assess-ment she recounted that she had been in a long-term relationship in which she had become very detached from her partner and from her own wishes and passions. She had met an exciting man, David, on a work trip abroad and after a short affair of two months, during which they had seen each other five times, he had asked her to leave her long-term partner, Michael, with whom she had a life and home.

Jayne was very keen to express all the excitement that David had brought to her life, and her fear of losing him if she was unable to make a decision very soon. She said that her relationship with Michael was very secure and that he was reliable and kind, but that she had always let him make decisions about even the smallest things, and she now looked at her life as being rather dull and quite different to the one that David seemed to be offering – something more exciting, dynamic, and alive. She said Michael had always chosen the restaurants they ate in and the films that they went to see, but now David was showing her a different kind of life, trying new foods and different cultural experiences, and this all added to her feelings of dissatisfaction with Michael. But she knew she liked reliability, and that she felt guilty about hurting Michael, and she thought it might all burn out with David if she were to leave Michael for him, and then she would be alone.

In the first session, Jayne used many devices to try to elicit my opinion of what she should do. Finding myself feeling her anxiety at making the wrong decision, I too felt a strong wish to resolve the dilemma of who would be the best partner for Jayne. I found myself trying to think about the relationship in which she would be most likely to thrive, and found myself, unwittingly, wanting to guide her towards thinking with me about these kinds of dilemmas.

I will now describe a striking realisation that occurred following a particularly intense session with Jayne, one in which I felt I had spoken far more than usual. Jayne had been particularly grateful for my engagement in her dilemma. I understood that in gaining my agreement to see her more frequently – in order to help her to make a decision – Jayne was recruiting me into a similar role to that played both by David and by Michael – one which allows her to be led and guided by the opinions and advice of another, in order to avoid making her own choices and acknowledging her freedom. I was struck by the degree to which I somehow had been drawn unconsciously into acquiescing to this, and how this had the impact of taking me away from a therapeutic method and established way of working. This was a helpful reflection, which enabled me to address directly with the patient her role in the unfolding transference relationship.

In the next session I put it to Jayne that she had wanted me to make decisions for her, and that this was also what happened in her relationships with the two men – that she allowed them to express their wish for her, and in so doing she was able to avoid the anguish of making a decision. This interpretation felt true to Jayne, and it offered her some temporary relief in the moment. She was able to see that whenever she experienced a set of competing demands from the wishes of others, this placed her in a terrible position and caused exhaustion, because she was unable to be all things to all the people she was trying to please.

Unable to be-for-herself, she sought out others to tell her what to do to resolve the conflict. She could see that when she was doing this with me, she was able to take some comfort from being-for-me, and she could acknowledge that she was, as a consequence, avoiding her own responsibility and freedom. It became clear that this pattern of being-for-others had led her to roles and relationships that had taken her so far away from herself that she felt disconnected from herself. Once this understanding had been established, we were able to begin the work of understanding what propelled her towards such a mode of being. The focus of the work then changed and she was able to begin the process of taking some responsibility for her therapy and for herself.

Analysis

The vignette describes the experience for the therapist of encountering a defensive echoist, whose primary mode of Being is for others and not for herself. It can be seen how the initial dilemma was brought about by an "other" whom the patient felt the compulsion to please. Jayne made a habit of being-for-others in the world and was unable to take responsibility for her choices and therefore sought out others to make them for her. This can be observed directly in terms of the role into which she attempted to recruit the therapist. In psychoanalytic terms we might also think about what is taking place in terms of projective processes. Jayne was available to others and their wishes or feelings, and was like a passive, permeable membrane into which projections could be pushed, and within which the wishes of others could be felt and met by her as an echoist.

At this point it is important to elaborate a little on what I introduced in the previous chapter concerning Sartre's notion of being-for-others as a specific defence in the echoist. For Sartre, the being-for-others is, for everyone, an ontological consequence of being-in-the-world with others. This state of Being is one in which our subjectivity is confronted through observing ourselves being *seen* by the Other. Sartre goes on to describe the annihilating nature of the gaze of the Other, as we are forced into the role of object in the eyes of the Other's subjectivity, and in that moment we lose our subjective position in the world and, indeed, in our own eyes – for we cannot make others see us as we might wish to be seen. It is worth pointing out here that I am making a distinction between Sartre's use of the term as an ontological state of being, to which we are all subjected, and my own specific use of it, in relation to the echoist, as a psychic defence.

Alice Holzhey-Kunz draws attention to this internal conflict brought about by Being-for-others. She describes how the individual's experience of seeing himself not as he sees himself but as the other wishes to see him, is an ambivalent one. She goes on to say:

> I suffer not only from the Other's freedom but also from my own freedom. This is why I need the Other, although he makes me anxious. He is to remove the burden of responsibility for my own life or at least to share it with me.
>
> (Holzhey-Kunz, 2014, p. 88)

This passage describes the type of conflict that is experienced as a result of the ontological conditions of existence for the human being, who must constantly succumb to the subjectivity of the other, and must regain his own subjectivity through an act of will. It is this experience that enables him to share responsibility for existence with others and relieves him of the burden of total responsibility. Thus, in doing so, the use of what Heidegger (1962, p. 158) refers to as "everydayness" relieves the ordinary individual of some of the ontological burden of being. In my experience this differs somewhat for both the echoist and the narcissist, who seem to operate a different system of defences to those of the ordinary individual, in relation to the phenomenon of the Other. Because the ordinary individual is not "specially sensitive", in the way that Holzhey-Kunz describes, she is not subjected to the same degree of ontological *angst* when presented with the other, as she has something of a cultural "shield" in place, which enables her to experience this as part of the everyday. The "specially sensitive" individual suffers more painfully with this unmediated ontological experience, and often she feels shame as a result of being seen, and, accordingly, she experiences traumatising anxiety in taking responsibility for her own freedoms.

Narcissistic defences against the ontological anxiety of The Look

As I describe in Chapter Two, the narcissist's colonisation of others as objects for himself, to some degree provides a narcissistic shield, which protects him from the pain and conflict of The Look, because in his mind he is not exposed to the potentially annihilating experience of The Look as long as he can maintain the illusion in his mind that there are no others. Neither does he suffer from the freedom of the other to *see* him. He can, through projective identification, make others see him as he wishes to be seen, at least to some degree; even then, however, in his mind these others do not hold the position of beings-for-themselves or subjects in their own right, because he sees them as beings-for-him. The gaze of the Other, if it is different from his own, has the effect either of being perceived to accord with the narcissist's view of himself, or else made not to matter, because the validity of the other as a subject is not allowed in the narcissistic organisation of the mind. The look of the other, therefore, does not produce the same level of anxiety or conflict for the narcissistic individual, as long as his narcissistic shield against relating to the other as an individual, separate from himself, remains in place. The reasons for this, and the way in which one approaches the difficulty of working with it clinically, are interesting but not a subject that can be taken further in this book. More relevant is what happens specifically in the case of the echoist.

Echoistic defences against ontological anxiety of The Look

In Sartre's sense of the term being-for-others, the word "for" refers to an ontological, and therefore unavoidable, state of having to share the world with others. In other words, our relational state is a consequence of being-in-the-world with others and this produces both anxiety and conflict. For the echoist, being-for-the-other is not simply an ontological condition of her existence, but a way of avoiding being-for-herself, and thereby avoiding her freedoms and responsibilities. The echoist remains subjected to the same ontological conditions as Sartre's individual, but, in common with the narcissist, she has in place a defence against this conflict. But in her case, and directly in opposition to the narcissist, she defends by substituting, in her mind, her own subjectivity for that of the other. Unlike Sartre's individual she is not plagued by her own freedom, and the struggle to maintain this in light of the other's freedom. Instead she hands both her own freedom and responsibility over to the other, as a way of avoiding being-for-herself. The narcissist, therefore, denies the freedom of the other and the echoist denies her own, and both manage to avoid the conflict of the exposure to the ontological state of being-for-others, in the sense described by Sartre, and to which Holzhey-Kunz also draws attention.

Whereas the narcissist experiences others as an extension of himself, we can extrapolate that the echoist sees herself as an extension of the narcissist, in which he is the subject and she is one of his objects. In this sense, the echoist is extremely permeable to the wishes and feelings of others and has, as we have seen above, learned to adapt herself to meet these. It is important to acknowledge how this might be experienced in the clinical situation and what the therapist might expect to encounter and feel, to alert her to this phenomenon of the echoist, rather than mistaking her for a presentation with which we are more familiar.

The "as-if" personality

My first thought on encountering Jayne was that she might conform to what has been classified in the psychoanalytic literature as an "as-if" personality. This term was introduced by Helene Deutsch (1942), who reported a series of cases in which, as she put it, "the individual's emotional relationship to the outside world and to his own ego appears impoverished or absent". In the paper she is concerned with "conditions bearing a close relationship to depersonalization but differing from it in that they were not perceived as disturbances by the patient himself". She uses her observations to demonstrate what she calls "a special type of personality", the "as-if" type. Using a case study, she writes of the "inescapable impression that the individual's whole relationship to life has something about it which is lacking in genuineness and yet outwardly runs along 'as if' it were complete."

Her patient appeared to adapt herself successfully to a variety of environments, teaching methods, and approaches with what Deutsch called "striking ease and speed". Her analyst was struck by the apparent normality and the ingenuity and creativity of the patient, along with her substantial intellectual abilities. Interestingly, it was through viewing the fruits of her creative labour in the form of a series of paintings made by the patient, that she became aware of what she described as a "repetition of a prototype without the slightest trace of originality". As a result of this, Deutsch was able to recognise that her patient conducted her relationships with others, "without the slightest trace of warmth … like the performance of an actor who is technically well trained but who lacks the necessary spark to make his impersonations true to life".

Deutsch went on to define the condition as a "real loss of object cathexis", making the interesting point that the lack of warmth brought about a dullness in her relationships. She also made the point that when a partner breaks off a relationship, the as-if individual tends to use her adaptive qualities immediately to seek out a new partner to replace the old, resulting in a renewed and repeated experience. Deutsch believed the as-if personality to be predisposed towards being morally unprincipled, and she felt that she could recognise them as the kinds of individuals who become attached to various groups and causes, and who serve to validate these through over-identification.

Britton (2003 pp. 147–149) refers to Deutsch's paper and makes two observations that are of relevance to my study of echoism. The first, from Winnicott (in Rodman, 1987) is how the as-if personality uses space in the consulting room as a type of transitional space, which is used not only as a way of keeping the analyst at a distance, but as a (not-self) space into which complete phantasies can be projected.

The form of relating being described would seem to offer little potential for insight or growth of the patient, and, as it stands, seems a clear contraindication for a therapeutic relationship. I do not, however, experience this with my echoistic patients, even when the space feels impenetrable and the patient seems on first impression to be unreachable. In the case of Jayne, her wish to identify with me might well, at first sight, appear to be an as-if presentation, but her ability to recognise her own absence of being-for-herself was both acknowledged and accepted.

The second point is that Britton has come to believe this type of presentation, the as-if, to be a third type of narcissistic disorder (alongside thin-skinned and thick-skinned narcissism). In Deutsch's case studies, where there are omnipotent identifications created as part of an ego-ideal that cannot be met by the ego of the patient, the as-if patient seeks the other – in the form of a series of replaceable partners – to realise this aspect of herself externally, as a way of propping up her omnipotent phantasies through identification with the other's ideal-ego. Britton refers to this phenomenon and gives examples of what he calls "twin-souls" (Britton, in Steiner, 2008, p. 22–34).

For the as-if patient, the idealised image of -the self becomes crushed when it cannot be sustained, and the patient resorts to weeping and rage, as described in Deutsch's paper. This behaviour is reminiscent both of the borderline patient and the thin-skinned narcissist when the self-image is punctured. It does not, however, describe the phenomenological encounter with Jayne, nor with the kind of patient I have come to call the echoist, whose lack of self is both known and (frequently) apologised for, rather than idealised.

Deutsch also writes of the suggestibility of as-if patients who might be incited to perform criminal acts, and she describes the patient giving off what she calls "an air of negative goodness, or mild amiability which, however, is readily convertible to evil". This suggestibility and potential for corruption corresponds strongly to that of the self-destructive echoist (described in detail in Chapter Five) who can be "acted-through" by a malignant narcissist.[1] We might easily mistake the defensive echoist's mild amiability for that of the as-if personality, and assume therefore that it too can be converted to malignancy. In my clinical experience, however, I have found the most evident negative trait in the defensive echoist to

1 See Chapter Ten.

be resentment, usually towards her narcissistic partner, or the others whom she has chosen to be-for. I understand this to be another form of denial for her own responsibility in the relationship, but not one easily convertible to destructiveness. Instead, what we are more likely to observe is an acting out of this resentment as a silent revenge against the narcissist. This can take the form of having secrets or indulging wishes, which might on the surface appear to correspond to the entitlement mentality of the narcissist, but is, in fact, something quite different. The following short vignette provides an example.

Vignette 4: Dr L

The patient, Dr L, aged forty-eight, was an attractive, successful scientist, who had spent his adult life with a narcissistic and bullying husband, Mr L, a CEO of a large corporation. The patient's attractiveness was prized by his husband and taken as a reflection of his own importance and power, and Dr L was expected to appear well-dressed and handsome whenever they were in public together. While he tried to perform this role to the best of his ability, he was often left feeling that he "never quite succeeded in pulling it off" as Mr L might wish him to. At the same time, Mr L's envy of Dr L's intelligence and natural curiosity resulted in the patient silencing himself habitually, silencing his thoughts and opinions to avoid his partner's sneering comments and aggressive reactions. As the relationship had evolved he had become more and more timid and would spend long periods of time unable to speak, for fear of provoking an attack, while trying to conform to the roles his husband prescribed for him.

Dr L described how he had, over the years, succumbed to Mr L's wishes, and had tried to adapt himself to how he felt his husband wanted him to be. His resentment had grown over the years and he shared with the therapist accounts of his silent acts of revenge, which he described as his "little secrets". These took the form of clandestine liaisons with lovers, smoking when he was away from his husband, and other activities that, while satisfying his need to have something for himself, plagued him with growing fear of discovery and abandonment. When some of these activities were, inevitably, discovered, Dr L was told by his husband that he had to go into therapy, and he found a suitable therapist *for* him. This very fact was further evidence of Dr L's echoism.

Analysis

Because the defensive echoist is more libidinal[2] than the as-if personality, the narcissist, or the self-destructive echoist, she is more likely to act out a wish for an affirmation of the self that she knows has been denied her in the relationship, even if it must be done secretly. This patient's wish to engage the therapist as a

---

2 In the sense of the term used by Rosenfeld (1971) and Britton (2003).

"co-conspirator" might have been understood as a wish to enlist the therapist, through projective identification, into a sense of narcissistic entitlement. Instead, I interpreted that it was necessary for him to share his "little secrets" as part of a (resistive) life force, so that they could be understood, and his entitlement to having a life of his own, could be acknowledged.

In time, this patient might be liberated from having to act out his rebellion against his internal and external object in ways that are hidden, and instead become able to take responsibility in a way that can be lived out openly. This pattern of relating must not be interpreted as narcissistic. Such a patient is not a narcissist, and neither is he a "twin narcissist". He is relating to a narcissist and cannot have any sense of a self. There is insufficient space in a relationship to a narcissist for him to have a self, and so his little acts of resistance, or revenge, are the only things that affirm to him that he is a self.

Growth potential in the defensive echoist

The feeling that the patient needs more and more from the therapist is also more observable in the defensive echoist, who seeks out the other to know how to be for them. She also tries to read ahead, uses incomplete sentences out of fear that they will be judged by the therapist, and seeks to please both the therapist and others in order to feel acceptable. She is, however, open to relating, and in my experience this is because a life source is sought out, and human relating can, to some degree, be achieved. When this is the case there is good potential for relationships and attachments. With the self-destructive echoist, however, there is a tendency to try to undermine or to destroy the therapeutic relationship, a feature which she shares with the destructive narcissist and which I describe in the next chapter.

Ontic fears and Ontological anxieties

The difficulty for the therapist is how to avoid being-for the echoist in a way that allows her own defences to stop the patient from being for-herself. I would argue that because the echoist not only seeks out narcissists, but attempts to recruit the therapist into this role, a distinction needs constantly to be drawn between me and not-me for the patient. This involves interpreting both the transference and the way the patient views external relationships with others. As we can see in the vignette below, this can have the impact of creating terrible anxiety for the patient, and it is in regard to this that it is so very helpful, necessary in fact, to draw upon writings and theories from existential and Daseinsanalytic schools in order to make distinctions between ontic fears, which can be acted upon through specific actions, and ontological anxieties, which have to be "*be-ed*[3] with" and which I go on to discuss later in more depth.

---

3 Bion too has used this term, which feels the most appropriate, even though the construction is not grammatically correct.

Vignette 5: Mary

A female patient, Mary, thirty-five years old and single, who had been attending twice-weekly therapy for just six weeks before the summer break, returned for her first session. There were many long silences, which, because of my awareness that the echoist looks to others to fill them, I did not. I wanted our space to be one in which she could hear her own-voice, but she grew increasingly nervous at not being able to know what I might want her to talk about, or how to use the session. She said that she did not know what to bring, and did I have anything. I asked her what she imagined. She looked very alarmed, and said she was feeling anxious and that she had disappeared from the room.

I tried to stay with her anxiety and to explore where she felt she had gone and what it might be that felt so painful to be with. She became frustrated with me and then with herself. She didn't know. She thought that she should probably bring me up to date with what she had been doing in the summer, and then I would have some questions for her. She seemed relieved by this decision, and filled the rest of the session with descriptions of the events of the summer, and "confessions" that she had "fallen into old patterns" of adapting herself to how she felt others wanted her to be.

Analysis

This session illustrates the patient's retreat into silence, and her wish for the other to fill the space left by her. On further exploration it became evident that the patient had somehow "lost her voice" over the summer and she had forgotten how she usually communicates with her therapist. The fear that she might say the "wrong thing", or that she would be judged for not saying the *perfect* thing, seemed to put her in touch with what felt like an ontological guilt for her own existence as she "disappeared from the room", and she was quite literally struck dumb as a result. One characteristic aspect of the patient's communications was what seemed like incoherent stops and starts, different thoughts and ideas, which petered out to nothing, leaving the patient feeling deflated and resentful towards the therapist who refused to speak for her.

While this patient has features of the as-if personality described above, she showed no narcissism in her idea of herself either in relation to the therapist or in relation to external others. What became evident through further sessions was the presence of an internal voice, which was much louder than the patient's own little voice, and this judged not just her words, but often her thoughts, before she even had a chance to utter them. This judgement was felt, through projective identification, to belong to the therapist, reinforcing the patient's fear that whatever she said would be judged and found unacceptable. I go on to discuss the role of projective identification and introjective identification later in the book, but for the purpose of this chapter it is important to state the following: the projections into the therapist are in this case *not* those of the patient, but of an internal superego object, who pretends to have authority over the patient to protect her from the criticisms of others. I go on to describe this in far more detail in Chapter Six, but suffice it to say, once the patient was made aware of the presence of this object's critical voice, and was able to communicate its impact on her own voice, much of the emptiness that had felt like an impasse, was able to be interpreted and understood in a way that freed her to relate to her therapist.

Against what is the defensive echoist defending?

In the final part of this chapter I interrogate the use of my own term "defensive" as a description for this type of echoism, as opposed to the more self-destructive form that I describe in the next chapter. I am therefore asking the question: against what is the echoist defending? I believe that she is defending against severe anxieties that can be understood from both psychoanalytic and existential perspectives.

From a psychoanalytic point of view, we are relatively familiar with the defences operated by narcissists. They show us their need, for example, to defend against anything that stimulates their envy. Defences are frequently mobilised against reality itself, through the use of paranoid-schizoid mechanisms, including splitting and projective identification, which results in the avoidance of perceiving the other as separate. In my experience, the echoist is usually found in a more depressive state, and, in fact, she is not as removed from reality as the narcissist, except when she is proffering the narcissist's view.

I have frequently found defensive echoistic patients to be extremely anxious that I will be, or have been, harmed by their narcissistic object, as well as by real or supposed bad parts of themselves. This can be aroused when the patient is told by her object that her therapist will certainly abandon her if she brings all of herself to her. In this case, the internal narcissistic object will appear to be protecting its host from the dread of being abandoned, whilst, in all likelihood, really functioning to prevent a more complete form of relating that might be possible in the therapeutic relationship, leading to potential integration and growth – an eventuality most hated by the narcissistic object.

The defensive echoist also experiences anxiety in feeling that she does not have the strength to protect the therapist, and the therapeutic couple, and that she cannot stand up to the object. This is experienced in the transference as the patient feeling ashamed that they are unable to protect the therapist and the therapeutic relationship from violent attacks.

If and when the defensive echoist is able to achieve a degree of liberation from the power of her narcissistic object, this creates a further, and more conscious, anxiety that she has become narcissistic herself. In having been enabled to experience a self, defensive echoists fear that they have become grandiose and omnipotent themselves, and because they have spent so much of their life experiencing the destructive harm caused by such an object, they become subject to the depressive pain of now feeling that they are a cause of suffering to others. This is another defence against growth, and it accords with Bion's (1965, p. 156) conviction that psychic growth is the most feared event because it is felt to be indistinguishable from megalomania.[4]

A common description given by the defensive echoist is of a relationship with a narcissistic object that keeps her barely alive,[5] feeding off her without letting her have a voice and a life of her own. It can be recognised as the real-life counterpart to the curse of Hera.

A further defence can be observed in the patient who has been in a relationship with a narcissistic partner. She will often seek advice and spend much of the sessions talking incessantly about him, and making him the focus of them. In so doing, she can avoid acknowledging her lack of an own-voice, and the severe anguish and dread arising from this. In fact, it is a central thesis of this book that such an anxiety is the prime cause of the hole in the literature in regard to echoism.

From the existential perspective there exists a defence against being a self and having an own-voice. The defensive echoist frequently presents as playing no active part in her relationship to the narcissist, considering herself to be a victim, and it manifests as a further defence against possessing and using her own voice. Because she is usually, on entering therapy, so enmeshed in her role in this dynamic, she can use resentment and blame to defend against acknowledging having at least some elements of a self with which she plays her part, and, as long as she does so, she can see herself only as subjected to *his* behaviour rather than contributing to it.

This defence against taking at least some responsibility for the reaction of the other is common, and it can take years of therapy to understand and effect any change. It is a defence that may also be used by individuals who are not necessarily in relationships with narcissists, but who recruit others into narcissistic roles and behaviours through their unwillingness to acknowledge their own being-in-the-world.

I experience the defensive echoist as fearing to make a footprint and unable to take responsibility for her own freedom and choices, and yet, even in her unconscious choice to be-for-another, it is she who undeniably makes the footprint at the instigation of the other. If the patient can be helped to understand this at some

---

4 "The transformation that involves 'becoming' is felt as inseparable from becoming God, ultimate reality, the First Cause. The 'dark night' pain is fear of megalomania. This fear inhibits acceptance of being responsible, that is mature, because it appears to involve being God, being the First Cause, being ultimate reality with a pain that can be, though inadequately, expressed by 'megalomania'".

5 This description of a person being reduced and kept barely alive, at the lowest possible level of existence, is strikingly close to the formulation of the death instinct in the writings of the British Kleinian analyst, Michael Feldman. "While there is certainly the threat of annihilation, it is important that his objects (including his analyst) remain just alive" (2003, p. 101). Feldman mentions Joseph's (1982) description of a state of near-death, in which "life is allowed to continue just so long as nothing is really alive and functioning".

point in the therapy, it can enable her to adopt more of a courageous attitude in freeing herself to act on her own wishes, rather than those of others.

Once she is able to remove herself from the grip of the narcissistic object, with its skewed positions on the world, she experiences and begins to display the libidinal wish to exist and to be in relationship to others. I would add, however, that the echoist also perceives the internal narcissistic object as protecting her from relating to others in a way that she fears they may find unacceptable. Whenever she is subjected to this anxiety it can lead her to reinforce and renew her alliance with the object from which she is trying to emancipate herself.

I had considered using the term "defended" as opposed to "defensive", as I felt her silence to be a form of defence that felt like armour, but I settled on the term "defensive", partly because it fits with the descriptions of narcissism that bear some resemblance to it at an initial glance, and because I think the term itself suggests more of an active defensiveness in the echoist than is implied by the term defended.

Chapter 5

Hosts and henchmen
The self-destructive echoist

> There's my life, why not, it is one, if you like, if you must, I don't say no, this evening. There has to be one, it seems, once there is speech, no need of a story, a story is not compulsory, just a life, that's the mistake I made, one of the mistakes, to have wanted a story for myself.
>
> Samuel Beckett, *Texts for Nothing*, No: 4., 1967

In this chapter, having previously defined the self-destructive echoist, I return to the myth, and focus on the feelings of resentment felt by Echo as Narcissus dies, and I explain the relevance of this to the clinical situation. I describe how I have come to understand the self-destructive echoist's way of Being in terms of her active introjection of the other, through a process that I illustrate through clinical vignettes.

Unlike the defensive echoist, who often experiences herself as a passive, permeable membrane into which projections are pushed, the self-destructive echoist, in order to animate her own barely existent being, draws the other into herself, becoming what I call a being-through-others. I suggest that this state of non-existence is, perhaps, the most painful of all states, and postulate that the self-destructive echoist will actively introject any object or life force available as a way of avoiding the pain of it. I then proceed to extrapolate further how the acknowledgment and experience of this in the clinical situation may be so unbearable for both patient and therapist, that evasion has ensued as a way of protecting them both. This relates to Strachey's seminal paper (1934, p. 158), where he discusses the difficulties for the analyst in the clinical situation in giving mutative interpretations, and it may form part of the explanation for why echoism has, until recently, had no place in psychoanalytic writing and theory.

It was, essentially, the experience of difficulty in being with a self-destructive echoist, and feeling that I was failing in every sense, that first led me to recognise the phenomenon of echoism as specific and distinct from narcissism, in spite of the presence of certain traits in the patient that appeared to be narcissistic. I write more about this in Chapter Six on mistaken identity, but for the purpose of this chapter I will be using a number of different theoretical models that help to explain or orient the therapist towards a particularly extreme and malignant form of echoism, which I describe as self-destructive.

Although this form of echoism is destructive to others, and can be experienced as destructive to the relationship between the therapist and the patient – for reasons that I go on to describe – it is the Being of the echoist herself that is destroyed repeatedly through a process of parasitism, and an experience of anxiety, which I refer to as "life anxiety", that keeps her imprisoned in this position. The chapter is called "Hosts and Henchmen"; the former refers to the idea of the echoist as host to the parasitic object, while the latter describes a situation in which the echoist acts as a henchman or conduit through which malignancy and narcissistic behaviours are projected.

The therapist's experience of projective processes

Vignette 6: Mrs P

The patient, Mrs P, came to me following an initial couples session, which she had attended with Mr P, her narcissistic husband, following the discovery of his recent affair, which revealed that it was, in fact, the latest in a sequence throughout their twelve-year marriage. He also had engaged in hedonistic behaviour on a regular basis, including the use of drugs, alcohol, and prostitution. In the session, he said he expected that they would be able to work towards healing the rift between them by "drawing a line under what had happened", and to start afresh. When asked what she felt, Mrs P looked heavenward and shook her head, silently appealing to me, but unable to express any wish of her own. I was unwilling to work with them as a couple on this basis, and he began therapy with an addictions counsellor while I agreed to see Mrs P for individual work.

In the first few months of therapy, Mrs P expressed her feelings of grief, and she began to tell me about the shame that she felt. She spent much of the session crying, and almost all of each session speaking about her husband, with whom she hoped to rebuild a trusting relationship. She phantasised and tormented herself with images of his infidelity, having found receipts from sex shops and lingerie sales, and she felt full of resentment towards him. She also described his unwillingness to speak with her about what had happened, or about his addiction treatment, and she became infuriated as the sessions continued, saying that although she was seeing me on a regular basis, nothing seemed to be changing in her life.

I found myself becoming frustrated in my wish to help her, and I felt inclined to fill the space left by her in the sessions, and to respond to her desperate attempts to pull me into telling her how she should behave with him. As each session finished I felt exhausted and as if I had barely given the patient enough ("enough what?" I wondered) to last until she got out of the door. I was drained and filled with feelings of inadequacy. I found myself frequently going over the time boundaries by more than a minute or two, and she became accusatory and resentful towards me. I began to wonder whether she too was a narcissist, because her behaviour felt full of entitlement and her wishes were expressed as needs. At this stage, my more cursory understanding of narcissism actually misled me temporarily, and I wonder whether I might have continued to follow this line of thought for some time, had I not met her husband and observed first-hand how she became silent in response to his narcissism.

Analysis

I was drawn back to thinking about the myth of Echo and Narcissus, and was struck again by the end of the myth in which Echo, watching the decline of Narcissus, is filled with angry resentment. I was reminded of my experience with Mrs P, when I had resisted filling the space, and particularly when she felt abandoned by me at the end of sessions. I was felt to be absent by the patient whenever I was not actively providing something. This seemed to trigger her resentment towards me, and made me feel I was somehow not giving the patient enough of something to last until she came back to see me. For both of us it caused an anxiety that I have since understood to be ontological in nature, though it was expressed in concrete terms through her complaints that nothing was changing, and that this was somehow felt, by both of us, to be my fault.

On considering what it might be that she could not have enough of, I was forced to consider my own countertransference, in order to attempt to understand what it was that I was trying to give her. I felt dismay at the extent to which my interventions were non-therapeutic. They seemed to be based upon my feelings of anger towards the narcissistic partner, while Mrs P seemed to feel a rather lacklustre self-pity and some resentment. I questioned why I might be feeling these feelings on her behalf, and – rather than trying to understand this with her – I found myself making suggestions as to how she might respond to him with a voice that could be heard to be resistant and powerful. It was a painful recognition when I realised that I was unconsciously trying to provide a voice for her to repeat and to echo, thereby re-enacting the narcissistic dynamic in which she found herself at home.

On further examination, and in further reading on projective identification, I assumed initially that the feelings of anger I felt must be those being projected into me by the patient, and accounts in the literature seemed to confirm this. It was in further questioning – of how these theories matched my experiences with my patient – that I was forced to notice something incongruous.

My experience of being with narcissistic patients often left me with the feeling that there was no space for me and that I was somehow unnecessary in the session – as if the narcissist had enough of a *self* for both of us. In the case of the echoist, I realised I felt that *I* had to provide enough self for both of us.

Mrs P, it felt to me, could not rouse enough of a self to exist at all in the sessions, and was somehow drawing the life out of me in order to provide a life source for her. (This view was further endorsed once I had discovered the presence of an ego-destructive object in all the echoists I have treated, and which I discuss in depth in the next chapter). For the purpose of this research, however, at the point at which I had this experience, I was drawn to some of Melanie Klein's thinking, in which she states that all forms of projection are followed by re-introjection.

Concerning introjection and projection, Klein quotes Freud (1915c, p. 135–136) as follows:

> Under the dominance of the pleasure principle a further development now takes place in the ego. In so far as the objects which are presented to it are sources of pleasure, it takes them into itself, 'introjects' them (to use Ferenczi's [1909] term); and, on the other hand, it expels whatever within itself becomes a cause of unpleasure....
>
> (the mechanism of projection).

Klein writes of the alternation between introjection and projection:

> When, as a small child, he first begins to introject his objects – and these, it must be remembered, are only very vaguely known to him and mainly through their separate organs – his fear of those introjected objects sets in motion the mechanisms of ejection and projection, as we have already seen; and there now follows a reciprocal action between projection and introjection, which seems to be of fundamental importance not only for the formation of his super-ego but for the development of his object-relations to persons and his adaptation to reality. The steady and continual urge he is under to project his terrifying identifications on to his objects results, it would seem, in an increased impulse to repeat the process of introjection again and again, and is thus itself a decisive factor in the evolution of his relationship to objects.
>
> (Klein, 1932, p. 202)

Klein (1955), in her paper "On Identification", includes a description of the internalisation of the external object as a defence against separation and as part of the developmental process.

Klein's description of a process in which introjection is followed by projection felt truer to my experience with my patient than the other way around but, in the case of Mrs P, it did not seem to correspond to Klein's description of a developmental process, as the patient was unable to keep anything nourishing that she appeared to introject from me. As I sensed her feelings of resentment at the end of each session, I began to feel that two things were happening, which I go on to explain. The first was that in echoism the more common order of the processes of projective identification followed by re-introjection was somehow reversed. And second, that whatever was being pulled out of me and into the patient was somehow being consumed before she had a chance to use it.

This led me to consider the idea of a consuming part of the patient, or else something within the patient, that prohibited any growth and which functioned as a parasite. This pointed to the conclusion that the patient must in some way be acting as a host to the parasite. It was this rather intuitive leap that led to further reading and discoveries in the clinical work, which I will attempt to convey.

Parasitism

Psychoanalyst Herbert Rosenfeld identified parasitical processes in his patients, which he felt as the overwhelming need of the patient to actualise an unconscious belief that it was possible to inhabit his analyst in order to live out a continuous existence inside him. In the early 1960s his colleague Wilfred Bion had described clinical interactions showing how functions of the mind could themselves be projected wholesale into the analyst, who was then supposed to carry out those functions for the patient (1962, p. 21).

By 1970 Rosenfeld was applying Bion's findings to his own work, observing how his patients, in operating powerful phantasies of parasitism, expected their analyst to function as the patient's own mind (1970, p. 8). Rosenfeld experienced just how difficult and painful it was to be with patients so depleted of their own agency, vitality, and capacity to function in the relationship. Of this experience he wrote that the parasitic patient relies entirely on the analyst,

> … often making him responsible for his entire life. He generally behaves in an extremely passive, silent and sluggish manner, demanding everything and giving nothing in return. This state can be extremely chronic and the analytic work is often minimal.
>
> (p. 9)

Here Rosenfeld could be describing an echoistic patient, especially as he went on to describe a similar patient who likened himself to an infant hardly made of living matter at all, resembling a stone that was so heavy and lacking its own life that his analyst would cast him aside.

We are reminded strikingly of Echo's predicament in the myth, described in Chapter One:

> As he (Narcissus) pulls away, Echo reaches and clings all the more, knowing that without him she will be again reduced to a non-being. She is left to pine, and as she does the life seeps out of her and her skin and bones meld into the rocks and shrubs where she lies, leaving her barely distinguishable from these insentient beings with whom she shares her existence.

Rosenfeld's patient clearly and accurately felt that he was sapping the life from his helper, who experienced him truly as an unrewarding and unalive "dead weight". That his analyst did, in fact, experience him in this way is shown by Rosenfeld's ambiguous but revealing remark in the paper:

> I often have the impression that patients like the one who I described, who experience themselves as dead, and are often experienced by the analyst as

so inactive that they might as well be dead, use their analyst's aliveness as a means of survival.

(My emphasis)

The patient would come to life, fleetingly and sporadically, but Rosenfeld felt, originally, that the failure to thrive after having gained some semblance of life through his phantasy of occupying his analyst, resulted from the patient's own hostile, envious feelings at being less alive than his analyst. Rosenfeld attributed this to the aggressive component of his patient's hostility, and the defensive component of the patient's requirement to avoid pain.

I am going to explore Rosenfeld's formulation further, in order to suggest an alternative possibility, one which I believe throws some light on the value of distinguishing between echoistic and narcissistic processes in the clinical situation.

Returning to Rosenfeld's account, it struck me that after understanding his patient to be in such a severely depleted and deadened state that he simply could not feel alive without drawing on the life force of his analyst, he nevertheless concluded that the subsequent failure of growth and life in his patient reflected the latent hostility and envy of the patient – aggression thought to be caused by, and directed against, the liveliness of the analyst and the treatment itself. He wrote that "[i]t is the patient's latent hostility that is responsible for preventing the patient from getting more than minimal help or satisfaction from the analysis".

A year later, Rosenfeld was to write that a situation similar to the one that he had observed in his 1970 paper could be brought about by the silent operation of what he called "omnipotent destructive parts of the self". It is worth noting at this point that what Rosenfeld described in the 1971 paper as destructively omnipotent parts of the self, are more commonly encountered in the echoist as destructive narcissistic objects *occupying* the self.

These entities, wrote Rosenfeld,

> are directed both against any positive libidinal object relationship and any libidinal part of the self which experiences need for an object and the desire to depend on it. The destructive omnipotent parts of the self often remain disguised or they may be silent and split off, which obscures their existence and gives the impression that they have no relationship to the external world. In fact they have a very powerful effect in preventing dependent object relations and in keeping external objects permanently devalued.
>
> (1971, p. 173)

Under the conditions of which Rosenfeld had now become aware, he was less inclined to identify the patient's own envious hatred of the analyst's life-instinct and capability as the source of the deadening of the analysis. The emphasis had moved, at least in some cases, to the possibility that the potential lifeline between analyst and patient could be threatened by a hidden, parasitic, omnipotent internal object.

Rosenfeld had undergone a shift in his thinking, from his original understanding in which he considered the patient to be functioning parasitically in occupying the analyst, to regarding the patient as host to a parasitical internal object. Rosenfeld now recognised the profoundly deadening effect on the analysis as seen in this revised formulation, and in particular the effects on the patient himself, who, as host, experiences the destructive type of colonisation that takes place when in the grip of such a parasite.

It is interesting to note that Rosenfeld went on to say that this process "accounts for the apparent indifference of the *narcissistic individual* towards external objects and the world" (my emphasis). It is this generalisation of the phenomena to narcissistic personalities that I feel may be unwarranted. I understand this as a leap that Rosenfeld has not fully substantiated by reference to the clinical experiences that he described, and that the situation corresponds much more closely and resonantly with the phenomena that I have encountered with *echoistic* patients than any experiences I have had with *narcissistic* patients.

When what Britton refers to as "triangular space" permits sufficiently careful observation of the total transference situation, we can perceive frequently, in the study of echoistic patients, that both therapist and patient are subjected to an experience of an internal narcissistic object that treats the patient's ego as its host. This object consumes for itself the vitality and mental resources of the individual that it colonises, increasing its own strength, influence, and scope.

By 1971, Rosenfeld was suggesting that the patient, in appearing "determined to satisfy a desire to die and to disappear into nothing", seemed to correspond to Freud's description of a "pure culture", or a "defusion", of the death instinct:

> … analytically one can observe that the state is caused by the activity of destructive envious parts of the self which become severely split off and defused from the libidinal caring self which seems to have disappeared. The whole self becomes temporarily identified with the destructive self, which aims to triumph over life and creativity represented by the parents and the analyst by destroying the dependent libidinal self experienced as the child.
>
> (Rosenfeld, 1971, p. 173)

Rosenfeld then took this idea further and related it to what he termed "narcissistic conditions". He stated:

> Generally the life and death instincts are mixed or fused in varying degrees, and Freud maintained that the instincts, meaning the life and death instincts, "hardly ever appear in 'a pure form'". While states of severe defusion of the instincts do resemble Freud's description of the unfused death instinct – for example, a wish to die or to withdraw into a state of nothingness – on detailed clinical examination we find that the death instinct cannot be observed in its original form, since it always becomes manifest as a destructive process

directed against objects and the self. These processes seem to operate in their most virulent form in severe narcissistic conditions.

(Ibid., p.169)

This general (and generalis*ing*) label, "narcissistic conditions", is both accurate and misleading. It is, of course, accurate, in that both narcissists and echoists suffer similar fates in their inability to relate to others, and as the vignettes indicate, there may be a presentation of certain narcissistic traits, such as entitlement, in both. The term is, however, a broad brushstroke, which does not take into account certain differences of which Rosenfeld himself was aware, but which he did not write about as distinct from a more general understanding of narcissism already in place.

We will see in Chapter Six how the ways in which Rosenfeld's ideas can be taken up may lend themselves to an over-inclusive and poorly discriminating use of the concept of narcissism, which then becomes a too readily available label to categorise anybody who demonstrates certain traits that may, in fact, be observed in both the narcissist and the echoist.

Some of Rosenfeld's detailed descriptions come very close to the clinical experiences described in this book, but because echoism was not recognised at the time, it came to be thought about within the extensive canon of writing on narcissism already published within psychoanalysis. Consequently, the echoistic patient's particular way of Being became caught up in the category signified by the term narcissistic conditions. Somewhat ironically, one consequence of this was that it had the unintended effect of colonising the echoist's individual experience in much the same way as the narcissist colonises his objects and the analyst, and the narcissistic object colonises its host.

Given that Rosenfeld was describing his patient as functioning at a very minimal level of existence, barely alive, and drawing his helper into a comparable near-death state of mind, another possible explanation is one that must be thought about from the perspective of ontological anxiety. It is clear from Rosenfeld's account that both patient and analyst were brought face to face with their own mortality and the unbearable anxiety resulting from this. It is helpful, therefore, to turn to the body of thinking taken up in Daseinsanalysis, in which the fact that human beings naturally shrink back from anxiety may well go some way to explaining why Rosenfeld, in his reference to the patient whom he described as one who "might as well be dead", interpreted destructive envy in the patient. I think we can infer, from Rosenfeld's way of expressing this, that he may well have had to endure extraordinarily difficult unconscious countertransference fears and wishes that the patient would indeed die. If we consider the role of ontological anxiety in this situation, in which powerful feelings of life and death have been stimulated, we would expect them to have been evoked in Rosenfeld. If so, an unconscious impulse to flee from it himself would constitute a natural defence against the *angst* evoked through being with such a lifeless patient, in relation to his own annihilation anxiety and the exposure to an existential sense of nothingness.

Interestingly, Rosenfeld himself was renowned in his later work for highlighting, often in the work of his colleagues, a serious kind of impasse, resulting from a natural defence against the pain aroused in the clinical encounter. We could speculate that the patient he described as one "who might as well be dead", may have produced unconscious anxiety too momentous to permit the attitude of negative capability to be sustained. Perhaps, at such moments, we are prone to misidentify phenomena by the pressure to identify it as the already-known. It seems possible that this may have been a factor in why Rosenfeld, in addressing the patient's anxiety in the absence of his own, appears in his 1970 description to cling to something known – theories of narcissism – rather than staying with the particularly painful individual experience.

In Chapters One and Ten, I refer to an experience of Bion's in which he seems momentarily to realise that there is an important part of the myth of Narcissus missing in his clinical understanding. Something seems to get in the way of seeing what that might be. Perhaps the nameless dread experienced by both patient and therapist, when they are closely in touch with the echoist's lifelessness, goes some way to explaining the reasons that have contributed to this phenomenon of somehow just missing it. The traditional literatures and their emphases are so compelling that many echoists consider themselves to be narcissists, in spite of their experiences at the hands of narcissistic parents and partners. I would argue that the self-destructive echoist is, at times, so identified with the parasitic object that there is no sense of a separate self that can exist without it.

In the following vignette, Anna, a patient who has been in therapy three times a week for two years, and who has some understanding of her internal relationship to a narcissistic object, made the link herself to the myth. She had been reading up on narcissism before coming into therapy, as she was trying to understand something of her relationship with a narcissistic parent. She had spoken of herself in relation to the characters in the myth in a number of sessions. She said that while she felt that she identified more with the character of Echo in the myth, in one session she reported an experience in which she felt intense envy, and described how she recognised this aspect in abundance in her narcissistic parent, and, on this basis, she considered some of her own feelings and judgements to be, characteristically, narcissistic.

Vignette 7: Anna

In the session, Anna spoke of a dream

> *in which she is having a drink with her brother and her best friend, who, after a while, begin kissing and talking together, getting on very well and leaving her out of the conversation. She feels jealous and upset that they are now closer together than she is with either of them, yet it is she who had brought them together. She is crying in the dream and is told that she is over-sensitive. She awakes whimpering like an animal, crying inside.*

She then spoke of how this dream to some degree paralleled an actual situation, in which she and two others, whom she had recently introduced to one another, had made her feel intense envy. She described having a meal with them during which, as they began speaking, she felt that everything they had to say was not only more relevant than what she had to say, but that if she were to speak she would somehow be spoiling the relationship. She described becoming physically self-conscious and blushing, and wanting to shrink, as a way of not wishing to draw further attention to herself, for fear that this might be seen. As the meal continued she began to feel intense resentment as well as a powerful sense of shame when her quietness was noticed and commented on by one of the others. She told me that in that moment she had felt powerful envy, and that this was the horrible and disgusting part of her that made her sure she was a narcissist.

Analysis

Whilst we can notice the more obvious Oedipal elements present in the dream, and in the events with which the patient associates (Anna feels excluded from the couple), the patient introduces and free-associates to the myth of Echo and Narcissus. It is in relation to this that we must, as Bion reminds us, also place our attention:

> Free association to a myth is the equivalent of giving the elements a value as if they were variables in a formula. The values are those that are relevant to a particular problem, and the particular problem is the personality of the person who produces the free associations. By attributing these values to the variables of the myth we understand that those qualities are, for that person, constantly conjoined.
>
> (Bion, 1992, p. 237)

I understood that there was something important to Anna in the myth of Echo and Narcissus that she wished to communicate to me. My attention was directed towards rage and envy as what I understood to be defences against the feelings of annihilation felt by Anna, described as she awoke whimpering like an animal.

Alice Holzhey-Kunz has highlighted what she describes as the analyst finding ways to listen to the ontological realm as well as to the ontic. I was reminded of what she described as "ontological guilt", a state in which the patient feels unable to accept her freedom (Holzhey-Kunz, 2017). It seemed to me that Anna, in the description of her experience, had felt unable to allow herself to speak, not least because she felt that what she had to say would be taking time away from the more important contributions of her companions. The feelings she described, of blushing and wishing to shrink out of existence, reminded me quite literally of a crushing of herself into a state of non-existence. I was present at that moment to the most dreadful feelings of deadness and annihilation, and this was felt not to have an intentional object, but was much closer to a state felt to be objectless, and of the human condition itself.

I interpreted that what she described felt closer to her own annihilation, from which envy had sprung as a product of seeing the others existing. At this point the patient burst into tears of pain and relief. She said: "That feels so true. It's not that I don't feel the envy and resentment, it's just that if they are the primary feelings, my object and I can use them as further ammunition to attack me with. I did feel annihilated, it feels shameful to admit, but I think the feelings of envy and resentment came after, and helped me to leave."

It struck me at this point that the envy, instead of being destructive for this patient, had been mobilised in such a way that it enabled her to retain a sense of self, so that she could leave without subjecting herself to further feelings of being annihilated by the experience.

This interpretation, which the patient then further interpreted, resulted in a shift in Anna that enabled her to attend her next two sessions without having lost her insight that she herself is not actually the narcissistic self or object, but is the conduit through which it expresses itself and the host from which it feeds, and also attacks. She understood that the result of such an on-going process is to keep her from having any growth of the tiny self that was very slowly trying to emerge and express itself, and was often felt to be evolving in our work, but which had been constantly consumed time and again whenever she left me.

The anxiety I felt when making the annihilation interpretation indicated to me that there was a psychological risk, but I felt it to be the only one that could relieve something of the anxiety of that which was, quite literally, unspeakable. It is what I believe Strachey was referring to when he described the giving of a mutative interpretation.

In his landmark 1934 paper, Strachey stated:

> there must be some quite special internal difficulty to be overcome by the analyst in giving interpretations. And this, I am sure, applies particularly to the giving of mutative interpretations. ... there is sometimes a lurking difficulty in the actual *giving* of the interpretation, for there seems to be a constant temptation for the analyst to do something else instead. He may ask questions, or he may give reassurances or advice or discourses upon theory, or he may give interpretations – but interpretations that are not mutative, extra-transference interpretations, interpretations that are non-immediate, or ambiguous, or inexact – or he may give two or more alternative interpretations simultaneously, or he may give interpretations and at the same time show his own scepticism about them. All of this strongly suggests that the giving of a mutative interpretation is a crucial act for the analyst as well as for the patient, and that he is exposing himself to some great danger in doing so.
>
> (1934, p. 158)

Like Rosenfeld, I was able to acknowledge the presence of envy in my patient, but I did not interpret this as the primary trait present, but as secondary to the feelings of annihilation. Holzhey-Kunz believes envy to be a necessary trait when working with patients whom she calls "reluctant philosophers" – those she considers to be specially sensitive or thin-skinned and permeable to the ontological facticity of their being and nothingness. These patients feel intense anxiety for living and taking space in the world. She argues that unlike the role of envy in narcissism, which is a destructive emotion, it can be a creative one for the reluctant philosopher (and, by association, the lifeless patient who is also presented in the echoist). I would add that because unconscious envy contains a wish to destroy or to possess something belonging to another, narcissism is the absolute defence against recognising envy, because the narcissist obliterates the idea that there is an object other than himself to be valued. This patient, however, is conscious of her own envy, and this in itself marks her out as different from the narcissistic patient. It is arguable that that this conscious awareness of envy in the echoist can manifest as the wish to authorise herself to take space in the world (as a self and a voice). In my experience the self-destructive echoist constantly avoids taking her space (living in the world) and making this wish manifest, but instead uses the life-source of another. In the clinical situation, this might be experienced by the therapist as being introjected by the patient (much as Rosenfeld describes in the earlier passage), in other words, having the life sucked out of them.

While it is clear from his account of the barely alive patient, that Rosenfeld, as both an expert and an authority on narcissism, was able to distinguish between very different presentations in the clinical work, it is less certain that the nuances have been fully taken up in writings that form part of his legacy. This may go some way to further understanding why echoism as a specific condition has until recently gone unrecognised.

In his discussions on narcissistic conditions Rosenfeld (1987) describes how projection and introjection are used by the narcissist to colonise the therapist:

> In the case of introjection the object becomes part of the self to such a degree that any separate identity or boundary between self and object is felt not to exist. In the case of projective identification parts of the self become so much part of the object, for example the mother, that the patient has the idea he possesses all the desirable qualities of the object – in fact that he is the object in these respects. I took the view that identification by introjection and by projection usually occurs simultaneously and emphasized that narcissistic omnipotent object relations are partly defensive against the recognition of the separateness of self and object.

(1987, p. 20)

My clinical experiences bear out very similar findings to those of Rosenfeld's, but Rosenfeld uses the ideas of introjective identification and projective identification interchangeably to describe a result in which the recognition of the separateness of the patient and analyst is obscured. He does not, however, distinguish, in the published account, between who is projecting into whom in this process.

The thick-skinned impenetrability of the narcissist was well known and documented by Rosenfeld. He was familiar with the difficulty posed to the analyst in giving interpretations that can be heard by the narcissist, noting how the narcissist will project into the analyst, and then introject anything good (including the analyst's interpretations), and will attribute all the value as coming from himself and not from the analyst. In the case of the echoist, however, the permeability of the patient is unmistakably different to that of the narcissist, and the willingness to take in the analyst's interpretations as her own thoughts and words can also result in a similar lack of separateness between subject and object. The difference, however, is that the narcissist claims responsibility and credit for anything positive, while the echoist can take responsibility for, and claim, nothing as her own. She is in this sense what I call a being-through-others.

Being-through-others

This term, being-through-others, links to the idea of a being-for-others in the specific way that I use the term to indicate a psychic defence in the echoist. In Chapter Four I describe how my use of the term being-for-others in relation to the echoist, is an extension of Sartre's use of the term as an ontological state common to all human beings. It is applied specifically to the defensive echoist's way of relating, wherein the echoist actively gives up her own wishes, thoughts, and choices, prioritising those of others. In the case of the being-through-others, however, the patient uses the life force of another as a substitute for her own – she does, in a sense, avoid living freely. In this situation, the echoist may do so completely consciously, particularly if she has had a narcissistic parent to whom she has adapted herself not simply to please, but to serve. What is experienced in the clinical situation is not just an internal introjected version of this in the form of the parasitic object described in the section above. It is a way of relating that can reveal itself through a series of relationships in which the self-destructive echoist is unable to take responsibility for any of her thoughts, words, or actions, because she does not recognise them as her own, nor does she feel any agency in expressing them; it is as if they must come out through a channel in which she sees herself as the conduit and not the agent. This may present in the form of telling the therapist what others say or think about her, rather than owning any thoughts of her own. Because she is quite literally a conduit for any projections, and because she is highly likely to have been in relationships with narcissists by virtue of her henchman-like orientation, it is not unusual for the therapist to hear words and thoughts that are actually coming from a narcissist (in the patient's internal or external worlds) and attribute them to the patient. The following vignette presents a patient who presented in a way that might easily have been interpreted as narcissistic.

Vignette 8: Jaz

Jaz, a married woman, employed as a pharmacist, was in her early forties. She came into therapy asking for an urgent appointment, saying she felt depressed and frustrated. Her relationship with her husband was breaking down and he, having felt that she was a bad influence on their three children, aged nine, twelve, and thirteen, had asked her to move out while she sorted herself out; he was giving her a last chance to address her behaviour. He had said that he found her destructive and aggressive, and that if she didn't attend to it they would have to separate permanently. She rearranged her assessment twice, then arrived late. When she asked for confirmation of my fees she said she had very little money to pay for therapy (which I thought surprising, given her profession) and she tried to negotiate with me. At the end of the assessment session she asked a series of questions in an attempt to go beyond the fifty-minute time boundary, and seemed reluctant to leave. Based upon this evidence, I wondered if she was the partner of a man who had decided to put a boundary in place and that this might be her narcissistic attempt to enlist my support against him. I suggested a second assessment session to determine whether I could find or reach a part of her with which I could work.

In her second assessment session, I became aware that the urgency of the request, the negotiating of fees, and the rearrangement of sessions were actually not at her instigation. The session proceeded as follows:

Jaz: I wanted to be on time and I've brought the money. I felt you were angry with me last time, that I had done something wrong. I kept remembering you saying that I seemed to think it would be OK for me to pay what I wanted and cancel appointments when I felt like it, with little regard for your time or work.

Therapist: That is what you heard me say.

Jaz: Yes. You did say that, didn't you? I hope I got that right. My husband asked me what you had said. I tried to say exactly what you had said. He was angry …

[Silence]

Jaz: He thinks I am planning on spending too much money on therapy. He wanted me to get some help and now he is angry that I came to you and he wants me to look for someone else. The times you mentioned that you are free for sessions are both times he goes to his club, and that means he would have to stay at home with the children. He likes to go to the club most evenings to wind down from the day. He thinks I could have found a cheaper way of getting help ... that I am wasting our money in coming to you when there is free counselling available through the GP, and he thinks it should be at times that would fit in better ...

Therapist: It seems you feel he is angry with you for not doing what he wants, and that I am angry with you because you understood from my comments that you had not behaved in a way that I found acceptable.

Jaz: Yes, it's dreadful really. I shouldn't have made him angry and I don't want you to be annoyed with me. I told him I would try to see if I could come at a different time, maybe early before I go to work in the morning. But maybe that is not possible for you?

Therapist: You have come in today and are trying to express a wish to see if we can make this work. I think you felt last time, that you were coming here with a set of conditions that you wanted me to meet and which you expressed as demands with some degree of entitlement.

Jaz: [Tearful] I'm sorry, I didn't mean … It's just that … I thought… My husband said … I'm …

Therapist: It feels difficult for you to finish a sentence, to be able to follow through on any of those wishes, expressed as demands …

Jaz: I feel like I'm disappearing …

[Long silence]

Therapist: I wonder if we look at what happened and try to see if we can understand what led you to that feeling that you were disappearing. I think it's a feeling you know well …

Jaz: Yes. I feel it a lot with my husband.

Therapist: When you made the provisional appointment and then rearranged the sessions and tried to negotiate the fees, you presented your demands as if they were coming from you. It seems that if I had gone along with them, your husband would have been pleased and you would not have experienced angry feelings from him or me.

Jaz: Well yes, that's what I was hoping at the time.

Therapist: And you wanted that so much that you delivered your wishes quite powerfully. And you hoped I would be suitably acquiescent that I would just agree.

Jaz: I can see how manipulative I have been …

[Silence – reaches for a tissue and weeps a little]

Jaz: Sorry I don't normally cry, my husband hates it when women cry. He says it's manipulative. I don't want to be manipulative any more.

Therapist: I think you felt that you had to express your husband's conditions as if they were your own … but when I did not simply accept them, you felt us both to be punishing you for not giving the right response. You spoke his words to me as if they were your own, and then my words to him.

[The patient nods and cries gently]

Therapist: It is hard to know what your own feelings and words are but you present the other person's as if they are yours, then you can't cope with the response, because you were not the originator of the thought or the demand.

Jaz: It's true … I couldn't take it, because I hadn't actually felt it, but when P said it, it sounded so reasonable …

Therapist: So, you disappear … Not being able to take responsibility for your words because they are in fact your husband's wishes, his thoughts, his demands, his words.

Jaz: It's true. I hadn't really seen that before. But he is so compelling and usually right and I can't say no to him. And he hates me to be weak … and here I am crying to you.

Therapist: Do you notice how as soon as I point out that you were not the originator of your own thoughts, you immediately serve a judgement or
criticism upon yourself. Is that your own view or is that also your
husband's I wonder?

Jaz: I don't know, my mum and sister say I'm strong when I'm not with
him …

Therapist: You are telling me about yourself through other people. I have no idea
what you actually feel about yourself.

Jaz: I don't know. But I do feel I have seen something today. And I would
like to keep coming. If you can see me. I know it is difficult and that
I might have to become a little stronger before I can go back to P and
say what I want.

Therapist: I think you feel you can say that to me, and to accept whatever
response I make to that, because that is your own wish.

Jaz: Yes. So will you work with me?

Analysis

The vignette illustrates the way in which the self-destructive echoist avoids
becoming a self in her own right, and attempts to recruit the therapist into the role
of narcissist. This is a clear demonstration of active echoism, where the patient is
doing something to the therapist. We can see, however, that whatever the patient
is doing, it has the effect of eliciting something *from* the therapist rather than putting something *into* her.

I feel there is some real hope for an echoistic patient when interpretations focus
on the therapist's and the patient's shared experience, in which the echoist can
have some understanding of her role in the dynamic. By drawing her attention to
her inability to take responsibility for the words she has uttered, the self-destructive echoist is made aware that she impacts the world, in spite of her deeply held,
but often unconscious, belief that she exists through another and not in her own
right.

In existential terms this reminds us that not actively choosing to live is still a
choice, and that it has consequences as far-reaching as any conscious act. If this
can be interpreted and understood, the patient has the potential for genuine and
observable progress in terms of growth and agency. The echoist's willingness
to take in the other makes her a willing recipient of both learning and care from
a good object, but only if and when her narcissistic object can be observed and
heard in its wish to steal and consume the goodness for itself. The following chapter goes on to consider the role of ego-destructive objects in much more depth.

Over-valued ideas, god-like objects, and faith

Part III

Over-valued ideas,
god-like objects, and faith

Chapter 6

Mistaken identity or what you will?

Internal voices, narcissistic objects, and the echoist

> Sebastian: A lady, sir, though it was said she much resembled me, was yet of many accounted beautiful: but, though I could not with such estimable wonder overfar believe that, yet thus far I will boldly publish her; she bore a mind that envy could not but call fair. She is drowned already, sir, with saltwater, though I seem to drown her remembrance again with more.
>
> Shakespeare, *Twelfth Night*

In this chapter I consider how to make a meaningful distinction between the echoist and the narcissist, who may at times present with similar traits. I do this by examining the echoist's relationship to internal and external narcissistic objects and explain how they can manifest in the transference.

I focus specifically on the voice, and its presence in the work, and how this can be understood as a symbol of both a mind and a self, as well as having a relevance in its own right. Using clinical vignettes I illustrate the particular presentation of an ego-destructive object in the transference, and specific traits that may be experienced in encountering an echoist with a narcissistic primary object. I draw upon examples of my countertransference, and how I make use of a clinical attitude of negative capability (Bion, 1970, p. 125) as a way of staying open to projective processes taking place in the clinical situation, to inform understanding.

I draw attention to the echoist's predisposition to use sessions to speak about an external narcissistic person, as avoidance of responsibility for her own self, and as a way of evading contact with the internal omnipotent object, which can cause even more terror than the external version. I describe my method and rationale for turning attention back on to the echoist through staying with what is uncomfortable in the here and now, and in not filling the space – an act so difficult to resist when it feels it is exactly what the echoist requires and yearns for.

In Chapter Two I introduced and defined the psychoanalytic term "ego-destructive object". This chapter explores the usefulness of that concept in recognising and understanding the echoist. It begins, however, not with the theoretical concept, but with the experience of being with the patient.

Voice and language

It is hardly surprising, given our knowledge of the myth, that the presence of such a critical object is communicated most often in the echoistic patient's relationship to voice and voices – her own, others', and internal voices. Because it is not always clear whose voice is being heard in a session, whether it is the patient's actual voice or an echo of another's, it can be easy to mistake the echoist for one of the voices she is echoing – most often, this may be that of the loudest or most authoritative voice she hears, and for this reason she can easily be mistaken as narcissistic herself. I have learned that it is important to listen out for unusual phrases and speech patterns that strike me as unfamiliar or not belonging to the patient. In my work with echoists, paying attention to voice is crucial in understanding and being with their plight. While many echoistic patients find it hard to speak or to have their voices heard in their relationships with others, they may present quite differently in the therapeutic relationship.

My experience of working with the most extreme echoists is that they can sometimes speak incessantly in the sessions, much like the early Echo of the myth on whom Hera places the curse, but this idle chatter is a block to being heard in way that can promote growth, and can often be an attempt to keep the therapist away from the pain that is so unbearable it cannot be spoken of.

I have observed a number of common features in the ways that echoists present. Surprisingly perhaps, a repeated experience is that the echoist does not want the session to end, and will begin to speak with some desperation in her voice as the session is coming to a close. It is often here that the pain of the echoist is most evident, much like at the end of the myth where Echo feels herself to be dying alongside the much-loved narcissistic youth, echoing his death-cries and drawing attention to *her* pain, using *his* voice. It can become difficult for the therapist to end the session because of a painful countertransference feeling that the patient may expire or be unable to survive until the next session if they are not given something by the therapist. This can lead to the therapist feeling the need to *do* something, and if this is not felt to be enough by the patient, the therapist often experiences resentment, much like the resentment felt by Echo at the end of the myth: "Echo had watched his decline, still filled with angry resentment …"

As a therapist, the most likely feeling that we will have is that we are being strongly projected into by the patient, and we might assume, too, that the patient feels entitled to more of our time. It is easy to see how we might, therefore, feel we are in the presence of a narcissist and on this basis a whole series of thoughts, preconceptions, and assumptions may unconsciously become activated in the therapist at the idea of working with such a patient.

I am also highly attentive to the language used by the patient to describe her experience. As we have seen in the previous chapters, the echoist often experiences what she feels to be an inner conflict of thoughts in which she is so convinced she is not going to be understood because she is not making sense, that she may give up trying to be heard. The patient who has lost her voice under such conditions can *seem* to be creating a stagnating impasse in the therapeutic situation, similar to that explored by Steiner (1993) in his work on psychic retreats, in which the patient appears unable or unwilling to make contact with the therapist because of an overwhelming need and pressure to protect herself, and perhaps the therapist, from psychic pain.

Steiner described how his studies of patients with whom he could not make meaningful contact, and whose analyses became characterised by stasis, led him to make closer observations that revealed that they made use of

> a variety of mechanisms to create states of mind which provided protection from anxiety and pain. They retreated out of contact with the analyst into these states which were often experienced spatially as if they were places in which the patient could hide.
>
> (1993, p. xi)

Steiner stated that he proposed to refer to the prolonged evasive use of such states of mind for the function of finding necessary "refuges, shelters, sanctuaries or havens", as psychic retreats (ibid.).

An alternative theory regarding the echoist, is that because the echoist is so familiar with trying to meet the competing wishes of others, she may be struck mute in the session when she feels these different voices to have conflicting wishes or intentions for her. I found, early on in this work, a strong wish to enable echoists to move beyond this impasse, and tried to encourage them to verbalise their feelings in relation to being unable to speak. This often resulted in a patient feeling under pressure to perform and supply answers, and even to try to read what she thinks I might want her to do or say in the session. Needless to say, this proved fruitless and I was forced to address how I was imposing my own desire upon the patient. I was reminded of Bion's caution to the therapist to withhold memory and desire. I realised I was somehow doing the wishing on behalf of my patient, and in so doing I was actually assuming a narcissistic omnipotent position. It is important in these moments to retain a capacity to reflect upon what is going on, to detect when we feel ourselves to be in an omnipotent role, and, I would add, to be able to consider whether we are in the presence of an echoist who is somehow drawing this out of us.

I realised eventually that I needed to stay as close to the patient's experience as possible, and when I was able to do this it became clear that the patient experienced the competing thoughts that shut her down as separate voices in her mind. In the following vignette I present an experience of a session in which the patient was able to describe the voice that she had come to recognise as the "Critical-voice", a term used by many of the echoistic patients in describing the most powerful internal voice responsible for shutting them down. Other terms used by the echoist to describe this particular voice, and which we go on to examine in more detail later in this chapter, include an authoritative, ridiculing, shaming, and even protective voice. These are all ways of describing what I understand to be the experience of having an internal ego-destructive object who is preventing the echoist from making genuine contact and receiving anything from the therapist. Much of my practice has become focused on exploring the relationship between the echoistic patients' critical-voice and what I have come to call their "Own-voice".

The following clinical vignette covers a whole session with a patient who had been in therapy for four years and who had significant insight into the relationship between her ego-destructive object and her own-voice. This patient had grown up with a malignantly narcissistic mother who had controlled her husband's and children's actions and, to some degree, through projective identification, their thoughts. When the patient had left home to marry she became aware that other families operated differently and realised that she looked to her mother to author-ise her in all matters and that this became an obstacle in her relationship with her husband. She was only able to recognise how much she had been colluding with her mother once she had managed to completely cut off contact with her. This vignette illustrates a number of the features described in this chapter. I will go on to examine these in some detail in the subsequent analysis.

Vignette 9: Lisa

My patient Lisa arrives and is silent. After about five minutes she begins to weep softly. She says that she had been feeling more and more full of self-loathing over the last few days. She is worried that she is a narcissist like her mother and that it means she is damaging her children. She feels sure that it could be true because she is being a "false self". When she speaks to me, her thoughts come out as quite jumbled, and she expresses herself with doubt, uncertainty, hesitation, and anxiety.

Lisa: I had an email from my aunt a few days ago, passed on from my mother. It said that my dad has breathing difficulties and he is in hospital and could die. I know this is possible because he has had a heart attack. I thought there is no way I can go and see him because she [Lisa's mother] will be there. I spoke to Fred and his mum about it and they agreed that I'm doing the right thing. Even though it may be true, and even possible that he is dying, I can't risk seeing him because I've got to stay cut off. ... [long pause while she thinks] ... It sounds so mean, but at the time there was no question of it, that I would go and see him. Then over the past couple of days I've been thinking maybe I'm really cruel and heartless to behave like this if my father might actually be dying. Then I've been remembering good times with him and feeling like I should go and see him, because when he was apart from *her* he was okay, and I always felt he cared about me [quite tearful].

Th: And part of you still cares for him ...?

Lisa: Yes. I think I do. The worst thing is that I now feel I have to hide that side from Fred and his mum because they have supported me. If I say I care they are going to feel betrayed by me. But now I hear the critical-voice in my head all the time, telling me how false I am, that I am lying to them and that I'm actually just as bad. A narcissist just like her.

Th: The voice tells you that you are like your mother or that you are a narcissist?

Lisa: Both, and then … [sobs]. I think perhaps I am doing so much damage to my daughter, and I don't even know I'm doing it or how to stop it. The part of me that feels bad for him, my dad, remembers the good times. When we went to the seaside at Brighton and he was away from her for a while and he took me on the pier and the slot machines, he was fun. Whenever she got angry or upset about something, he used to come and make me apologise but as if he was on my side. He would say "You know what she's like, apologise and then it will be okay and we can all move on and forget it". That's the him I remember when I feel I should go and see him, but it's not the real him because the real him has been taken over by her. I didn't really believe he would choose her over his own daughter, grandchild and even his own sister, but he has. Now I can see he's totally under her spell and has become one of what they call her flying monkeys, doing her bidding and acting on her behalf. He's her main one actually. He could have got out and taken my brothers with him, that is really the only way I could see him and them, but I can't go back or she will take me over again. Then I think perhaps I'm the problem if they have all stayed, and maybe I'm just serving myself.

Th: It feels like even when you are away from her you are persecuted by the kind of criticism you received from her.

Lisa: My critical-voice says to me, "You're terrible, and you can't be trusted to make your own decisions".

Th: From what you describe, it feels that if you stick to your resolve not to have anything to do with any family members whom you feel she controls, then the critical-voice tells you that you are heartless and cruel, but if you have any warm feelings of care or sadness about your father then you can't share it because you have betrayed members of Fred's family whom you feel you have manipulated and dragged in to support you. Then the voice tells you that if you don't share your conflict with Fred and his mother that you are a false self.

Lisa: That's exactly it.

Th: I wonder what that critical-voice makes it all mean?

Lisa: Sorry. What do you mean?

Th: You are apologising for not understanding my ambiguous question.

Lisa: I thought it was me.

Th: It feels as if your critical-voice is here now telling you that you must be stupid.

Lisa: [Smiles] Ha yes, that's exactly what it was saying. And that you must think I'm not listening or paying attention properly. It's saying "You are too obsessed with yourself to listen to anyone else".

Th: You think this all means you must be a narcissist, like your mother.

Lisa: Yes. I think if I listen to the critical-voice it's inevitable. And then I think, but what if it's right. Then my poor daughter is going to end up like me. I've noticed when I wasn't here over the summer that I was focused on events outside, threats that my mother might get in at any moment, and then I was not really noticing the critical-voice. Since I came back to therapy last week I'm not sure if the voice is more critical or I'm just noticing it more. Whatever I do I end up thinking I am like her if I listen to the critical-voice. Then I feel I'm such a fraud coming here and talking about her when I'm just as bad.

Th: Yet I think you feel that when you can bring the critical-voice here and we can actually hear what it has to say, we can both see that you can't win whatever you do if you listen to its criticisms.

Lisa: Yes. It's so easy to believe it. It's only when I spend time with my aunt and my mum's younger brother James, who have both managed to escape, that I feel I'm not going mad. She used to drive past James's house to check up on which women he was seeing, and James changed all his relationships to suit my mother and to make sure he had her approval. For over twenty-five years he put up with it – she made him sabotage relationships with really nice women because she was so envious. James knows now that he was taken over by her and understands how difficult it is to escape, because he tried loads of times and got pulled back in. I think nobody understands unless they have been one of her people.

[… Cries a lot]

[I feel sad and sit with her feeling that she is not understood]

Th: You feel I can't really understand, Lisa.

Lisa: I feel you do. I don't know how. Even if my father dies I wouldn't be welcome at his funeral. Because I feel he doesn't exist anymore and that she has taken him over, so because she hates me and he didn't get out, she exists in him, and he hates me so he would not want me there anyway. He has had chances but he didn't get out.

Th: And you, Lisa, feel very angry and betrayed by him for being too weak to leave, because you know how painful it is because you did get out.

Lisa: [sobbing gently] I know what it feels like for him too – because before I got out I didn't really have my own thoughts. I was so horrible to my aunt when I was younger, laughing at her hobbling about with her white stick as she walked down our drive because my mother said her partial blindness was just put on for sympathy. I feel so bad because I believed the things she said about her and joined in.

[I recognised a possible transference communication at this point, in which Lisa's object was mocking the therapist for her blindness. Lisa, may well have joined in were it not for the considerable work already undertaken in which Lisa had become aware of the influence of her mother on her own thoughts, and on her susceptibility to join with the object in a devaluation if she did not remain vigilant. I remained silent concerning this possibility, but held this in mind as she continued]

Lisa: I actually don't know what it is like to have my own thoughts … [sobbing gently] … and I think everybody just expects me to be over it now because it's four years ago that I cut all contact with her. But sometimes I feel so confused and I don't know what to believe about my own childhood, what was actually true or what she made me believe, because it all felt normal. [Cries. Takes second tissue from an almost full pack]

Lisa: Sorry I've used all your tissues. [Blows nose] I just listened to my mother and I think I thought whatever *she* thought.

Th: And now you have to try to listen and think for yourself.

Lisa: I don't know what to trust.

Th: … and it's very hard coming here because I don't tell you what to think or do or give you any reassurance. It is so painful, not knowing what feels OK for Lisa.

Lisa: Yes. I don't trust my own-voice. The critical-voice is so powerful I just doubt myself all the time when I'm not here.

Th: But I think when you are here and we can listen to what the critical-voice says, you can have some understanding of its intentions.
[Lisa nods]

Th: We have to finish in a moment. I wonder how you feel about leaving here?

Lisa: It's quite hard. The session goes so quickly, it feels safe here, like a refuge where nobody can come and get me … even the voice doesn't sound so convincing when I say it aloud to you. I realise that when we can look at my internal world and that critical-voice, in our sessions, I actually I feel I have a bit more strength to say something back to it and I feel a bit more powerful [little smile].

Analysis

Perhaps the most striking feature of this session is not simply its illustration of the critical-voice, but the importance of being able to hear it speak in the here and now of the session. It seems that if we can allow it to speak with the therapist present, not only does it lose some of the power it has when constantly criticising the patient, but that its intentions might be exposed in a way that can be thought about by the patient and the therapist together. This creates what Britton (1989, p. 86) has called triangular space, in which the patient can observe the impact and intentions of such a critical-voice. In Lisa's case she feels that she has a helper with whom she can think about it and, in the moment, gain some emancipation from it, even temporarily, as described by Lisa above in her final statement. Britton describes how the early oedipal triangle in the family can be used to tolerate pain and separateness in a way that can then be utilised in the analytic relationship and related to internal objects as well as external ones. He states:

> The acknowledgement by the child of the parents' relationship with each other unites his psychic world, limiting it to one world shared with his two parents in which different object relationships can exist. The closure of the oedipal triangle by the recognition of the link joining the parents provides a limiting boundary for the internal world. It creates what I call a 'triangular

space' – i.e., a space bounded by the three persons of the oedipal situation and all their potential relationships. It includes, therefore, the possibility of being a participant in a relationship and observed by a third person as well as being an observer of a relationship between two people.

The primal family triangle provides the child with two links connecting him separately with each parent and confronts him with the link between them which excludes him… If the link between the parents perceived in love and hate can be tolerated in the child's mind, it provides him with a prototype for an object relationship of a third kind in which he is a witness and not a participant. A third position then comes into existence from which object relationships can be observed … This provides us with a capacity for seeing ourselves in interaction with others and for entertaining another point of view whilst retaining our own, for reflecting on ourselves whilst being ourselves. This is a capacity we hope to find in ourselves and in our patients in analysis.

(Britton, 1989, p. 87)

In my work with echoistic patients I have discovered the importance of creating a space in which the patient is not simply subjected to the tyranny of the object or critical-voice, but is able to witness its presence and think about it in the relationship with the therapist. This affords the patient the opportunity to observe not just how it relates to her but also what it has to say to or about the therapist. The creation of such a space enables the patient to see the similarity of the object in its functioning and relating, to that of the external narcissist. In the same way that Lisa cannot remove her narcissistic mother or alter her behaviour, she can alter her relationship to her mother so that she is not a recipient of her judgements and projections, and she has a space to think about her responses to them and to be able to start to judge them for herself. She has determined, "I am not in agreement with my mother's judgements and so I will not listen to them or subject myself to hearing them and acting on them in the same way my father continues to". In her internal world she finds this more difficult, and in breaks from the therapy the judgements of the narcissistic object govern and subjugate her, until she returns to her therapist and can have some space between her and it, within which to think about her view of its criticisms and authority.

Judgement and emancipation

Britton (2003, p. 107) considered the relationship between a powerfully oppressive superego object and a subjugated self, by making use of the biblical story of Job, on the basis that, as he put it, "the study of the nature of the superego in psychoanalysis had been preceded for centuries by the study in theology of the nature of its external representation, God".

In Britton's account of Job's predicament at the hands of the tyrannical god, he writes of the need to gain emancipation from the cruel object, "by the reclamation of his rights to form *judgements*" (p. 107, my emphasis). The counterpart to this in the therapeutic situation is the help we give to the patient in revealing the super-ego object as an unsuitable pretender to that role and task. Britton's close reading of the story of Job reveals in detail many aspects of the internal object relations involved in emancipation from such a dominant internal figure. He shows how Job begins to have a mind of his own, so that he becomes able to perceive God as "unrelenting and incapable of change … these would be serious faults in a man" (p. 109). Having found his voice, Job "begins to imply that God is deficient, that he lacks empathy, that he is less than a man" (ibid.). This reversal is important for our purposes in considering the plight of the echoist in her fraught relationship to the dominant narcissistic object in her world.

The idea of being able to see and judge an ego-destructive object is an impor-tant and liberating experience for an echoist who has been under its power and felt constantly judged by it. In the triangular space the patient is in the position not just of being judged by a god-like object but, as Job is able to judge God, they are able to judge the intentions of such an object and its treatment of them.

As Britton goes on to say:

> Therapeutic effect can follow from deposing a cruel internal object from the authoritative position of the superego, even if it remains substantially unmod-ified as an internal threat.

The presence of such an object is very familiar to me in working with echoistic patients, and the same tactics, intentions, and persuasive narratives, used by such an object as the one described in the vignette above, are commonplace. One key feature is that when the object speaks it often refers to the patient as "You", taking not just an accusatory tone but separating itself out from the patient and attacking the little ego or self. The value of triangular space in working with the echoist is of particular interest because of the dominance of such an object in the mind of the echoist. In my experience, the ego-destructive object acts in much the same way as the actual narcissist. It is authoritative and envious and fills whatever space is available, including colonising the thoughts of the individuals that it objectifies. Lisa gives a very good description of her experience of being colonised by her narcissistic mother, and of her observations of those around her who continue to be under the spell of such an individual until they can escape and get some dis-tance from the narcissist.

The destructive behaviour of the external or internal version of the narcissist can only be seen for what it is once some psychological distance has been gained. Only then does it become possible to perceive how it exercises power, not only over the actions but also the thoughts of others, by its concerted use of projective identification.

This, of course, has no impact on the behaviour of the narcissist or his belief that he is right, but the individual who has escaped is able to liberate himself in a way that allows for some growth of his own thoughts and voice. This can, of course, feel very intimidating for the echoist who has not had the experience of having an own-voice heard, and who may find it very difficult to take responsibility for sharing her own thoughts, and for the responses and consequences that flow from them. As I have shown in Chapter Five, when the patient is a self-destructive echoist, it is hard for her even to acknowledge that she make an impact on the world and this can result in blaming others for every choice and decision made, and the effect it has on other individuals.

In the vignette above, however, it can be seen that this patient does have an own-voice that, with the help of the therapist, she is able to have heard. In this example, Lisa is able to acknowledge not just her own voice, which is demonstrated by the agency she takes in making the decision for herself not to have contact with her father, but a sophisticated reasoning process, which helps her to make her decision. What is of particular interest here is that she demonstrates, while she is in the session talking through her dilemma, that she has an internal dialogue between different objects that are (good) ego objects within her. She is able to remember, with some love, a father who had cared for her, as well as being able to understand that this father is under the power of the narcissistic mother and would therefore be unable to meet her as himself.

These internal dialogues are parts of her mind that are able to inform her, and enable her to take agency and responsibility for her actions. She is, ultimately, as Sartre says, "condemned to freedom", and through the process she undergoes in deciding not to see her father she demonstrates here a healthy part of herself in which thinking and agency can occur. It is vital, therefore, that the therapist does not reassure or even validate the patient's decisions, as this would threaten the patient's autonomy, which she is developing very cautiously, as if still a very small child, filled with anxiety at making decisions in the world. The therapist may feel very proud of the patient's ability to think and take responsibility for her own voice, and may wish to congratulate or affirm the patient and relieve her of the anxiety that any choice she has will have consequences. I would argue that this is not just unhelpful to the patient because the therapist is somehow stepping into the role absented by the all-knowing mother, but also that the therapist would be avoiding being with the patient's anxiety. In fact, the absence of reassurance is likely to contribute to and increase the patient's anxiety. While it is speculative to interpret the patient's early situation, it is possible to infer with some confidence, that a mother who is narcissistic in the way that this patient's mother is, would have been unable to provide the container-contained relationship into which the baby's anxiety can be taken and felt by the mother, in a way that relieves the patient. The therapist must, therefore, be willing to do this, and to bear the patient's anxiety with her so that she is not overwhelmed by it or left alone with it during or after the session.

The account above illustrates how the patient has managed to take in an object relationship where she has space to think and hear different opinions and influences from good objects in the self who want to support her to do what is best for her. For a patient like Lisa, who had at this point been in twice-weekly therapy for four years, this is a hard-won and very positive development in terms of being able to internalise such a relationship and to draw upon it under difficult circumstances. Where she suffered, however, and what constantly sought to undo the work, was the critical narcissistic object that not only judged her for every choice she made, but also tried to rob her of any security she felt in having agency and making decisions that helped her in the world. The therapist must be willing to listen with the patient to this object, and to help her discern and distinguish the healthy parts of the self that are emerging in spite of its dominance. Furthermore, the patient needs our support to accept responsibility for the presence within her of the ego-destructive object in her personality, and in relation to which the healthy self must continue to be aware, to guard against, and to speak back to.

As we can see from the example, psychic space promotes psychic growth, and, as Bion has demonstrated in his model of container-contained and alpha function (see Chapter One), psychic growth depends upon psychic space (in particular, the triangular space defined above by Ronald Britton). This space is the core condition for growth and it is particularly important for therapists working with echoists, who have never fully developed a voice or a self, to understand the significance of this. This has further implications for patients at the assessment stage, who may be deemed to have an as-if personality, or not enough of a self to receive or be able to benefit from therapy. I would suggest that many echoistic patients have been overlooked and may continue to be so if this phenomenon is not widely acknowledged and understood.

Self-diagnosis

The question of mistaken diagnosis occurs frequently, and echoistic patients often feel that something is wrong, but because there is no category for echoism, they misdiagnose themselves. I have seen a number of patients who present as self-destructive echoists while diagnosing themselves with borderline personality disorder after taking one of the plethora of online tests available. There are traits that are similar, and those that overlap. The tests, however, make no distinction between certain borderline traits present in a narcissist and those in an echoist. I worked with one patient who had two narcissistic parents and who came into therapy with no voice of her own. She had seen other therapists in the past, to treat a range of symptoms, and had tried to think of using *their* words in social situations or when trying to speak to others. She pictured the therapists in her mind and tried to recall what *they* might say so she could repeat it and feel acceptable to speak. Interestingly, when she arrived in therapy with me she said she had very little hope, as this technique had failed her when she was forced to face the consequences of her words through the reactions of others.

In one session following a break, this patient described how she had been heavily persecuted by her critical-voice. We had had a number of breakthroughs before the holiday, during which she had been able to recognise the tyrannical nature of her object and its wishes to sabotage any developing relationships in her life. Although she had acknowledged feeling both love and care for me, she had become convinced during the break that she was with the wrong therapist. After taking an online test she was certain she had borderline personality disorder and was recommended to find a "dialectical behavioural therapist".

Later in the same session she acknowledged how she had noticed some areas of growth, early on during the break. For example, she had enjoyed a meal during which a discussion was taking place, and she had felt a desire to join in. Faced with the dilemma of not speaking and appearing distant and awkward, or possibly "saying the wrong thing", she had thought: "What would I say to my therapist?" This had helped her both to think of something she wanted to say, and to quiet the object who was taunting her that she would make a fool of herself if she spoke. She had decided to speak in the group and said she felt it had "gone down well". I pointed out that I had heard a distinction between what she had said about her previous therapist – that in a difficult situation she had thought about what that therapist would say to her – and how she had thought in this case about what she might say to me. She was astonished by this, and realised that in the previous case, after speaking the words of another and being ridiculed by her object, she had no recourse, whereas with me she had been able to draw upon an internalised relationship in which she had a voice of her own, and in which triangular space could be created in her own mind, leaving her less at the mercy of her destructive object. While the object itself showed no signs of changing, the patient was able to change, at least temporarily, her relationship to it. This is an example of what I referred to earlier as Britton's finding that it is the dislodging of a bad object from its position of authority in the personality that can be the decisive therapeutic factor in such cases.

This particular session revealed not just the problem of misdiagnosis and the "do-it-yourself" nature of online tests, but, more importantly, the issue of an echoist seeking a form of therapy where she is told what to do and say and think. Such an approach reinforces her dependency on another to provide the words to echo back and renders the patient unable to take responsibility for her own words and actions, while trying to find somebody to blame when she must face the consequences of speaking aloud. The act of blaming was itself enough to convince the patient that she was demonstrating "borderline behaviour", and that the critical-voice "must be right". This powerful session revealed the internal unconscious dynamics that accompanied her external actions and allowed the patient to break the cycle of always accepting the object's authority.

Summary

At the outset of this chapter I indicated the importance of voice in working with the echoist. I have shown the power relations of internal voices and, in particular, that of the internal critical-voice or narcissistic ego-destructive voice to the own-voice.

Other areas to which I pay attention are descriptions of the effect of external voices on the echoist. This may present as her telling me what other people think, feel, or have told her about herself. In the transference I am conscious of trying to listen for different voices in the patient's mind through the way they express themselves, and how certain tones and nuances of language and power appear in her various communications with me. In drawing attention to these we can begin to learn about the patient's own-voice and the various objects in her mind. This includes listening out for an internalised version of me.

As the therapy continues, the quality of the patient's own-voice and its strength provide significant indicators for understanding growth in the echoist.

As I have demonstrated, the presence of the narcissistic or critical-voice can silence the patient, as it does in the above vignette. A common experience in the early stages of the work with the echoistic patient is to feel that the patient is bringing not herself, but another into the session. The following short vignette gives an illustration of this.

Vignette 10: Peter

Peter, twenty-six, a psychology student, had been in therapy for two months. He had found making contact with the therapist and staying present in sessions difficult, unless he was talking about his partner Josie. Josie was, he said, incredibly beautiful, much cleverer than him; she was sophisticated and decisive, and when he felt loved by her it was the most amazing feeling in the world. Unfortunately, however, much of the time she was unavailable; she would say she loved him, then – when he began to feel relieved – she would say she was not sure that was true or that she could really love anybody. He had found lists where she had written his name at the top and the things she felt were positive and negative about him. He had tried to change some of the negative things but others were impossible to change, such as her feeling that he came from a less affluent and influential background than her. She made promises and broke them constantly. When they went out together she would turn her attention away from Peter and smile and gaze at other men in a way that made Peter feel insecure and inadequate. When he tried to address it with her she became angry and said if he didn't like her as she was he should leave. Peter felt growing desperation, he was constantly changing his life to fit around Josie and do what she wanted, and although there were moments of genuine pleasure these were becoming fewer and fewer and he had begun to feel that a good day was a day when they had shared a pleasant moment, a brief lull in amongst what felt like an ongoing storm. He was, he said, hungry for just a morsel of affection, and receiving this was just enough to hold on to until the next. He said his energy was depleted, his friends were becoming angry with him for neglecting them, and he felt hopeless.

In the first two months, Peter spent almost all of each session talking about Josie. When the relationship was not changing and his unhappiness was felt to be increasing, Peter became very resentful towards me. He said he was spending all this money and nothing was improving. I suggested that in bringing Josie to our sessions each week, rather than bringing himself, perhaps Peter was hoping that she might somehow be treated vicariously. Peter heard this as a criticism. He said he thought I was criticising him for talking about the wrong things in the session. He didn't know what else to talk about. He said there was no him without Josie, that he had lost himself and that I was not helping him to get himself back.

I had a strong countertransferential reaction to Peter. I thought I could see what he was unable to see, and my attempts to get him to speak about himself seemed to fall on deaf ears. He brought no dreams, no communications from the unconscious, and wanted to stay only with what was concrete for him. In fact, whenever I tried various tactics to get him to speak of himself, or of himself before he met Josie, or looked for indications as to what led him to play such a role in his relationship with Josie, he maintained that his life and childhood had been perfect before his relationship her. He felt that I was "one of those therapists who thinks that everything goes back to your childhood", and he felt a strong need to defend his own against my perceived attack on it, and on his parents who were, he said, perfect.

Analysis

I use this vignette to illustrate the difficulty for the therapist in working with an echoistic patient who has become colonised by an external narcissist and who, unlike Lisa in the previous vignette, is still subjugated and under the narcissist's power. While I may make many accurate assumptions about the patient's state and relationship based on my experience of working with fellow-sufferers, I would be doing so in what Bion calls the domain of K, whereby I have knowledge about the patient that he may not have about himself. In the case of the echoist, however, an interpretation from this position produces a very particular reaction. The patient feels criticised and silenced by the therapist and the feelings of inferiority are reinforced. In fact, the patient feels as tyrannised by the therapist as by the narcissist to whom he is shackled.

This realisation produces a difficulty for both therapist and patient. The patient feels he is not allowed to speak about his narcissistic partner in the sessions and therefore feels he has nothing to speak about at all; his concrete world is *her*, as he feels he is nothing without her.

As we have seen in Chapter Three, when the patient feels he is nothing, he is, in an existential sense, in touch with a reality that actually exists. As Alice Holzhey-Kunz (2016, p. 21) states:

> But when I take my patients as ontologically traumatized, I take them as suffering from an experience which 'is likely to cause pervasive distress in anyone'. So the problem of the neurotics is not a lack of mental capacities, (nor) respectively a lack of psychic maturity, but a *special sensitivity* (*Hellhörigkeit*) for the ontological truth of their own being …
>
> … the sensitivity I want to introduce here is a special sensitivity for what is disclosed not by interpretation, but only by Angst. This special sensitivity for the truth about one's own being disclosed by Angst is a gift and at the same time a heavy burden, because it exposes people to what is – in its 'naked that' – hardly bearable. Therefore being especially sensitive is a quality which

singles out and overcharges these people at the same time. That is why I call my patients *reluctant philosophers*. Albeit they do not philosophize about their life in the usual sense, they are philosophers in so far as they are exposed to the philosophical truth about human existence. But they are only reluctant philosophers because they cannot bear this truth and are therefore in a desperate revolt against it.

The echoistic patient who is hypersensitive to the ontological truth of this state of existence will feel completely vulnerable to the threat of extinction. The need to stay in the concrete world of the object to whom he feels his life force is dependent makes Peter feel protected from the reality of his actual state. (Although the patient has given no indication of an internal object at this stage in the therapy, this external object provides a good example of how the internal narcissistic object can also make the echoist feel protected by its presence). In this case, Peter left therapy before we were able to establish a safe enough relationship to be able to overcome this barrier.

Silence

The therapist may well feel drawn to fill the space rather than to leave the patient alone with her anxiety. When this is done through hasty interpretations or by leading or guiding the patient, the therapist fulfils the role that keeps the echoist dependent, by providing a voice to echo back. The experience of staying with the patient in the most unbearable silence, which can feel interminable for both patient and therapist, causes genuine anguish for the therapist. The patient's resentment becomes more and more evident as she feels she is not being helped by the therapist, and the therapist realises that if she is unable to give the patient anything, this will become the very obstacle to the therapy that will stop the patient coming. Getting past this impasse is a challenge made particularly difficult for a patient who feels she doesn't have a right to therapy in the first place.

I have found that the only relief that might be afforded both therapist and patient is to try to stay with the patient's experience of the here and now of the session – to be able to speak of the anxiety felt in the silence and feelings of threat and fear of annihilation. The therapist must be willing to be experienced as the bad object, and to acknowledge and speak of how disappointed the patient feels to have a therapist who is not helping her and who makes her feel that she is wasting her money. If this experience can enable both therapist and patient to speak of the haunting feelings of anxiety, and the state of barely existing without the presence of the narcissist, they may be able to make enough contact for the patient to continue with the work. Sometimes this is not the case and the patient ends the work, leaving the therapist feeling inadequate and frustrated.

Finally, as I go on to discuss more fully in Chapter Eight (Groups), the quality of the patient's voice itself can be indicative of the amount of self that is present in the patient. I have come to use the terms voice, self, and ego interchangeably; however, linked to the very nature of Hera's curse and what it represents, the voice itself, and its symbolic significance, cannot be underestimated in this work. It is important to stay attentive to changes in the voice, its tone and depth, and the confidence with which it is executed, as these all indicate aspects of the patient's state of Being, and the degree to which they are present at any moment.

Chapter 7

Hera's curse

Faith and reason – a complex paradox

Wait without hope

> I said to my soul, be still, and wait without hope
> For hope would be hope for the wrong thing; wait without love,
> For love would be love of the wrong thing; there is yet faith
> But the faith and the love and the hope are all in the waiting.
> Wait without thought, for you are not ready for thought:
> So the darkness shall be the light, and the stillness the dancing.
> Whisper of running streams, and winter lightning.
> The wild thyme unseen and the wild strawberry,
> The laughter in the garden, echoed ecstasy
> Not lost, but requiring, pointing to the agony
> Of death and birth.
>
> T. S. Eliot, "East Coker", 1959

I had little idea, when I set out to write this book, of the journey on which I would be taken by the clinical work and the ideas that developed from it. I did not expect that I would venture into theological philosophy, and yet this chapter is about how the work has led me to this very area as a way of trying to understand not just the echoist's plight but her relationship with an internal object and how she manages to remain in therapy. This chapter brings together Hera's curse, passages in the writings of Kierkegaard in which he interrogates his theological faith, lines from "East Coker" by T. S. Eliot, and my work with one particular patient who taught me about the importance of faith. I will argue that hope is hope *for* something; love too has its objects but faith, in the way I will consider it, is ontological and thereby of the human condition and not *in* something.

Hera's Curse

Hera's curse, as I discussed in the first chapter, takes the following form:

> Echo, a young and talkative nymph, leaves a clearing where Zeus, the thunder
> God, ruler of the gods on Mount Olympus, is cavorting with other nymphs.
> Suddenly she encounters the goddess Hera, wife of Zeus. Known for her

loquaciousness, Echo uses her verbal prowess to charm the unsuspecting Hera with words, distracting the goddess from sounds of laughter emanating from her husband's antics in the glade. On learning of this, the jealous goddess wreaks vengeance upon Echo, cursing her: "You shall no longer use your tongue to manipulate and deceive, from this moment you will be struck mute". As an afterthought she adds: "Since you are so fond of having the last word, I will grant you that. You may repeat the last words of another, and your echo shall be a reminder to all of the power of the gods." Echo is immediately struck dumb and loses the ability to communicate her original thoughts in words. Horrified at her loss of identity she hides away, unable to express her pain in words, with increasing resentment towards the goddess. Over time she begins to withdraw and fade from forest life. Without another with whom to converse, she begins to forget the sound of her own voice, and the ability to make her thoughts manifest, and in so doing loses her connection to humanity. As she does, her life force dwindles and she starts to fade away.

Engaging with the character of Hera has been one of the most difficult tasks in writing this book. It is as if thinking about her, and the reason behind her curse, is somehow taboo and, as such, not quite available to consciousness. I have found it important to retain some curiosity about this state, and to be able to bear it without being able to understand it fully. I realised that "understanding" it too quickly would be likely to lead to missing the most important and elusive aspects of it. Accordingly, this chapter may render a reader who is impatient for an explanation frustrated. It does, I believe, come down to having faith that meaning will somehow be revealed through being with the phenomenon.

In this chapter I draw upon some passages from Søren Kierkegaard's *Fear and Trembling* (1843), in which he struggles between his devotion and his philosophical interrogation of faith, and in which he describes faith as "a tremendous paradox". Writing under the pseudonym *Johannes de Silentio*, Kierkegaard, the devoted Christian, is silenced in a creative split, enabling Johannes to adopt the role of interrogator and sceptic:

> faith is … a paradox which is capable of transforming a murder into a holy act well-pleasing to God, … which no thought can master, because faith begins precisely there where thinking leaves off.
>
> (ibid.)

The paradox for Kierkegaard is made evident in his explication of the biblical story of Abraham's response to God's test in which he is required to sacrifice his son, Isaac. Johannes feels painfully this *horror religiosus*, and while on the one hand he admires Abraham's unquestioning faith in the divine, he is also appalled by it, and unable to understand it from a philosophical and existential perspective.

In pinning his faith on to something concrete, in this case God, who takes away the struggle for truth and understanding, I would argue that Abraham is able to avoid the ontological anxiety of the situation through having faith in an entity in the ontic realm. This is what Holzhey-Kunz would describe as an ontic illusion, in which the concrete is used as a defence against the anguish of the ontological realm of being. For Johannes, who uses the myth of Agamemnon as a comparable idea, in which a deity requires him to sacrifice his beloved child in return for victory in the Trojan war, Johannes is able to have sympathy for Agamemnon who suffers the pain of the choice yet acts for a higher *telos*.

Although I move freely between Kierkegaard's text and my own notion of faith, these should not be thought of as one and the same, but as faith in relation to two different realms, the ontic and the ontological. In this chapter I am interested in the relationship between belief in an authority who takes away the need for responsibility for action, and the doubt that ensues in questioning it or turning away from it. In light of this terrible struggle, symbolised in the two opposing parts of Kierkegaard, I ask: what keeps the echoistic patient in therapy? This I conceptualise as faith, yet I refer to a faith that is in the ontological realm. It is necessary for the patient to have this faith in order to stay in therapy, but this is not in the realm of the concrete – a faith *in* something. Neither must it be mistaken for hope which is *for* something. It is a faith that creates the conditions in which terrible truths can be revealed and borne without fleeing to an illusory wish for a god-object who takes away the anguish.

The struggle is with the ontological, and the fear and trembling incurred in having to hold on to faith when its objects and agents are absent and cannot be conceptualised. This is illustrated beautifully in Britton's (1998) commentary on the relationship between doubt and terror in John Bunyan's *Pilgrim's Progress:*

> Seriously questioning the calm mutual regard and the virtues of untroublesomeness releases a destructive force which purports to be a moral force. It has the judicial powers of conscience, with the punitive methods of the Inquisition. Like Bunyan's judge and jury it resembles a destructive, envious super-ego and super container of dissatisfaction. By its intervention faith in the analytic situation is quickly destroyed, and resort is taken to hope as a substitute for faith, optimism deputising for confidence. Faithful is executed and Hopeful takes his place. This harsh force of a quasi-judicial kind was never far away, but while the analytic pair could remain mutually hopeful it was believed that it could be kept at bay and never encountered. What was really needed for progress in the analysis was a long enough period imprisoned in Doubting Castle to explore it and not simply escape from it.
>
> (Britton, 1998, p. 88)

Faith, in the ontic realm, is different for each person according to his or her own experiences and attitudes to god-like figures (both internal and external). In relation to our patients we cannot generalise in our speculations about the state of the objects in the internal world but must learn from each individual the specifics of her own, and in doing so offer some understanding to relieve her from her isolation and to lessen her feelings of inner persecution. This comes about not through *knowing* or attempting to *identify* with our own particular relationships, but through experiencing a shared human state in which we give up focusing on our own suffering in order to prioritise that of the patient. The importance of this shared human state appears in Freud's writings as early as 1895. Freud (1950a) had stated that the helpless infant, faced with mounting inner tension, requires the attention of the experienced person, the mother. A little later (p. 331) he writes:

> Let us suppose that the object which furnishes the perception resembles the subject – a fellow human-being … it is in relation to a fellow human being that a human-being learns to cognize.

Freud is suggesting that this experienced other may be perceived as sharing a basic common humanity. Freud calls this the *Nebenmensch.*

The following lines from Kierkegaard offer a touching description of the kind of provision that can be offered by the fellow-sufferer in the case of the tragic hero that the man of total, unquestioning faith is unable to receive:

> He visits the man whose soul is beset with sorrow, whose breast for stifled sobs cannot draw breath, whose thoughts pregnant with tears weigh heavily upon him, to him he makes his appearance, dissolves the sorcery of sorrow, loosens his corslet, coaxes forth his tears by the fact that in his sufferings the sufferer forgets his own.
>
> (Kierkegaard, ibid., p. 30)

Kierkegaard in this short passage puts us in mind of a state of human suffering common to all mankind, one requiring a human being to meet it and to take it on with compassion for the fellow sufferer. Johannes (Kierkegaard) distinguishes between the choices made by the protagonist in the Greek tragedy and the plight of Abraham in the Old Testament. What they have in common with one another, and with Echo in the myth, is that the one "beset with sorrow" is acting in relation to a deity. Kierkegaard's descriptions, and Freud's emphasis on the understanding of the *Nebenmensch*, orient us and direct us towards a way of being with the struggles of the echoist with her god-like objects.

Kierkegaard and Greek tragedy

In his discussion of faith and duty, Kierkegaard refers to the predicament of Agamemnon. In the Greek tragedy, *The Oresteia*, this tragic figure, a tortured king, is asked to sacrifice his daughter Iphigenia on the altar to appease the goddess Artemis. The outcome of the Trojan War is determined by sacrifices to the gods made by individuals on both sides. These gods squabble and behave omnipotently, using the humans as pawns in their power games. Their immense power over the mortals is both frightening and absolute. In addition to fearing Artemis, Agamemnon has a particular interest in seeing justice served, as his brother Menelaus has faced the loss of his beautiful wife Helen to the Trojan prince, Paris. He sees it as his duty to meet Artemis' wishes. In order that the Greek ships might sail and bring about justice, returning Helen to her rightful place with his brother, he has to consent to the agonising sacrifice of his beloved Iphigenia as the enactment of duty.

Kierkegaard tells us:

> He who denies himself and sacrifices himself for duty gives up the finite in order to grasp the infinite, and that man is secure enough. The tragic hero gives up the certain for the still more certain, and the eye of the beholder rests upon him confidently... The tragic hero has need of tears and claims them, and where is the envious eye which would be so barren that it could not weep with Agamemnon.
>
> (1843, p. 29)

Agamemnon's decision to sacrifice his daughter, for what he believes to be the greater good, is opposed by his wife, Clytemnestra, questioned by the chorus, and suffered agonisingly by the protagonist himself, who, knowing that his actions will have tragic consequences, makes the decision to obey the deity for reasons he believes to be necessary. Kierkegaard goes on to say:

> I am now on the subject of the tragic hero ... Agamemnon must sacrifice Iphigenia. Now aesthetics requires silence of Agamemnon inasmuch as it would be unworthy of the hero to seek comfort from any other man, and out of solicitude for the women too he ought to conceal this from them as long as possible. On the other hand, the hero, precisely in order to be a hero, must be tried by dreadful temptations which the tears of Clytemnestra and Iphigenia provide for him ... The tragic hero displays his ethical courage precisely by the fact that it is he who, without being ensnared in any aesthetic illusion, himself announces to Iphigenia her fate. If he keeps silent, it may be because he thinks thereby to make it easier for others, but it may also be because thereby he makes it easier for himself. However, he knows that he is not influenced by this latter motive. If he keeps silent, he assumes as the individual a serious responsibility inasmuch as he ignores an argument which may come from without. As a tragic hero he cannot do this, for ethics loves him precisely because he constantly expresses the universal. His heroic action demands courage, but it belongs to this courage that he shall shun no argumentation.
>
> (Kierkegaard, ibid., p. 161)

I refer to this passage in order to introduce a number of themes related to the plight of Echo in the myth. Artemis' request of Agamemnon is a curse, in which he is required to place duty before personal gain. It is also one that sets in motion a set of tragic consequences, which once activated cannot be stopped. The subsequent murder of Agamemnon at the hands of his wife Clytemnestra and her lover Aegisthus, must then be avenged by Orestes, Agamemnon's exiled son, and it is he who is then persecuted by the furies for committing the act of matricide. While Agamemnon may have foreseen the potential for this nemesis, he nevertheless made the decision to do what was required of him, to sacrifice his own life and his family for duty. As Aristotle writes in *The Poetics*, the arousal of pity and fear in the form of catharsis is what brings about our deep connection to the protagonist. We pity him for the choices he is faced with, and the degree of responsibility he must bear. We place ourselves at the heart of his predicament and along with our pity, fear is aroused in us that, like Agamemnon, our actions must and always do have consequences, which we must bear, even when we choose not to act.

In this case we are reminded of Echo. She is cursed by Hera in the most terrible way. Her very being is withdrawn from her, condemning her to live in the lowest state of existence, barely animate, while being forced to bear the knowledge that she lives thus. Why does Hera curse her so? It appears in a cursory reading of Ovid that it is a fitting punishment for Echo's endless talkativeness and prattling. But, as I suggested in Chapter One, Echo's actions conceal the narcissistic activities of Zeus, the most powerful of all the gods, whose wrath she might rightly fear. It is as if she is programmed to defer to the most powerful object from the beginning, and while we cannot know the reason for it, the realisation of it is made manifest through Hera's curse. Could we interpret Echo's action as being comparable to the destructive echoist, in that Hera enacts the will of a powerful narcissist upon a fellow sufferer? For this, she is cursed to have no free will or speech of her own. She suffers in silence because she is cursed to repeat only the words of another, for whose words she can take no responsibility.

How might this manifest in the clinical situation for the echoist, who has, in the character of the therapist, a space in which her own voice might be heard? It seems to me that while she might have some relief in speaking, the author-ity of the god-like figure within brings about a feeling that she is unworthy to seek comfort from a fellow human being. It is as if the echoist has entered into a pact with her omnipotent object and feels she would betray it, and unleash its wrath on any individual to whom she exposes its antics. It is this relation-ship in the myth, already manifested in Echo's encounter with Hera, that raises the question of guilt. In ontological terms, Echo is perhaps the most damned creature, for to have an own-voice means to betray a god and to subject the lis-tener to persecution by the authority figure. This draws attention to the difficulty faced by the echoist, and the therapist, in coming into therapy; each time the echoist speaks her true feelings she risks the feeling that the wrath of her god-like object will be unleashed upon the person who is willing to hear her voice. Because the echoist naturally functions in the mode of the depressive position, the fear of damaging the therapist serves as another reason to hold back and to remain in servitude to an object that cannot be damaged by her, as long as she pretends that it *is* her.

Silence

In *Fear and Trembling*, the role of silence is important in many different ways but is central to the plight of each of the protagonists and to Kierkegaard himself. In the case of Agamemnon, the tragic hero is forced to struggle between his feeling that he should silence his anxiety so as not to receive comfort for his dreadful actions, while at the same time voicing his intentions so as to be fully exposed to the pain and suffering he is causing to his daughter and wife. It is in this choice of where to use his voice and where to exercise silence that he demonstrates his nobility, and, as Kierkegaard states, we can truly and straightforwardly offer him the compassion of the fellow human being through our own cathartic response.

In the case of Abraham, the silence is of a different nature, in which there is nothing to be said, as the whole context is one in which the Word of God is the only word. Kierkegaard argues that "Abraham cannot speak, because he cannot say that which would explain everything". Furthermore, as noted by Stewart and Nun (2010), Kierkegaard made a note in the margin in his first draft of *Fear and Trembling*, that:

> There is also another reason that Abraham cannot speak, for in silence he is continually making the movement of faith.

Interestingly, Kierkegaard's creative split is the enacting of the silencing of the two different parts at different times. In order to understand Abraham, Kierkegaard must silence Johannes the philosopher, whose enquiry can be met with no answers from the silent Abraham. Yet in order to keep the spirit of curiosity and the questioning of a god-like object, the ontic faith of Kierkegaard must be silenced. In the case of Echo, the silence is imposed upon her by a deity. In the clinical situation we encounter a god-like object in the echoist, to whom she gives authority, and by whom she is cursed to silence. The purpose of the therapy is to retain something of Johannes' stance, to bear witness as a fellow human being, and in so doing to expose the authoritative object to scrutiny, especially concerning its motives. The therapist and the patient must struggle together not only with the anxiety produced by such a conflict, but they also need to face the loss of the ontical god-object, which hitherto had offered a sense of certainty and security. We are able to appreciate something of this in the clinical vignette that follows.

Vignette 11: Lucy

Lucy, a twenty-two-year-old physiotherapist, came into therapy with me following years of depression. She had attended a group residential weekend that I had co-facilitated, with the title, "Finding your Own-Voice". Lucy had found it unbearably difficult to stay present in a group, fearing being seen and heard by others. She hoped to embark upon intensive individual therapy with me because she was suffering what she described as social anxiety, an inability to speak in company, a self-consciousness that produced blushing if anybody looked at her, and a belief that she had no friends. Her overwhelming preoccupation was with a phantasy of her funeral, to which nobody came except her mother.

I saw Lucy three times a week and for the first year it was difficult for her to speak during sessions. As she began a sentence it either faded out or she undermined it immediately through negating it herself or telling me that I must be thinking how irrelevant it was. I became aware of an internal drama taking place in Lucy's mind, in which a god-like object judged her words before she even spoke them. This made her feel that it was not worth speaking them, or that if she did venture them forth, they would be judged before the sentence was even finished.

I drew her attention to this, and we were able to share in the experience of hearing this object speak. Lucy maintained for a long time that it was not an object but a part of herself that she called the destructive horrible part. She said when she was in company it judged others very harshly, and it told her not even to try speaking to them because she was above them, and that it was best not to have them as friends anyway. It was what made her such a terrible person, she felt; in fact it made her feel that she must be a narcissist, and if so then it was best that she didn't speak. If she did go out and join in a conversation it usually resulted in her feeling that she had been awkward or caused an atmosphere, and if that didn't succeed in silencing her, then she would suffer what she described as the post mortem once she got home and into her bed. This would involve a long night of suffering, in which the minutiae of every sentence would be put on trial, judged, and found to be excruciatingly shameful.

I had the idea that her object, which appeared as god-like, persecuted Lucy, and left her in a state of isolation where it could then claim to be her only reliable companion. It assumed authority over her not just in terms of knowing exactly what went on in her mind, but it claimed to be able to interpret the actions and thoughts of others and to deliver to Lucy the shortcomings of her performance each time she risked social interaction. As we came to know the object better, she was able to notice certain things about it. It was a critical object. It usually addressed her as "You", and it seemed to know what was best for her. It had, she said, been present for as long as she could remember, and it had had such an impact that she spent much of her time alone. She had developed a phantasy life, much like that of a child, in which she was a very popular person whose presence was coveted by many fascinated friends, and this she could maintain in her mind while sitting silently in the bathrooms at school in her lunch breaks, and even in a quiet corner when she was out and required to attend events such as family parties. Yet still the object retained the power to carry out the post mortem, an act over which she felt she had no agency, but which she experienced as persecution from within.

I felt that the level of interrogation and internal dissection was a post mortem in every sense; a procedure that could not be borne by a living mortal, and one which was only tolerable to a dead body who cannot feel the pain wielded by the knife, or one who has been anaesthetised. It was as if she was being kept in this state by her object at the lowest level of existence, like that of the Echo of the myth. When I interpreted this, Lucy became very emotional. It felt, she said, as if somebody might, for the first time in her life, have some understanding of the persecution she experienced.

Following this observation, we experienced what felt like an obstruction beginning to move, similar perhaps to the idea of a curse being lifted, and Lucy began to speak to me. We agreed to let the object speak aloud while she spoke her own feelings and thoughts, her wishes and fears. We listened to its counsel and criticisms and I felt I was getting to know its ways, and to begin to understand its motives. As I shared this with Lucy I was reminded of Ronald Britton's writings on Job, which I described in detail in Chapter Six. The reader will recall that Britton explained that Job is persecuted and punished by God, but, unlike Abraham, he puts God on trial and judges *His* actions. While Job cannot change God, he changes his relationship to him and decides not to act like him.

Somehow, Lucy and I came to some shared yet unspoken agreement to put her object on trial, at least in terms of its intentions and motivations, and as we did so, these became more exposed. The problem, however, was that any exposure of the object's activities created such anxiety in Lucy. She felt guilt for betraying it to me, and shame when she allowed it to speak its feelings towards me. These frequently contained strong criticisms of my work and of the value of our relationship, which might be expressed thus:

> She is only listening to you because you pay her. She isn't there when you need her, especially in the middle of the night or when you are out in a group and you can't speak. She isn't there at all the important times, just on her terms. It isn't a *real* relationship.

Whenever she was able to use her own voice, the most striking thing I noticed about Lucy was her passion. Once she knew she had a space in which she could be heard, I was present to a life force that felt full of potential, but whenever we made contact in this way it was as though it was stolen before the next session. It became evident that Lucy's object did not want her to have anything from me or anybody else, as this threatened Lucy's state of dependency upon it. And yet something of it was gradually retained, and resulted increasingly in the evolution of a tiny self that she came to regard as *Me* – a subjective state of being that previously she had not been able to allow, or even to imagine for herself. This led to her having a voice that she began to be able to use outside as well as in the room with me.

In internalising me Lucy stood to lose the sense of certainty induced by her object, which sought to reclaim her allegiance by telling her that ours was not the real relationship, and that she could rely upon "it" in the darkness of the night when she was tormented and alone. In a partial sense, her object was right in its "reasoning" – I could not give her persuasive reason to transfer her faith to this process, this relationship. And yet it was only by listening to her object that I knew this, because I had been with her in the experience of listening to it speak. Her object was in fact more "reasonable" in the concrete world than anything I could offer the patient.

In one session, when Lucy was suffering terribly from the anxiety produced by rebelling against the object's certainty, we shared a meaningful experience through a dream that she brought. She described lying on a chaise longue with her feet out, and wearing high heels, facing a man whom she liked. They enjoyed being together and she described the following details:

> *It was a very nice feeling lying opposite him, and then we did this strange movement which is not really possible, as if we contorted our bodies towards each other and touched but not in a sexual way and in a way that is physically actually impossible.*

I replied:

> The image on the sofa where you connect in a way that you know is not humanly possible reminds me of something that happens here. You feel something very powerful, where you feel touched and seen, but you can't believe it is real, it is an impossibility, and it often gets taken away from you when you leave. And yet the experience is undeniable.

On further discussion, Lucy agreed that nobody could possibly understand this relationship with me, that it was easier to consign it to the realm of "professional" so she could put me in a box, and not have to acknowledge this as a real relationship. Indeed, all reason told her that it was impossible and that any sane person would say that it is in fact an impossible relationship and yet, she says, while it would be so much easier to follow reason, each time she comes she chooses the impossible over and again and in every instance because the experience is undeniable.

I say to her:

> The object cannot understand the realm of experience, because that is where reason ends.

It is here that she teaches me about faith, faith in a process that has no certainty, where there are no universals nor is there the promise of a special relationship, like the one she must forego with her object by coming here.

In foregoing the protection of her object she is exposed to the emptiness and nothingness of the ontological. It is an expression, as in the words of T. S. Eliot, of her willingness to hold on to faith:

I said to my soul, be still, and let the dark come upon you
Which shall be the darkness of God. As, in a theatre,
The lights are extinguished, for the scene to be changed…
[…] you see behind every face the mental emptiness deepen
Leaving only the growing terror of nothing to think about;
Or when, under ether, the mind is conscious but conscious of nothing –

Analysis

In the vignette above we are able to understand something of the echoist's relationship to what I have called in this chapter her god-like object. It is, of course, the same object that we have referred to elsewhere in this book as the critical-voice, the parasitic narcissistic object, and what Rosenfeld (1987, p. 88) calls an envious, destructive superego, and Britton (2003) refers to as an ego-destructive superego. Bion (1959, p. 312) had earlier described clinically the formation and establishment of such an object in the mind, resulting from the denial of normal degrees of the projective process, as I have mentioned earlier in the book. I have chosen to represent it as a god-like object in this chapter, as it brings together certain ideas that are relevant in both the myth and in the clinical work.

As we saw earlier, Freud (1950a, p. 331) speaks of the mother as the *Neben-mensch*, the fellow human being. He added that she is the original caregiving object, and one, moreover, who first addresses anxiety, stating that she is "simultaneously the [subject's] first satisfying object and further his first hostile object, as well as his sole helping power".

In the case of Lucy, we might wonder who her first object was, and when in fact such a curse was placed upon her. Like Echo in the myth, it is as if Lucy is programmed to defer to the most powerful object from the beginning, and while we cannot know the reason for it, the realisation of it is made manifest through her having been silenced.

In the myth, while Hera places the curse, she is in fact punishing Echo for the actions of her own narcissistic partner, Zeus, and it is as if the god is somehow acting through Hera, as she projects his omnipotence along with her own feelings of envy and rage into Echo. We cannot ignore the god-like appearance of this in Lucy's object.

This begs the question of the origins of a god-like object who not only acts tyrannically within the mind of the patient but who requires of her a pact of silence, of isolation in which no other human interaction is allowed, rendering her both dependent upon and subjected to the whims of such an object and its calls to action, and a feeling of being barely alive as a result of this. As I have suggested above, it is only Abraham's faith that enables him to set out to commit such a dreadful act, and not to speak of it because it is beyond words, and so it is one in which he appears, because of his faith, to have no agency.

In the vignette above, the problem for Lucy was that each time she achieved some emancipation from the object she suffered a complex form of guilt. This is further illustrated in Britton's explanation of the impact of such a move away from the object's enslavement. He describes it thus:

> What I am asserting here, I believe, is implicit but not explicit in Klein's account of the move from the paranoid-schizoid to the depressive position. In that transition, the accent moves from the superego to the ego, as the individual moves from the position of feeling praised or persecuted to feeling responsible. The nature of guilt changes: it moves from punishment by the superego, through reproach, to arrive at remorse, an affect of the ego accompanied by a wish to make reparation.
>
> (Britton, 2003, p. 72)

Lucy's fear of somehow damaging me grew as the work progressed and she was able to take more responsibility for her own voice and self in the world. As she felt she had more opportunity to reflect upon our sessions and her interactions with others, the feelings of attack and the power of the post mortem began to diminish, but she had to take more ownership of her feelings towards me, and these were both positive and negative.

When Lucy's hostility was aroused, for example, during my breaks or when she encountered a particularly difficult situation where I was not present for her, she was forced to struggle in an internal battle between her gratitude for our relationship and her feelings of pain and antagonism towards me. The guilt feelings this produced were painful for both of us to be with but were necessary for growth to take place. One important component of this guilt is the imposition of the ontological pain of having an own-voice, in which the patient bears the responsibility for her own observations and criticisms of her therapist.

Finally, I return to the quotation from T. S. Eliot at the beginning of this chapter, and to Hera's curse. We remember that Lucy's object claimed supremacy not just in terms of knowing exactly what went on in her mind, but in its claim to be able to interpret the actions and thoughts of others. Is this not a form of madness and omnipotence that must be questioned? And yet it is evident that it cannot be seen while one is under its power, and that it might feel quite normal until such times as one is removed from the spell – or what we might think of as Hera's curse upon her.

Eliot writes:

> … Wait without hope
> For hope would be hope for the wrong thing; wait without love,
> For love would be love of the wrong thing; there is yet faith
> But the faith and the love and the hope are all in the waiting.

We cannot rush this process, and a curse cannot be undone through a wish, or a further spell. It is only in withholding hope for something, in doing what Bion calls withholding memory and desire, that we can begin the process of enabling the emancipation from the curse towards the growth of the tiny ego in the echoistic patient. To do away with hope for a particular outcome, to abandon the reason that might seem to be the only tangible form to which to cling, makes the process of therapy seem impossible. To expect the patient to withdraw from the object that has established itself as an essential and only companion, feels like inflicting cruelty upon one who is already suffering. To ask for faith in a process that has an unknown outcome, in a relationship that is impossible, is what we ask of the echoistic patient in taking her into therapy with us. And yet, it seems, the patient can teach us something of that faith, and in the case of Lucy, whose dream communicates an unconscious belief in the impossible, I have learned that it is within all of us; faith is ontological and paradoxical, and therein of the human condition and not *in something*. To have this faith is necessary if we are to have any impact on the power of the curse of Hera as we meet its counterpart in the clinical situation; we must therefore wrestle with this paradox.

Part IV

A dynamic understanding of an echoistic-narcissistic complex

Chapter 8

Characters in search of an author

Echoistic-narcissistic complexes and group dynamics

> Father: For the drama lies all in this – in the conscience that I have, that each
> one of us has. We believe this conscience to be a single thing, but it is many-
> sided. There is one for this person, and another for that. Diverse consciences.
> So we have this illusion of being one person for all, of having a personality that
> is unique in all our acts. But it isn't true.
>
> Pirandello, *Six Characters in Search of an Author*, 1968

In this chapter I analyse the presence of both echoistic and narcissistic traits and behaviours in heterogeneous and homogeneous groups, and in my work with couples. I draw upon Bion's theories relating to basic assumption phenomena and container-contained ($\female\male$), to understand and illuminate projective processes taking place. Making reference to the work of Klein as well as Group Analytic theory, I use vignettes to illustrate how these may present, and consider the role of the therapist/analyst/conductor in the group analytic situation in the presence of echoism.

The previous chapters are based on the experience of being with the echoist in individual therapy. As we have seen, it is essential for the therapist to use her own feelings and experiences to reflect on her countertransference and any roles she feels she is being recruited into, in order to offer some understanding to her patient. When the therapist is confronted with similar feelings and experiences when exposed to a number of patients suffering symptoms common to each other in their lives and relationships, this heuristic approach provides insight into the phenomenon that is echoism.

I have also been afforded the opportunity to work with patients presenting as echoistic in group therapy and couples therapy. This provides other contexts within which to experience the echoist in relation both to a partner, who often presents as narcissistic, and to others in the world. Having the opportunity to observe, as well as relate, affords an interesting perspective and some new insights.

This chapter uses clinical vignettes to illustrate some of the findings and how they correspond, and what they add to understanding gained in the experience of individual therapy. In this instance, the term "heterogeneous groups" describes any group in which the patients are not selected on the basis of suffering similar issues. The second vignettes are made up of the therapist and two others who are in therapy as a "couple". In the final vignette a homogeneous group of patients are selected on the basis of a similar presenting issue or diagnosis. I will consider the presentation of echoism in each of these groups and analyse what might be inferred.

The heterogeneous group

Group A is a heterogeneous group comprising seven patients and a group conductor. Selection was based on referrals from individual therapists whose patients shared a common wish to learn more about themselves in relation to others. Patients had all been in individual therapy and all joined at the same time. In the first instance the group met for six consecutive weekly sessions, but continued after this period for four years. All patients in the group had chosen to attend. Suicidal ideation had occurred in a number of patients, although none were deemed to be at risk at the time of joining. Two patients had mental health diagnoses, two others were recovering from a life-crisis that had brought them into therapy; most had suffered from anxiety or depression at some time, and difficulties in relationships with loved ones was a prevalent issue for a number of members.

In amongst the more obvious preoccupations of a new group in coming to terms with itself as a group, and the individuals' struggle to find a place within it, I noticed a specific relationship developing between two members, Amanda and Elizabeth. This dynamic, which I call the "Echoistic-Narcissistic Couple (ENC) was present to a lesser extent between other members of the group, depending on the degree to which their narcissism and echoism were evoked, but was very striking to observe in the couple Amanda and Elizabeth. Once this couple had formed, it felt less penetrable to the projections, interpretations, and movements from and within the group than the other individual members who comprised the group. This had the dual impact of protection from perceived threat, alongside prevention of growth, for both individuals within the relationship. What we might infer from this is that the forming of the couple gives both the echoist and narcissist the illusion that they are safe from external threats, while at the same time making growth, of either, impossible, whilst the relationship remains in place, and unless the relationship can somehow be interrupted or penetrated by an external source.

Vignette 12: Elizabeth and Amanda

Elizabeth, an echoistic thirty-year-old unemployed woman who lived with her ageing parents, described being unable to tell her mother that she wanted to go away to university to study for a Master's degree in Theology. Elizabeth had suffered a background of severe depression and had been unable to study for her A-levels when she was eighteen, due to paralysing anxiety attacks whenever she went into school. She had lived at home ever since, taking part-time and menial jobs in spite of her very high intelligence, which had been demonstrated in her first-class marks in her distance-learning degree. Her mother worried about her doing anything out of the house, for fear of her relapse, and had advised her not to holiday with friends or to try to find a partner. Prior to joining the group, Elizabeth had been in individual therapy for two years, where she had come to feel she had gained some autonomy in her own thoughts and wishes. Through the triangular space created by her therapist she had been able to think about her own voice in relation to her internal narcissistic object as well as to her mother. She had moved into group therapy as a way of trying out her own voice in a safe and protected space that also offered opportunities for reflection. In individual sessions Elizabeth had tried to think about her feelings about her mother, whom she reported as oppressively anxious about her ability to leave home and to manage without her, yet claiming to be motivated solely by protectiveness. Once in the group, however, Elizabeth found it very hard to speak about this.

Amanda, a fifty-six-year-old woman who had worked as a teacher of psychology, spoke with authority when Elizabeth was asked by Eddie, a fellow group member, what she felt might be stopping her from telling her mother of her wishes. Amanda made a habit of jumping in to answer questions on Elizabeth's behalf, and to theorise as to the reasons why Elizabeth found it difficult. Feeling she had to justify herself whenever she was challenged, Elizabeth deferred immediately to Amanda's theoretical explanations. In effect, she sought out another narcissistic object, or a substitute mother, and introjected her ideas to colonise her own hard-won, autonomous thoughts.

Drawing upon her intellectual knowledge of psychological theory, Amanda explained to the group that Elizabeth's mother was aware of Elizabeth's vulnerability following her history of depression and a previous suicide attempt, and that these were still real threats to Elizabeth. Amanda said she understood how it might look as if the mother was holding Elizabeth back from independence but that from her experience, Elizabeth was still incredibly vulnerable. She feared that Elizabeth might go to a new environment, feel isolated and unable to cope, and, as a consequence, return to her former suicidal state. Elizabeth was, Amanda said, "in the vulnerable state of needing those who understood and could support her". Elizabeth nodded as Amanda spoke, and the group members were drawn into what felt like both an unremarkable exchange between two group members and a certainty that Amanda had somehow provided the perfect interpretation.

The conductor asked both Amanda and Elizabeth if they were aware that Amanda had spoken for Elizabeth. Their surprise was evident, as was the group's. Once this had been established, both members were invited to explore what had taken place and how each had played a part in it. Unsurprisingly, Elizabeth, the echoistic patient, found it difficult to acknowledge her role in it – a common defence in the echoist who frequently sees herself as passive. This inability to take responsibility for her role in a pair or group is particularly pronounced in a self-destructive echoist, whose state of being-through-others can leave the echoist with the impression that she walks through the world without making an imprint upon it (I give a detailed exploration of the self-destructive echoist in Chapter Five).

Analysis

As the vignette shows, in this group the intervention came from the conductor, but it can come from any group member. Due to the power of projective identification, however, which becomes amplified by the seemingly concrete nature of the ENC, it is often hard to notice it is even taking place. This serves as an example of what Bion (1961, pp. 148–149) describes as the "numbing feeling of reality", which influences the affected group conductor and group members away from realising what has happened, and what is happening, under their noses. Their unwitting participation, affected as it is by the powerful projective processes, is to render something remarkable as unremarkable and too commonplace and obvious to warrant attention or comment, let alone interpretation. The group conductor comes to feel, simultaneously, powerful emotions and serious doubt about her questioning attitude, or even curiosity itself. She, and indeed, any member of the group, may feel anxious about disturbing the sense of "normality" in the proceedings.

Without some awareness of the processes described above occurring in groups, and particularly with the ENC, the conductor too might have been under the influence of this convincing pairing, and therefore unable to intervene in a way that was helpful to both members.

Bion suggested that when group members and the group analyst have become drawn in to being participants in a shared phantasy situation, it is hard to recognise. The awareness of playing a role, a part, in someone else's drama or phantasy, disappears under the influence of this mesmeric use of projective identification to produce a sense of "business as usual". This notion is particularly interesting in terms of the interrelatedness of the psychoanalytic and the existential perspectives. The projective identification and numbing feeling of reality places each member of the group into a role that is deemed to be "normal" and not worthy of comment or analysis. The roles give each member a fixed sense of themselves within the group and the feeling of identity: "I am the member who…" This effect includes the group conductor and generates the kind of feeling Sartre describes when he refers to the "waiterliness", a paradigmatic situation I have discussed at length in Chapter Three. In existential terms, we can see how this sequence of projective identification, amplified by the concrete certainty produced by the consensus of the ENC in their fixed roles, produces a situation of bad-faith in the members of the group. This has the effect of rendering them beings-in-themselves, enabling them to feel protected from the exposure to their own nothingness. Unless the group conductor, or an alert and curious member of the group, wakes up to this feeling, the consequence is that this prevents the growth of the individuals within the group. The result is a macrocosmic expression at group level of what is happening within the microcosm of the ENC.

Eventually, with the help of the group, Amanda resisted the urge to speak for Elizabeth quite so often, and allowed other group members' observations to be heard and considered by Elizabeth. Elizabeth was able to speak more easily in the group as Amanda removed her protective hold around her, and although it took a number of years, eventually Elizabeth left the group. This was seen as a very positive step for her, as it coincided with her taking a responsible and challenging job, with study involved, and a salary that would enable her to leave home and share a flat with a friend. Her emancipation from Amanda, and then the group, was a powerful experience in finding a self, and an own-voice, which contributed towards her eventually freeing herself from her mother's projections.

Interestingly, it may have been that the actual situation of finding herself in a group re-evoked the anxiety she had felt in the original situation when she had been unable to continue at school. The group therefore provided conditions for a transference relationship that would not have been produced in individual therapy.

Pairing

It is striking to notice the dynamics in the echoistic patient's internal world, and the degree to which she unconsciously seeks to recreate the manifestation of this in her external relationships. A newly forming heterogeneous group is an excellent opportunity to observe such a phenomenon as it is taking place, and gives some indication of the echoist's way of relating in the world. Where the pairs that form are less distinct, or the degree of echoism or narcissism is less pronounced or there is no natural partner, it is interesting to observe aspects and traits of both, and the degree to which narcissists cannot help but project parts of the self into the group in a way that attempts to turn other group members into echoists, or which exploits echoistic potential. Interestingly, echoists can also play a similar role in groups, drawing advice and agency out of others and attempting to find a protective other, even where there is no obvious narcissist to form the couple. Because the echoist is quieter and does this through active introjection, it is harder to observe. In the heterogeneous group, this may take the form of the other rescuing, soothing, or over-interpreting, as well as filling the space to hide the echoist's discomfort at having to be in the group without a narcissistic partner.

Bion's writing on "Basic Assumption" phenomena is valuable here, particularly in relation to the forming of a pair. He describes basic assumption phenomena as: "activity requir[ing] no training, experience or mental development. It is instantaneous, inevitable and instinctive" (Bion, 1961, p. 153). In its simplest form it can be understood as the unconscious phantasy life of the group. These basic assumptions concern hidden beliefs and phantasies about the purposes for which the group members are assembled. Pairing is one of three states in the group alongside the other two main basic assumptions of dependency and fight-flight. This inevitable process is one that naturally occurs in group life as a way of carrying hope for the survival and creativity of the group. Bion likens pairing to a sexual liaison in which the group invests its hope symbolically, to produce a messiah (a baby who holds the bountiful gifts of the future of the group). As long as this messiah is never actually produced, the group continues to hold it as a symbol of survival and hope. The emergence of such a pair is invested with the latent sexuality of the group members, although in the example given by Bion (1961, p. 150) he makes it clear that "the sex of the pair was of no particular consequence to the assumption that pairing was taking place". Any group analyst will be aware of this phenomenon and the impact it can have on the pair, the other group members, and herself, and the usefulness in directing attention towards it, as and when it can be seen to be emerging.

I would argue that while this is a necessary observation for all groups, it is not sufficient in understanding the specific dynamic of the echoistic-narcissistic couple and its impact on a group. This might be thought of more specifically in terms of the container-contained relationship, in which under normal circumstances the formation of a couple in a group is a necessary stage in the process of the group's wish and willingness to reproduce and effectively grow. The ability to observe the pairing of such a couple within a group allows the group to take ownership of the phantasies that belong to the whole group, but which have been projected into the couple as the symbolic embodiment of the messianic hope. This observation provides the conditions for a *symbiotic* container-contained relationship (see Chapter Two), from which springs the possibility of growth for all members of the group, and for the group as an entity in its own right. Conversely, if the couple is an ENC, the likelihood is that the container-contained relationship becomes a *parasitic* one (see Chapter Two), unless the conductor or another member of the group wakes up and notices what is being lived out under their very eyes in a drama in which they are also playing a role.

This raises the question of how to work in a way that allows growth within a group and in the individuals in the ENC pair. This is not the only type of pairing that may have a parasitic impact on the group – two members forming a pair to bully and intimidate others is a good example – however I suggest that other pairs may be far more transparent than the ENC pair, and therefore visible to both the conductor and other group members. Because there is something that feels so natural about the echoistic-narcissistic couple it is more likely to create the numbing feeling of reality described so beautifully by Bion. This raises a number of important questions concerning noticing it as it is happening, and then how to work with that information once the therapist, or an alert group member, has woken out of the un-noticing state Bion describes.

We know, from our work with individual patients, that the creation of triangular space is a necessary process to enable some observation of the dynamic relationship between internal narcissistic objects and the ego. I suggest that something of this method might be facilitated in group process, first by noticing the relationship emerging, and then separating the pair through helpful and supportive interpretations and interventions.

The echoistic-narcissistic couple and the therapist

As we have seen above, the echoist-narcissist couple is a phenomenon that seeks to realise itself wherever possible through projective and introjective processes. In couples therapy and in groups, in parent-child relationships or wherever this couple may appear, because of the naturalness of the union it can be difficult to observe, particularly when the couple have become co-dependent in an established relationship. These are the relationships we often see in couples therapy, and the narcissist can be so colonising of both the echoist and the therapist that it may seem that he is the victim. Alternatively, the long-suffering echoist may have come into therapy with her partner because the narcissistic behaviour has reached a level that can no longer be ignored. In the following short vignettes I draw attention to two different presentations of the ENC. In the first the narcissist is obviously dominant and the echoist presents as a victim, with a clear delineation of echoistic and narcissistic traits – in this example the libidinal narcissist is paired with the defensive echoist. The second vignette illustrates a disturbing relationship between a malignant narcissist and a self-destructive echoist.

Vignette 13: Mr and Mrs F

Mr and Mrs F came into therapy to address what they described as Mr F's mid-life crisis. Primarily, this had manifested in an affair with a woman he had met abroad. Mrs F was very upset and felt betrayed by her husband, who admitted he had not seen anything wrong with the affair until he was caught and his wife threatened to expose it to the children (aged twenty-one and sixteen) unless he came into therapy. Mr F agreed that he would attend but said that he refused to take all the blame.

In the course of the therapy I attempted to provide a space to explore their feelings towards one another, and how they had experienced the events and feelings leading up to the crisis. Mr F showed a willingness to speak about himself and his formative experiences as a way of understanding what might have caused a change in recent behaviours, while Mrs F took every opportunity to express her resentment towards her husband. She refused to consider her own background or whether she had played any part in the problems, stating that she had had a perfect childhood with loving parents and that it was her husband who was "screwed up".

I noticed how Mrs F attempted to recruit me into a role of being able to show and tell her husband what he had done wrong, and sought to coerce me into taking her side and even speaking for her. As I attempted to make an equal space for each of them to speak and to explore their own feelings, Mrs F became withdrawn, maintaining that her husband was the problem, not her. She said she needed me to tell them what they must do, and said that each time they left a session she felt I had not managed to make him see the errors of his ways. I agreed to see each member of the couple individually and this proved very illuminating.

In the individual session with Mr F, although his narcissism was evident, I was able to make contact with a healthy part of him. He said he loved Mrs F and wanted to understand what drove him to destructive behaviours. He said he felt she behaved as if she had been a perfect partner, but in the course of the relationship she had always relied upon him to bring any interest or excitement into the relationship. He was, he said, tired of having to provide all the energy and interest in their relationship, and the woman he had met had been spontaneous and creative and he had been excited by her. He had stopped all contact with this woman and wanted to make amends but he also wanted his wife to take a role in bringing some fun and pleasure into their relationship, especially now their children were so independent and they found themselves alone together more often.

In my individual session with Mrs F she found it difficult to speak to me except to complain about Mr F's behaviour, and to seek ways to help him recover from his destructiveness. Whenever I mentioned that this session was for her, she became uncomfortable and annoyed and reiterated that *she* was not the one who needed therapy. Interestingly, she took no responsibility for her role in the relationship and said she just wanted things to go back to how they were before.

Vignette 14: Ms M and Mr V

One of the most difficult and painful relationships for the therapist to endure is being in the presence of what I describe as the malignant couple – the couple comprised the destructive narcissist and the self-destructive echoist. I worked with one such couple, where the female partner, Ms M, was particularly dominant and critical of her partner Mr V, during early sessions. Ms M had instigated the therapy after her husband had been sent by her on any number of self-help workshops for assertiveness training, enabling him to say "No" and to empower him to express his masculinity. He had, it seemed, disappointed on all levels, and she sought therapy with me to help try to ascertain what he was doing wrong in the relationship. I watched as Mr V tried to adapt himself to meet Ms M's demands week by week, and how no matter what he changed, she found fault with everything he did. Although I attempted to provide a space in which his needs could be heard, and to draw attention to the balance of forces within the relationship, the demands made upon each other and the levels of acceptance in the relationship, both partners closed ranks and kept my voice out of the sessions.

Mr V, even when helped by me to have his own voice, capitulated immediately his partner raised a counter-argument. Whenever I drew attention to any narcissistic aspects of Ms M, her partner defended her. Effectively, he echoed her every word, and, in an attempt to colonise me, both partners joined together in complaining about the sessions when we made any progress in understanding something of their dynamic.

This relationship demonstrated a similar dynamic to the one taking place and described in the heterogeneous group above. In this instance, however, both partners were completely aware of their interactions and complicit in them. At times, I felt I was making progress in showing them the way in which the projective processes manifested in the couple, and the evidence for this, which was ample and obvious in the sessions. What was less obvious to me was how their envy of me having any insight manifested as destructive attacks on my work with them. The whole process was fruitless and painful and the level of complicity between them made their relationship impenetrable in every sense. I now understand that the united force of the penetrations into me – directly from Ms M, the narcissist, and through Mr V, the echoist – forced me into an echoistic position in which I not only lost my own voice but was required to repeat their joint assertions. As a result the work could not continue.

Analysis

Ronald Britton's contribution on the role of twinning, a collusion between two narcissists, is valuable and striking, particularly in the examples he gives (see Steiner 2008, pp. 28–33). In the above vignette, I would argue that while this may resemble twinning between narcissists, closer observation reveals it is a collusion between the two members of the echoistic-narcissistic couple, something the group and couple vignettes reveal more explicitly than in individual work, where the therapist must rely solely upon her own experience of being with the patient.

In both the heterogeneous group vignette and in the two couples' vignettes above, we can observe how the echoist and narcissist work together in a very specific way, forming a sealed unit where external projections seem almost to bounce off them, reinforcing their dependency upon one another. This goes some way to explain the difficulty for the echoist in leaving a relationship with a narcissist. Because, as I believe, this process is highly effective, due to the predominantly projecting nature of the narcissist and the predominantly introjecting nature of the echoist, it was of great interest to work with a homogeneous group of echoists together and to observe what would happen.

The homogeneous group

The homogeneous group of echoistic patients that I had the opportunity to work with and experience first hand proved a fascinating study within which to capture and gain some further understanding of echoism.

In the following account I use a vignette to describe an experience of weekend residential courses for women who felt they struggled to have a voice of their own, and who had been in a relationship with at least one narcissistic partner, or who had at least one parent who was narcissistic. Unsurprisingly, there was a correspondence between both, with a majority of members in the group having had a narcissistic parent and then having gone on to find a replacement with narcissistic partners, some habitually. This led, in many cases, to the patient group feeling they lacked importance, with individuals finding it hard to speak up in other relationships, both personal and professional. Often this resulted in forming relationships with friends and work colleagues who fitted the same pattern of relating as the narcissistic other. Because this confirmed previously formed ideas resulting from the individual and couples work, in addition to providing a space in which these women might feel some comfort from others suffering similar problems, a colleague and I were also interested to observe how the introjecting nature of the echoist might manifest in a group in which there were no narcissists. We agreed, beforehand, on a set of key principles, which resulted from the observations made from the individual work, and the evolving ideas emerging from couples and group work. This was to provide a mode of Being considered to be suitable for group therapists working with homogeneous groups of echoistic patients. These were as follows.

Key principles in treating the echoistic patient

- Development of an own-voice is the primary focus. While modelling a different voice to that of the ego-destructive internal object's voice, this should not overtake the key aim of developing an own-voice.
- Therapists should hold back and allow the space. Do not fill it, even though this will feel uncomfortable.
- Allow the internal objects a space to be heard. Any voices belonging to narcissistic and ego-destructive objects can be captured by the therapist and reflected back to the echoist for what they are. Enabling the echoist to distinguish between ego-destructive superego voices and a developing own-voice is imperative. Allowing dialogues between these different entities provides a powerful way of creating awareness for the echoist of her internal world, and why she seeks to replicate this in her external relationships. This also has the direct impact of creating triangular space (see Chapter Two).
- Do not reassure the patient. In particular, do not tell the echoist she is not a narcissist. Explore, and use interpretation when the patient has recognised something of this for herself.
- Recognising one's own narcissism and exploring it in supervision or with a peer helps to enable awareness of projective identification from a narcissistic object within the internal world of the echoist. Therapists should be alert to this in groups.
- A common experience for the therapist working with the echoistic patient is to be left with feelings of not being able to give enough, or feeling drained and exhausted. This characterises the very real phenomenon of being actively introjected by the life-hungry echoist (functioning very much as Echo does in the myth). The therapist should try to be aware of and monitor her own energy flow and reflect upon its significance.

- Fears of penetration, siege, a threat to safety and imminent attack appearing in sessions, reported or in dreams, are common. These should be taken as real threats in the echoist's world.

Vignette 15: Residential

Evidence from individual and couples work had indicated real difficulties for echoists in verbalising their thoughts and speaking aloud, especially in the company of others. In setting up a residential course, this element was considered carefully and it was decided to use arts therapies alongside the more traditional talking therapy, to provide opportunities for the patients to express themselves in other ways.[1]

Planning a programme with a group-analytic process group as the core of the course, allowed for a range of other exercises. These included using dramatherapy to allow opportunities for recruitment of others into particular roles, dynamic interaction in the external world to reflect internal processes, and expression through non-verbal forms. The aim was to be with the patients in a non-directive way in the process group, and to offer shape and a container in the creative exercises. The first priority was to set up a demarcated safe space where the process group was held, and to which patients could return at any time during the residential with a therapist on hand, available to be with them.

The two facilitators of the group, a psychotherapist and a dramatherapist, met the participants for the first process group. The patients were invited to introduce themselves and to share their conscious reasons for attending. Even at this early stage of the process they barely spoke of themselves, showing instead a marked tendency to speak of their narcissistic parents or partners, describing what they were left feeling as a result of these experiences. This then led into the first process group, a form to which we returned throughout the weekend.

In the first creative exercise patients were asked to choose a shell, stone, or natural object, which we called a "piece", from a collection wrapped in a large linen cloth. This piece was to represent them in a constellation exercise that would be used throughout the weekend to observe and record emotional presence and absence in the group, when it might not be able to be voiced, and to project on to the piece what might otherwise be unsayable.

---

1 Interestingly, having discovered that the centrality of the verbal component in talking therapies constituted an insurmountable obstacle for some echoists, I had, on a number of occasions, made use of art materials and symbolic and abstract images to help the echoist to express her feelings. This bears a similarity to the decision made by Klein in her work with children, to use toys to enable them to find other ways to express feelings and ideas hard for a child to verbalise. It begs the question as to whether some of Klein's techniques for use with children may well be appropriate for some of the time in work with some individuals who have never developed a voice (see final chapter).

Pieces

Following introductions, the group members spoke of what had attracted them to the particular shell or stone they had chosen and were asked to place their piece on a tray in relation to those of others, including those of the two facilitators. They spoke, if they were able, about their choice of piece, and what they understood about where they placed it, whether near to that of one of the therapists, another group member, on the outskirts of the group, or hiding in the centre amongst others. These pieces very quickly became symbols for the group members themselves, as they were invited to move them during certain sessions over the course of the weekend, to express how they were feeling in relation to other members of the group and to being in a group.

In the practice of dramatherapy use of pieces in this way allows the pieces themselves to become part of a dynamic process. The pieces "stand in" for self. For long periods of silence patients moved their pieces, and then others moved their pieces in relation to what had just happened. Individuals moved their pieces in response to feeling abandoned, exposed, forced into a central position, or separated from somebody they wanted to be close to. They were able to invest in the pieces as extensions of themselves, so as to be able to interact symbolically and freely in a way that they were unable to do verbally.

One member found herself unable to function when the group leader moved her piece away from hers. She said: "This doesn't mean anything to me anymore. It's just a tray of shells to me", and she withdrew from the exercise, which had become too painful for her, due perhaps to it having moved from a symbolic activity to a more concrete one, comparable to a symbolic equation[2] as described by Segal (1957).

At other times, after an exercise where individuals had shared a powerful reaction, or after meal breaks or in the morning after sharing a room with somebody, they moved their pieces to reflect this. They also used their pieces to indicate a conscious or unconscious wish to get to know others, or at times, with newfound independence, to be in the centre of the group after always remaining on the outskirts in group situations. The opportunity for the patients to analyse and interpret this as a group proved powerful and is discussed in the analysis below.

Process group

Perhaps the most compelling evidence for the phenomenon that is echoism came from this experience. The group met at various points, six times in total, for a therapeutic process group of ninety minutes each time, at various points in the weekend. From the first

---

2 "The early symbols, however, are not felt by the ego to be symbols or substitutes, but to be the original object itself. They are so different from symbols formed later that I think they deserve a name of their own" (Segal, 1957, p. 393).

group onwards, participants looked to others to speak, and then to the therapist facilitators. It is common in group therapy to observe rivalry and wrestling for space, as was seen more typically in the heterogeneous group above. Silences are also not unusual and are meaningful when they do occur within the normal flow and rhythm of group activity. A group dominated by silence, however, is significant in terms of the meaning of the silence and the relationships between group members. As Andrea Sabbadini states:

> If we believe silences to be meaningful, it follows that one of our functions … is to understand the meanings of our patients' silences: learning about their inner worlds involves listening to their silences, not just to their words.
>
> (Sabbadini, 2014, p.106)

He goes on (ibid., p. 109) to quote from Freud's 1919 paper, *The Uncanny*,[3] where he highlights the connection between silence and anxiety:

> Concerning the factors of silence, solitude and darkness… we can only say that they are actually elements in the production of the infantile anxiety from which the majority of human beings have never become quite free.
>
> (Freud, 1919h, p. 252)

Sabbadini suggests:

> Perhaps one of the main functions of silence is to transform unconscious anxiety, concerning some as yet unknown or unworked-through inner conflict, into more manageable, though often more painful, conscious anxiety …"

The therapists held in mind the notion of the "Leaderless Group" (Bion, 1946) as a group analytic concept that allows unconscious material to present itself in the space that is created through the absence of direction from the group analyst. This meant that while the therapists could and did use the space to interpret the silence, they did not fill it or direct the patients in the group. Because there were no "leaders" to follow, individuals became agitated and upset. One patient said in feedback: "Silence in process groups was difficult to stay with and sometimes felt wasted and unproductive. I wanted the leaders to be more directive."

What was valuable for research purposes was the opportunity to notice the active echoism, which seeks out another to fill the void. Some patients were very keen to explore their roles in this and to gain some understanding that they were not simply passive responders in the process. They found they were often unable to access this thinking during the process groups. In a more directive exercise, however, when they were invited by the therapists to reflect on what was happening in the

---

3 *unheimlich*, literally "unhomely", or "undomiciled"; sometimes translated as "unnatural", or "uncanny".

process group, they could analyse and understand more of their unconscious wish for a narcissistic and authoritative other to speak for them or tell them what to say. This in itself was interesting. In recognising their need for permission they could also acknowledge their relationships to an internal authoritative figure, who judged their words before they spoke in a group where there was no obvious "task". This "judge", which we have come to understand through this book as an internal narcissistic object, became the focus for an exercise below called "The Monster".

The Monster

In this exercise, the dramatherapist talked the patients through a guided imagery process to create a state of openness and a quietening of internal voices. They were then asked to imagine a monster standing just behind them, to visualise in their mind's eye the characteristic details of this monster, and to notice their reactions to its presence. There was a strong sense of fear, particularly because the monster was always behind the individual, and its voice, its breathing and footsteps, smell and touch were all brought to life in the patients' inner theatre of the mind. The final stage of the exercise was for patients to turn around and face the monster, and to see it and remember it and to listen to anything it had to say and the way it spoke. This caused powerful reactions and one patient ran from the room in tears. The point of dramatherapy is that patients should not be overwhelmed by their experience but can enact and experience what might be overwhelming in the "real" world but which is safe in the arts-based container. This implicit understanding enabled the patient to return soon after to the safe space to continue with the process.

The group members were then given art materials to represent the monster visually, and many added speech bubbles or wrote words to capture its voice and discourse. When all patients returned to the safe space with their drawings to discuss the exercise, they described how powerfully they had felt the experience.

Some found it difficult to look at their drawings, as it reproduced the fear they had felt during the exercise. For many they were able to acknowledge that it had a familiar voice and that the things it said were familiar in their internal world. One patient had drawn an actual man who had assaulted her as a teenager, and she had the realisation that he had somehow been internalised in this monstrous figure that was ever-present as a voice in her mind. Another patient had drawn herself, feeling that although she had recognised the voice of the monster as a loved parent who had betrayed her as a child, on seeing his face, her guilt was evoked and she had to make *herself* the monster. As a consequence of having told someone about his behaviour, he had been forcibly removed from her life. She had been left, since childhood, with the feeling that speaking or revealing the monster caused terrible loss of a loved one and intense guilt, and had made herself the monster to avoid developing an own-voice, as she considered it to have devastating consequences.

This exercise was highly effective in giving form to an internal object in a way that the patients could conceptualise it and talk about it as a part of themselves that had been somehow put or projected into them, but was not a part of the self or even a split-off part to be integrated. Instead, it was a malignant object in the inner world that did not want them to develop an own-voice, and it used a variety of strategies to steal anything they might have, particularly the space to be heard. This realisation then enabled more light to be shed on what was happening in the process groups.

Instruments

The next practical exercise after the group had had time to process the previous one was a group exercise using musical instruments as a mode of expression to externalise the relationship between internal objects and the self. The members were invited to choose a musical instrument and to find a quiet space in the room. They were asked to close their eyes and this time rather than quieting all the voices in the inner world they were guided to stay open to hearing them. As they began to listen for the voice that might be the monster's they also heard other voices, those of their therapists, and others who were felt to be good objects in their inner worlds. They learned something of the relationships between these voices as they listened and began to identify them.

After some time, they were asked to listen for their own voice to see if they could hear it. They were told when they could hear it, to tap their drums, ring their bells, shake their tambourines or maracas, or to strike their triangles, keeping their eyes closed.

Very tentatively the room began to resonate with the occasional sound of a percussion instrument, weak at first and becoming stronger, as some heard their own-voice and were able to express it. Gradually the sounds began to fill the room, creating rhythms and swells as more instruments joined in. At one point the sounds reached a crescendo and a number of the patients were hitting their drums or shaking their bells furiously, tears streaming down their faces. One described it afterwards as hearing her own voice for the first time. Eventually the therapist brought the exercise to a close and asked them to place their instruments on the floor. They were then given coloured pens to write down the internal dialogue, with one colour for their own-voice and different ones for the monster's and the voices of any other objects.

When they had completed this task, all members were invited to share aloud something of their dialogues. This produced much anxiety, and many felt exposed and fearful at having their own thoughts and voices witnessed by others. It produced powerful reactions, as they could acknowledge agency in their choice to have their voices heard, and feelings of privilege in hearing others share their own thoughts in a way that felt new and exposing.

It was in one of these reflective sessions that a group member likened herself to the character of Echo in the myth, and introduced the idea, and the myth itself, to the group, before the group therapists made any mention of it, or did any work on it. In fact it led perfectly into the dramatherapy work, which included acting out and working with the myth, in the activities described below.

Enacting the myth of Echo and Narcissus

In this exercise the patients split into groups and, using a script written in verse, rehearsed and performed the myth to the other groups. This was acknowledged by the patients as being very powerful, not only because of each individual's process of enactment, but also the repetition of being witnessed by others and of witnessing other versions, which meant that they were really able to think about their identifications with characters in the myth. They were given a range of props and some described experiencing pleasure in putting on sunglasses and posing in the mirror, and taking a role different from their usual role in relationships. Many felt strong identification between the character of Hera and a narcissistic parent upon whom they modelled their performances. Members also described a fear that they might really enjoy the narcissistic role and how seductive and alluring it was. Perhaps the most powerful response, however, was that of sadness and even grief when they watched another group's performance, and felt strongly not just for Echo's plight as she fades away but – for some members of the group – their own.

As a way of finding the essence of each of the characters, of deepening understanding of the central dilemma of Echo, we used an activity in which the group worked together to create a moving tableau for each character in the myth. Somebody called out the character's name, and one group member stepped from the circle into the centre and struck a pose or created a movement that symbolised something of that character, and repeated this movement as other members joined the tableau, adding their own movements to it. Participants were able to use sounds and even instruments if they wished, until all those wishing to join had done so; then one of the therapists replaced certain individuals so they could step out of the tableau to walk around it and observe it as a piece of performance art. This was very moving, particularly when the character of Echo was made into a machine, with a silent scream and a desperate drum-beat at the centre of the machine, characterising the appalling state of the curse of silence. Many members were deeply moved as they stepped out and saw a powerful representation of a state they lived with daily.

Analysis

The weekend residential was both educational and therapeutic, with patients reporting greater awareness of their own states, which they could take back to work on in individual therapy or analysis. Moments of the course had been challenging and emotionally demanding for some members of the group. The presence of two therapists was felt to have been essential for patients who needed a quiet and safe space to work through some of these painful states when it felt too exposing to stay in the group.

The safe space was used by many individuals at different times in the weekend, as many previously unconscious or repressed feelings emerged through the creative exercises. Patients were given a space to verbalise them, often for the first time. The pieces exercise proved invaluable as a way of symbolising the dynamic internal theatre of the objects in the mind. Patients were able to show something of the inner workings of their minds and their relationships to good objects and to narcissistic objects in terms of the roles into which they recruited members of the group, and the group therapists. For almost all members, the ability to reflect on how the pieces exercise took on symbolic meaning was a rare opportunity to be able to share their common experiences.

At the end of the weekend the two therapists listed and discussed the experiences common to the echoistic individuals they had worked with in the homogeneous group. These were synonymous with experiences of echoistic patients in both individual work, heterogeneous groups, and in couples work. They were, however, particularly pronounced and observable in the homogenous group, where they were highlighted by the absence of narcissists or participants willing to occupy the narcissistic role.

Chapter 9

Is there anybody in there?

The therapist as echoist

Christianity has done its utmost to close the circle and declared even doubt to be sin. One is supposed to be cast into belief without reason, by a miracle, and from then on to swim in it as in the brightest and least ambiguous of elements: even a glance towards land, even the thought that one perhaps exists for something else as well as swimming, even the slightest impulse of our amphibious nature — is sin! And notice that all this means that the foundation of belief and all reflection on its origin is likewise excluded as sinful. What is wanted are blindness and intoxication and an eternal song over the waves in which reason has drowned.

Friedrich Nietzsche,
Daybreak: Thoughts on the Prejudices of Morality, 1997

In this chapter I consider the importance of the therapist's awareness of her own echoism, and her responsibility for acknowledging its presence in the clinical relationship. I recount the experiences of other therapists who have attended my training workshops on echoism, and I explore the acknowledgments made by these participants of their own echoistic traits, which may even have led them into the work of therapy. Illustrating how the skills of listening, repeating, reflecting, and providing a container for powerful projections are requirements of the clinical practitioner, I ask how this might predispose the therapist to making particular interpretations if these are unknown defences in her own personality. I explain how an echoistic disposition in the therapist might make toleration of the echoistic patient difficult, as well as leading to the therapist experiencing countertransference problems produced by the echoist's difficulty in staying in therapy, where the focus of attention lies uncomfortably fixed on her. Finally, this chapter highlights the requirement for reflexivity, the willingness to address difficult countertransference experiences in supervision, and a call for the therapist to have as much awareness of the impact of her own echoism as she does of her narcissism.

Permeability

One active aspect of echoism to which I have become alert is what I experience as permeability in the patient. In the defensive echoist I may be aware of the patient's more conscious attempt to draw me in, for example, by asking me how I am, or by inducing me to speak, but what is much less tangible is the unconscious process taking place in which the echoistic patient is appealing to me to do or to say something through actively introjecting me. This can result in the therapist feeling impotent, sometimes creating high levels of discomfort and anxiety in the ensuing silence, and producing an unconscious wish, behind the more conscious urge to fill the empty space, to "fill" the patient, as an attempt to flee from this anxiety. In attempting to understand this I find it useful to consider Samuel Beckett's *Waiting for Godot*, in which the recurring wish to quell the existential anxiety felt by the two main characters, Vladimir and Estragon, is *to do something*, in order to avoid the *angst* produced by endless waiting. The line "There's nothing to be done" reflects a painful state that must be borne by both in coming to terms with the absence of another to fill the emptiness, and to provide a focus away from the truth of their predicament.

Aspects of echoism, like narcissism, are present in every individual, but, as I discussed in Chapter Four, these become problematic when they dominate the personality. It is essential, therefore, that all therapists continue to monitor and reflect upon their own echoistic tendencies. The requirement to actively introject the other as part of a willingness to accept their projections, in order that they can be thought about and, eventually, understood, is a normal part of clinical practice and it is one in which the therapist's echoistic tendencies can go undetected.

I have, as part of my method, made use of *epoché*[1] (the bracketing of the therapist's own feelings). What has surprised and interested me is the way in which echoistic patients have somehow managed to pick up these bracketed feelings. Echoists seem to pick up anxiety and other feelings in the therapist in a way that can feel uncanny. This leads me to believe that the echoist has some of the qualities that can take some therapists many years to develop. For those echoists who decide to work as clinical practitioners, there is a risk that what appear to be skills could actually be being used unconsciously as defences, and it is essential that these are detected and worked on during training and supervision.

The therapist as echoist

It is widely accepted that therapists should have a commitment to an evolving understanding of their tendencies towards specific responses in stressful emotional situations, so that they may function in their role in the best interests of the patient. The necessity for the therapist to acknowledge and to explore, in her own therapy and supervision, any narcissistic traits she may possess, in order to understand the communications of the patient and her own countertransference reactions, is well documented. As this book shows, the impact of echoism on the other and the predisposition for the echoist to form a couple, and to play particular

---

1 *Epoché* (ἐποχή) means "suspension". It has been used in the philosophy of Descartes and Husserl to refer to the suspension or "bracketing" of judgement in relation to matters felt to require a completely open attitude towards phenomena, to examine them as they are originally given to consciousness, before "the synthesis of the understanding" (Kant). The term was popularised in philosophy by Husserl, who developed the notion of "phenomenological epoché", the bracketing principle. He also called it the procedure of "phenomenological reduction".

roles in relating, makes the necessity for such open acknowledgement and exploration of echoistic traits in the therapist, imperative.

As I say, echoistic characteristics can be found or elicited in all of us and not simply in echoists. Readers will now be familiar with these traits from the observations made in this book. Without having had the opportunity to explore these in their own analyses or therapy, however, they may be less conscious of them in themselves and in their practice. In the writing and researching of this book I have worked with many practitioners and had the opportunity of learning about their experiences with echoistic patients. One subject of lively discussion relates to the defences found in therapists in terms of engaging with echoism, if and when it resonates with aspects of themselves.

In many of the humanistic therapy trainings, practitioners are required to demonstrate a range of skills, including listening, mirroring, reflecting back, and repeating the patient's words. As the clinician develops further, other ideas are introduced, including openness, *epoché*, and a willingness to take patients in and to allow their projections to reside within them as a way of resonating with and understanding their feelings. It is not difficult to see that these requirements, common to all therapists, regardless of modality and training, are also aspects of echoistic relating. We can see how they also correlate with the behaviours of Echo in the myth.

In the case of what we have called the ordinary individual, the echoistic behaviours listed above may be regarded as the very important skills required to perform the work effectively. If, however, an echoistic therapist is working with aspects of narcissism in a patient, or with aspects of echoism, or with an echoist, then the lack of awareness of the therapist's own potential for the echoistic use of primitive defences may lead to the very opposite of growth in the patient's mental life and, indeed, actual life.

Earlier in the book I described the nature of echoism, and I considered the behaviours that can be attributed directly to the echoist as active rather than passive. In their thinking about narcissism, therapists are less focused upon traits common in the narcissist, than to how they interact with us, and act upon us in the clinical situation, as well as the ways in which they relate to others in the world. The same applies to echoism, and I believe that we need to pay as much attention to our own echoism as we might to our narcissism, and to retain a capacity to differentiate between our own echoism and that of the patient.

In working with the patient's narcissism the echoistically inclined therapist may be unaware of her own permeability and therefore not as alert as she might be to the projections of the narcissist, which will tend to feel natural, making them harder to interrogate and interpret. Another hazardous situation to which the echoism of the therapist may contribute, is an invisible power relationship in the room, in which she becomes intimidated by the narcissistic patient or flattered by his seductiveness and his assertions that the therapy really is working and helping him. She may also feel responsible and inadequate if the patient asserts that it is *not* helping him. Being able to account for the unconscious role her own echoism is playing in this process enables the therapist to identify what the patient is doing more clearly, and, in the supervisory relationship, to help her supervisor to gain a detailed understanding of the processes in which she is involved. This insight may prevent a repetitive recycling of a hidden mode of relating that I have described as ENC pairing.

The consequences may be quite different if the therapist is working with an echoistic patient and is unaware of her own echoism. A patient who is unable to speak about herself may be experienced by the therapist as resistant when the silence becomes too uncomfortable. If an echoistically inclined therapist feels actively drawn to fill the space produced by the passivity of the echoist, she may consciously or unconsciously become resentful towards her patient, frustrated at what might feel like the patient's punishing use of a psychic retreat.

Reflexivity and supervision

In the course of training many practitioners have come to recognise some of their patients as echoists, having previously conceptualised them as narcissistic, as-if, or borderline personalities. Collating the thoughts and experiences of these therapists has produced fascinating insights. In these discussions a major concern that has emerged is the danger of encountering what might present as a lack of self, or a false self, and concluding that the patient is unsuitable for therapy.[2] This emphasises the need for the concept of echoism to be regarded seriously. In order for therapists to be able to consider the impact of their own echoistic traits on their clinical relationships, it is also vital for supervisors to be aware of the concept and alert to phenomena that the therapist may be less conscious or even unconscious of in herself, and which is only available for understanding afterwards and with another.

If the therapist herself possesses echoistic traits but is not conscious of them, she is in danger of using them unwittingly and with little or no awareness of the consequences. This is made more likely in terms of the numbers of individuals with strong echoistic behaviours whose natural habitat might easily be found in the therapist's role, where she can exercise these aspects of herself. These can pass largely unnoticed by herself or even a keen supervisor, who, without having an explicit awareness of the processes of echoism, may be unable to make the requisite observations in amongst what looks like the natural run of a clinical session. I think most supervisors would be equipped to identify and to explore narcissism being enacted by the therapist, but their supervisee's echoism is likely to remain far more elusive.

One real danger is that a therapist unable to take responsibility for her own echoism might inadvertently project echoistic aspects of herself powerfully into the patient. Such an event is likely to result in the therapist's denial of the anxiety

2 And see Chapter Six, about mistaken identity.

at being with another who reminds her of herself, anxiety that may elicit narcissistic defences in the therapist. In consequence, she may unwittingly enact the very same relationship that the echoist seeks in the world but, being unable to observe it, she would therefore fail to interpret it, because it would remain unconscious. I have conceptualised this dynamic, with which I have become familiar, as the forming of an echoistic-narcissistic couple (ENC,[3] see Chapter Eight). If this interactive process goes unnoticed, the patient's pattern of echoistic relating can be further reinforced.

My work suggests that another aspect to which the therapist needs to be alert, and open to experiencing, is the role of an ego-destructive object – particularly if she herself has such an object. When I run training events on echoism, I ask therapists to listen to the different and dominant voices of the objects in their minds. This interactive exercise, which usually takes place near the end of a course, once there is some trust in the group, can elicit powerful reactions and valuable insights.

Vignette 16: Serena

Serena, a person-centred therapist who attended an event on echoism and narcissism, took part in the aforementioned exercise. She became concerned that she could herself be an echoist. She also reflected on the method of therapy in which she had trained, and she became aware that specific features of her approach might well have lent themselves to colluding with, and to reinforcing, certain defences in her patients, rather than challenging them. She described using mirroring and echoing back the patient's own words, and she said her approach encouraged offering "unconditional positive regard"[4] to the patient. Serena explained that her ability to offer these skills had led her into her profession, and that they were very natural for her. She reported, however, becoming aware throughout the day of the dangers of offering these to a narcissistic patient, one of which was her fear that she would collude with him and, in all likelihood, be susceptible to forming an ENC relationship with him.

The group members asked her how she felt her own echoism might affect echoistic patients, and wondered whether she had worked with any that she would now consider to be echoistic. Serena remembered a patient with whom she had started work, and whom she now regarded as echoistic, but who had left after just seven sessions. She recalled the crushing feeling she had experienced in long and painful silences, and described how her attempts to stay attuned to the patient resulted in feelings of inadequacy and incompetence, as the echoist asked her what she should do and threatened to leave as each session drew to a close, stating that she felt she was not being helped. The therapy had ended, somewhat to Serena's relief, after her supervisor had felt that the patient was not yet ready

---

3　ENC – an echoistic-narcissistic couple who form a complex dynamic of relating.
4　One of Carl Rogers' core principles of client-centred counselling.

to engage in the work of therapy. What was so interesting, in the context of the work in this book, was that Serena shared with the group the circumstances under which the therapy actually came to an end. She explained that her supervisor had suggested to her that the next time the patient spoke in the way that had become routine, Serena might say that she understood the patient may not be ready. She said she simply had echoed the words of her supervisor at the very next session, and this had brought the therapy to an end.

Analysis

The discussion that then took place raised important questions about the suitability of "echoing back" the patient's words when working with echoistic patients, and the withholding of this with narcissistic patients. Actions used to convey "Unconditional Positive Regard", when expressed to a destructive narcissist, or a patient with a destructive narcissistic object, proved to be both problematic and contentious, and led to further discussions about how supervisors might help therapists to deal with the specific and difficult demands of working with narcissistic and echoistic patients. Serena concluded that she had been made aware that she was practising a method that felt very natural to her, but which may have largely been based on a defensive organisation of her mind, one that until then she had been unable to acknowledge, and which her supervisor had not detected.

Acting through the therapist

I have found that the self-destructive echoist has a narcissistic object from whom she cannot always differentiate herself. The presence of such an object, when the therapist herself is echoistic to a significant degree, makes understanding the transference and countertransference in the clinical situation incredibly complex. The following short vignette depicts an experience shared by one therapist, who attended a training course. She identified in herself a largely narcissistic object, and she shared a clinical experience in which she was able to understand something of the role this object played in her own mind, and its impact in the sessions with a self-destructive echoistic patient.

Vignette 17: Catherine

Catherine had been practising as a therapist for many years and had decided to attend a training on echoism because she thought she recognised aspects of herself in the description of the workshop. Throughout the day, the concept of a critical-voice resonated so strongly with her that she expressed some relief in the workshop at being able to share it, and to feel that others had experienced something similar. She expressed a secret fear that if she had mentioned this on her training or to a supervisor, they might think she was schizophrenic. This turned out to be a common fear, and could be seen as a barrier to being able to talk about the work openly and transparently, with further consequences for the patient. In a clinical seminar later in the workshop Catherine presented her work with a patient whom she now believed to be echoistic. She described a situation in which something led her to be defensive in supervision, and protective of the patient whenever the supervisor detected hostility. She described repeating the patient's own words to the supervisor, and reported that these were often delivered with some force and judgement that the supervisor detected, but that Catherine could not see.

Analysis

The group had powerful reactions to Catherine's clinical descriptions and were able to recognise the presence of a particular feeling of *certainty*, both of the patient – who Catherine described as echoistic and unconfident – and of the therapist. This resounding certainty, present in the atmosphere, seemed, on discussion of the case, not to belong to the patient, nor to the therapist – who was generally felt to be tentative and halting in her communications – but seemed instead to be the property of a narcissistic object in the patient, one which operated and projected through Catherine.

When the therapist's own object, which was less malignant yet more critical than the patient's, had the chance to impose judgement on Catherine, she experienced crushing feelings and thought herself incompetent as well as arrogant, and feared that she herself was a narcissist. The group felt that they were able to help Catherine understand something of what might be taking place in the sessions, based on their own countertransference reactions to the material and to Catherine's session with her supervisor. This relationship, in which the self-destructive echoistic patient's narcissistic object is projecting through a defensive echoistic therapist with a critical object of her own, revealed a highly complex process, which required a good degree of understanding of echoism.

Conclusion

This chapter raises further questions as to whether specific clinical approaches may be more appropriate than others for working with echoism and narcissism. It not only indicates but confirms the need for training in echoistic phenomena and relating, for all therapists and supervisors.

The next chapter takes this further in considering how the concept might be developed both theoretically and clinically, and how the balance of attention given to narcissism over echoism might begin to be redressed.

Conclusions and future directions

Chapter 10

Prometheus' fire

Being and becoming: an approach to treatment

Titan! to whom immortal eyes
The sufferings of mortality
Seen in their sad reality,
Were not as things that Gods despise;
What was thy pity's recompense?
A silent suffering, and intense;
The rock, the vulture, and the chain,
All that the proud can feel of pain,
The agony they do not show,
The suffocating sense of woe,
Which speaks but in its loneliness,
And then is jealous lest the sky
Should have a listener, nor will sigh
Until its voice is echoless.
　　　Prometheus, Lord Byron, 1816

In this final chapter I summarise the reasons that echoism is prone to being missed, marginalised, or completely ignored. I draw together the findings of my research and provide a clear working definition of the term echoism as a clinical phenomenon within a theoretical framework, for recognition and further exploration by therapists of all orientations. The findings described in this book reveal the necessity for a dialogue regarding shifting the existing paradigm of narcissism towards an acknowledgment of what I call an "echoistic-narcissistic complex". I go on to describe an evolving approach to treatment of the echoist in individual, couple, and group therapies, and the requirement for a dual approach that includes existential modes of being-with the phenomenon, combined with a psychoanalytic approach, both of which are important in studying it adequately. The chapter considers the therapist's experience of working with echoistic patients as the work progresses, and discusses some of the clinical implications of recovery. The final section is an invitation to fellow practitioners and theorists to consider ways in which the concept might be developed further in terms of treatment, method, and training. It offers an acknowledgement of the debt that I owe to literary theory, which has functioned for me as a beam of light enabling me to penetrate aspects of echoism that otherwise may have been missed. Finally, I propose ways in which the imbalance of the previously existing paradigm, in which the echoist was invisible through the dominant lens of narcissism, might be redressed.

Echoism as a clinical and theoretical concept

This book began with a close reading of the myth of Echo and Narcissus as a way of introducing the phenomenon of echoism. One of the most interesting and important questions posed in the introduction is why this phenomenon has been missed and overlooked. I posited at first that it may have been be due to dominant discourses in literature, in which patriarchal and phallocentric narratives are prioritised over marginalised voices. This chapter also considers another, less conscious, factor – the possibility that there has been a deeply unconscious repulsion, amounting to a denial. As I have discussed, the fate of Echo in the myth expresses a primal and horrific loss of voice, corresponding to identity at the most fundamental level. I suggest the possibility that what has been operating, in the field of theory and practice, has been an innate defence common to humanity, against acknowledging echoism in the self and in others. Perhaps this is the worst state to bear – that of being barely alive, rendering the individual unable to be a self, except as a cipher[1] in response to or through an other. This has resulted in her becoming predisposed to a painfully dependent relationship with a narcissist.

In 1933, Samuel Beckett wrote a story, "Echo's Bones", which he penned in a short space of time to complete a collection of stories, published under the title, *More Pricks than Kicks*. Prentice, the publisher, received the manuscript and, on reading "Echo's Bones":

> recoiled from the story, and decided to print the collection as it had originally been conceived [omitting this story]. "It is a nightmare", began his letter in which he apologetically rejected the story. "People will shudder and be puzzled and confused; and they won't be keen on analysing the shudder".
>
> (Lezard, 2014)

The story was eventually published in 2014, over eighty years after its inception, offering an interesting parallel to the exclusion of Echo's story from a myth

---

1 etym. a. OF. cyfre, cyffre (mod.F. chiffre) f. Arab. çifr the arithmetical symbol "zero" or "nought" (written in Indian and Arabic numeration), a subst. use of the adj. çifr "empty, void", f. çafara to be empty. (The Arabic was simply a translation of the Sanscrit name śūnya, literally "empty".)

   1. a.1.a An arithmetical symbol or character (o) of no value by itself, but which increases or decreases the value of other figures according to its position. When placed after any figure or series of figures in a whole number it increases the value of that figure or series tenfold, and when placed before a figure in decimal fractions, it decreases its value in the same proportion.

   2. fig. a.2.a A person who fills a place, but is of no importance or worth, a nonentity, a "mere nothing".

in which she had an equal role. John Pilling remarked of "Echo's Bones", that there are:

> So many echoes that they seem to multiply to infinity, and yet they are little more than the bare bones of material without any overarching purpose to animate.
>
> (Beckett, 2014, p. xvi-xvii)

This critique of Beckett's startling book echoes, poetically, the plight of the echoist herself, and I cannot help but wonder if this is yet another example of the unconscious dread that seems to evoke endless defences against engaging with Echo in any form.

We can see that the character of Echo, and the lived entity that is the echoist, seem to defy acknowledgement as subjects worthy of interest – in history, culture, and in our theories in psychoanalysis. I have shown in this book that patients who resemble more closely the character of Echo than Narcissus are also subjected to this in our consulting rooms.

In trying to understand the communications of one particular patient, Wilfred Bion found himself remarkably close to recognising that there is, in fact, a forgotten and elusive aspect in what he calls "The myth of Narcissus". In one of his undated notes he describes beautifully in the following words what we might think are his own processes of defence, obstacles that enable him to just miss it. He begins, in considering a patient with a narcissistic presentation, by suggesting that the way to make use of a myth is to associate to it. He writes:

> The values are those that are relevant to a particular problem, and the particular problem is the personality of the person who produces the free associations. By attributing these values to the variables of the myth we understand that those qualities are, for that person, constantly conjoined. ... I would say that, listening to the free associations, one would think something like this: the patient is wanting me to agree with him; it is obvious from the way he is putting forward a suggestion that he has a beautiful personality. It appears to me that it is a morally beautiful personality; my personality is likewise beautiful; in fact I am to be a mirror of his excellence.
>
> (Bion, 1992, p. 238)

At this point, as I described in Chapter One, Bion then questions his own use and understanding of the myth, and goes on to say:

> But there is more of this story, the myth of Narcissus: there is a god who turns him into a flower. What is the patient saying that corresponds to this? There *must* be something because my myth tells me that these elements are constantly conjoined; or perhaps this is not the right myth ...

And in his frustration, and perhaps to justify his reasoning to himself, he goes on to say:

> I can see objections. It will be argued that no analyst could possibly have such a store of myths available in his psychoanalytic armoury as this procedure would seem to desiderate.

This self-recorded instance of a "blind spot" by such an experienced clinician, known for his courage, seems to add weight to my thesis that there is something at the heart of the phenomenon itself so dreadful that we tend to shrink back from recognising its existence. If we can acknowledge that such an innate system of defences is in place in all of us, we need a clear definition of echoism to enable its recognition by therapists, as a way of overcoming these defences and seeing what is actually there.

On recognising the echoistic patient – a definition

Echoism is a condition, whose name derives from the myth of Echo and Narcissus, in which a curse is placed upon Echo that stops her from having her own voice, and forces her to repeat the words and thoughts of another as her own. In its clinical counterpart, the echoist, it creates a state of *absence of being*, in which the individual forgoes being-for-herself in favour of the other, and is thereby reduced to a being who is barely alive and without agency or a sense of self. Always found in relation to narcissistic objects, the echoist is a recipient for projections and communications that dictate how she should be. She forgoes developing and becoming a self, and the conditions within which this could be done are withheld from her as long as she is in relation to a narcissistic other in her external or internal world. For this self, to develop a voice is an achievement that relies upon the active loving help of others. When the primary source of constriction or destruction of that voice is the dominant narcissism of the other, or others, we speak of echoism – the silenced response to narcissism, following the fate of the cursed nymph in the myth of Echo and Narcissus.

The therapist must be the guide for the echoistic patient, yet it is important to recognise that at no point is she a fully experienced helper who has previously navigated this terrain herself. Instead she is the fellow-sufferer who, having demonstrated the capacity for having survived familiar and similar territories over and again, must be able, first of all, to bear, and then, subsequently, to communicate to the patient, a direct understanding of her actual predicament, to help the patient to stay in treatment.

The writing of this book has been a similar process, in which I have encountered new ground, and I have attempted to map it for the reader. The clinicians and theorists to whom I am indebted have provided experience and guiding help that has enabled me to stay on the path, without knowing what lies ahead.

Existing paradigms, dialectics, and theoretical re-synthesis

As we have seen, something obscures Echo's narrative from being heard, and yet, while the echoist may not have been considered a subject in her own right, we do meet her in the consulting room. This book shows that if we misdiagnose her or consider her unsuitable for therapy, we consign the patient not only to further echoistic relating but, as a result, more subjection to narcissism.

We therefore need to begin with the paradigms that are in place in orienting us towards the phenomenon of narcissism, and to consider what theoretical revision and re-synthesis needs to take place in order to allow for additional information from the research into echoism to be incorporated into an existing theoretical framework. This would then reposition both echoism and narcissism in a more balanced relationship, revealing an echoistic-narcissistic complex rather than favouring a narcissistic complex through which echoism is viewed.

In order to do so it is necessary to dialogue seamlessly between both the psychoanalytic and the existential, as I have allowed myself to do in this book. This will also heighten our awareness of the feelings of naturalness of the echoistic-narcissistic couple (ENC), and help alert us to the actual phenomenon.

If we begin with Rosenfeld's experience of his parasitic patient (described at length in Chapter Six), we see that he describes a very similar clinical experience to those I have encountered when working with echoistic patients, but he interprets it according to an existing body of theoretical ideas on narcissistic projective identification. He acknowledges, however, experiencing the introjecting nature of the patient, and also the feeling that the therapist can never give the patient enough (see Chapter Five). Rosenfeld, as we saw, then went on to interpret the patient's silence as a form of hostility and a defence against emotions that caused him to feel pain.

If, however, one interprets from the perspective of an understanding of echoism, this powerful experience – that the patient can never be given enough to sustain him – can be thought about differently. Once the patient has taken in the therapist's vitality, it is stolen by a parasitic internal object who consumes and strips out from it anything that can be of nourishment to the patient's ego, rendering growth unlikely.

In the case of patients who may to some degree have emancipated themselves from the enslavement to such an object by attempting to understand its motivations and intentions, there is a further problem for the echoist, which I consider to be a defence against living. Being released from the object is only the beginning, because it was, in a way, another shield from ontological guilt, in which one can no longer not act because of one's imprisonment to another. This is again similar to Rosenfeld's interpretation, but instead of interpreting pain I would argue that it is a defence against anxiety – fundamentally the anxiety that the patient is exposed to in choosing to live at all, a defence against any emotion or relationship that constitutes being alive, because to live, or to be-for-herself is the most audacious and anxiety-provoking action of all for the echoist.

In psychoanalysis much has been written of the death instinct and it has been discussed widely in relation to destructiveness in narcissism. As this book demonstrates, in echoism a state of barely-aliveness is commonplace, particularly in self-destructive echoists. The echoist, therefore, feels ontologically and ontically guilty for having a voice and must therefore go through an "anxiety barrier" in order to harness her life instinct. Interpretations that routinely and automatically treat aggression as attacks on the therapeutic relationship can themselves function as a barrier to growth, if the therapist interprets attacks on the therapy as destructive without recognising the patient's predicament in being exposed to the anxieties of the human condition itself – *life anxiety*. This dreaded state is experienced by the echoistic patient whenever there are any signs of growth in the therapy or in the patient. I maintain that this state is the hardest to bear because the echoist has to risk the anxiety that she *can* bear it in order to *live*, rather than accept the state of "non-living", which is both her natural state, and one which keeps her bound in servitude to the narcissist. We might say that the very thing that keeps her in servitude to the narcissistic object is the need to avoid the anxiety that arises through daring to *be*.

As therapists, when we are subjected to such dread, and put in touch with our own nothingness, we might reach for fact and reason as a way of avoiding it. By staying with the *ontic* version of guilt we may unconsciously resist that which is so much harder to bear. The nameless dread that the echoist feels each time she allows herself to wish to exist, or acknowledge that she makes an imprint on the world, faces her with ontological guilt whenever she attempts to "gather the fragments" to become a self.

This book raises a number of speculations about the situations of early infancy. Based on existing paradigms, many of its findings reinforce and accord with current understanding of the figures in the internal world of the patient – those whom we may meet in the transference – particularly in narcissistic patients. The echoists with whom I have worked all have a critical-voice or ego-destructive object. They have also had narcissistic partners. It is not clear whether *all* have had narcissistic parents but there is much evidence of them in the transference and in the patients' memories, and a common feature described by echoists when they first come in to therapy is an uncertainty in being able to distinguish between what are their own and what are their parents' thoughts and wishes for them.

If we consider the use of normal degrees of projective identification in the early infant-parent situation, we can see how the discharge of raw unprocessed experience into the primary carer, "beta elements" (Bion, 1962, Ch. 3), enables a process called alpha function to take place in the infant, creating the conditions for growth of a self and of a reliable good object in the internal world.

Klein recognised the value of introjective identification as a developmental process, and we can see how this is the case with a normal (non-narcissistic and non-echoistic) patient, who is not only able to experience a representation of the analyst in his inner world, but to use the vitality of the analyst to enrich his internal world and to promote mental growth. In the case of narcissism, it is well documented that due to the colonising nature of the narcissist this vitality is used not for growth but as more ammunition in the armoury that defends the already huge and omnipotent self against the need to relate to others in the world. In the case of the echoist however, if the concept itself had not been somehow obscured or avoided (for reasons that this book seeks to understand), the introjected life force cannot, as I have described, be used in the normal ways because of the parasitism of the object.

We can hypothesise that a baby whose parent is narcissistic will forego his natural predisposition to project, and – in what results in a parasitic container-contained relationship – will, in order to survive, introject a highly projecting narcissistic parental object, who steals any life force from the baby. We meet the latest version of this object in our consulting rooms daily when working with echoistic patients.

There are many theoretical concepts that have an established place in our knowledge, based as they are upon years of experience, careful study, and considered analysis. Those concepts that have been so widely understood in relation to narcissism present the greatest risk of being misinterpreted in the echoistic patient. Signs of movement towards elements of the depressive position are usually thought of as a sign of growth in the narcissistic patient, while the opposite may be the case in the recovering echoist as she begins to take her place in the world alongside others. Different aspects of envy form the theses of many publications and papers, and whilst envy is almost always considered destructive, elements of it, such as possession and entitlement, may be evidence of the beginnings of a self in the echoist.

Anyone who has ever cared for a toddler will be aware of his frustration as he tries to establish a sense of self that can be recognised as separate from, and which can co-exist with, others in the world. For the echoistic patient, a state similar to this must be endured as she finds her own voice, and learns how to use it powerfully, and to moderate it in particular settings. A harsh therapist may be quick to interpret entitlement as envy or hostility in a way that further subjects the echoist to her own ontological guilt, and which enables her harsh superego object to further subjugate her under the threat that one of her greatest fears may be realised – that she herself could be a narcissist, when she knows the suffering caused by such individuals in the world.

There are many other questions, which arise naturally and which cannot be answered in this book but which do, I believe, require deeper understanding if we are to redefine existing paradigms. These include:

- Is echoism a pathological organisation of the personality like certain forms of narcissism?
- Do all echoists have a narcissistic parent or early childhood influential figure?
- What can we learn about narcissism if we consider it through the lens of echoism?

- Are all echoists "reluctant philosophers"?
- What motivates the echoist to stay in therapy if being in therapy at all raises so much anxiety and guilt?

This leads us on to a question to which the next section does attempt to provide some initial answers: Should the clinician adapt her way of working for the echoistic patient?

An evolving approach to treatment

In allowing ourselves to draw upon different theories to orient us towards the phenomena of echoism, we are able to offer and communicate a type of understanding that is not limited to a particular modality but which gets to both ontic and ontological truths in the realms of being and thinking. This involves being open to the echoist's particular needs in treatment, which may differ from those of other patients. As the group chapter illustrates, the echoist, in a group of echoists, presents in a much more defensive way when there is no natural narcissistic other to fill the void, making it easier to observe her behaviours. This is more difficult to observe in individual work and requires sensitivity and openness in the therapist to understand the patient and to allow her to find ways to express herself.

Psychoanalytic perspective

There is much to be retained of the psychoanalytic approach, described at length in this book, in terms of having an in-depth understanding of the patient and an alertness to the processes taking place in the echoist and her relationships with others (internal and external). An awareness of projective processes and an ability in the therapist to reflect on her own countertransference experience is essential. Observing the presence of an ego-destructive object in the patient's internal world, and its projections into the therapist of narcissistic envy as well as other malignant emotions, can lead to further understanding and to helping the therapist not to reach for received wisdom or overvalued ideas and, in so-doing, misdiagnose the patient. In Chapters Six and Seven I have discussed examples of how putting a parasitic ego-destructive object, or god-like object, residing in the patient, "on trial", as it were, can result in what Ronald Britton describes as a degree of "emancipation from the object". Attempting to differentiate between the patient's often tiny and emerging self and the object's projections is central to doing so.

The role of interpretation is important in psychoanalytic therapies, to relieve patients of their deep-rooted unconscious fears and enable them to feel understood. When working with echoists it is important to consider carefully the uses and ways of giving interpretations to this particular group, so that they might become meaningful and owned as part of the self and not just another echo of the other to be taken in and repeated. The dangers of over-interpreting or "knowing" the patient more than she does herself can reinforce the dependency on the relationship and hinder the slow and lengthy process of finding an own-voice, and rather than creating space for a self to emerge, the therapist can become another replacement or substitute for a narcissistic other, from whom the patient may have managed to achieve some degree of liberation or emancipation. This is particularly difficult when the patient is both consciously and unconsciously attempting to pull the therapist into the space to relieve her of the anxiety she feels.

Existential and Daseinsanalytic approaches

In thinking about the reasons that make it difficult for the echoist to have a voice, Alice Holzhey-Kunz considers ontological anxiety to be central. She reminds us of Heidegger's important observation that we are always in flight from anxiety. Every time the echoist attempts to rouse a sense of self she is exposed to this anxiety. The aim for the therapist is to bear this with the patient, to increase her capacity to tolerate it so that she can repeatedly risk developing an own-voice and experience being alive. There is a constant temptation to transform the anxiety into concrete fear in the ontic realm as a way of avoiding it. Because the ontological anxiety is dreadful, the echoist might seek to avoid it by manifesting symptoms and concrete fears in order that she feels she has some control over it in the realm of action.

One patient's need to control her anxiety whenever we encountered a break, was met by an urge to spend her money on buying a house rather than continuing to come to therapy. This concretisation took her into the mode of enactment, and on one level it enabled her to flee from the anxiety she felt at being abandoned by the therapist to her own raw feelings about existing, anxiety to which she was highly sensitive. She was able to stay in therapy and acknowledge this tendency when she realised that the house she was considering purchasing was in fact hundreds of miles away from her therapist, her small network of people, and her job – and that it would in fact serve to isolate her further. As she found it so difficult to speak in new situations, she was quite literally considering choosing to act in a way that reinforced her echoism, and took her further away from relating to others, including her therapist, who at times was the only person to whom she felt connected.

Holzhey-Kunz also describes the ontological guilt felt by the echoist at having a voice that is not, nor ever can be, perfect. This voice, or self, is a being who fears to tread and make an imprint on the earth, for in doing so she must acknowledge and take responsibility for her existence. The phenomenological approach aims at staying with the patient's experience and not leaping ahead (Heidegger, 1927, p. 158), and instead encourages them to describe their experience. If, however, the patient is unable to verbalise feelings or express them in the moment, despite the attempts of the therapist to stay with the patient, the echoist may feel impelled to flee the room, either literally or by withdrawing emotionally from the therapist. If we imagine a very small child who feels unable to articulate his feelings, or to express them because he is certain that they will not be met, we are put in mind of an echoist who may not have developed an own-voice, nor had a parent who can contain or bear her feelings.

Creative expression

In Chapter Eight I discussed a combined approach to using art therapies alongside traditional talking therapies in the work with homogeneous groups. In the vignette discussed, this setting provided opportunities for patients to express a self through other means than voice alone, which could then be thought about and spoken about with the therapists. Melanie Klein, in her work with children, developed a technique using toys and drawing materials to enable children to communicate their innermost anxieties and deepest phantasies.

Echoists often describe not being able to articulate feelings verbally, and many point to their throat and say that words are stuck there, unable to come out, or that the words and thoughts are not connected to each other so the patient cannot form coherent sentences. For some echoists who have had narcissistic parents there is a sense that they have never had a chance to develop or even to hear their own-voice. Some of these patients show evidence of a self through more creative expression, and it is not unusual to discover that echoists have studied creative writing, play therapy, dance, or painting, or that they have pursued careers in these areas.

If I were to articulate any specific goal I have in working with the echoist I would say that it is to enable her own voice to be heard in a way that feels safe enough for her to utter it, and to find ways to provide the conditions for growth.

If the first stage of this is enabling the patient to communicate an aspect of a self, even before she can *speak* of it, I think it is important for the therapist to stay open to any form through which it can be expressed.

I would argue that if any means can be found for an expression of a self in the echoist, the therapist, regardless of modality, must endeavour to stay open to this and to provide a container for the patient's communication, so that it can be thought about and transformed. The ability to utter words may be reached at a much later stage of the therapy, and I have worked with some patients who cannot speak but who can draw or write poetry which they can share with me, in a way that feels safe enough for us to establish a communication. The implication of this for therapists and supervisors is that a greater degree of flexibility is needed when working with this newly discovered patient group.

Recovery in the echoist is a long and painful process, and brings its own new problems, which I summarise in the section below.

The recovering echoist

It may be too soon to speak of recovered echoists, but in my work I have observed signs of growth that indicate a process of recovery in some of my echoistic patients. Recovering echoists are often able to begin to speak of negative aspects of their relationship with the therapist that go beyond the more commonly expressed resentment when they have not been able to receive enough in the sessions. A familiar experience for the recovering echoist is her sudden exposure to grief once she is able to recognise the loss of all the years in which she was unable to have her voice heard, or her existence validated. The newly experienced loss can lead to wishes for the kind of naivety experienced prior to therapy, in which the echoist could use defences against the pain of not-being through an unhealthy attachment to her omnipotent object or to an external narcissist.

The pain of liberation from such an object is easy to underestimate given the therapist's wish to help emancipate the patient from such a destructive pairing. Staying with the patient's experience and not imposing this wish upon her is challenging for a therapist who wants the best for the patient, but who feels frustrated at the rate of progress. The process of recovery is long and difficult, and the early stages are marked by a falling back for every gain made, and both therapist and patient can feel themselves to be locked in an unbreakable cycle. In the course of my work I am often helped to bear some of this pain by internalised objects from my theatre and literary background, and the wisdom they have imparted.

In a recent production of *No's Knife*, Samuel Beckett's prose from *Texts for Nothing* was put into the mouth of a character who in consecutive scenes was bound in a rock-face, enclosed in a cage, and abandoned in a wasteland, and who resembled strongly my experience of the speech patterns and feelings of the echoistic patient. In one scene during her eighty minute monologue she asks:

> Where would I go, if I could go, who would I be, if I could be, what would I say, if I had a voice, who says this, saying it's me? …

After an interaction with a man who, she says, "comes and goes", and whose role appears to resemble that of a therapist, the unnamed protagonist replies to herself:

> Yes, there are moments, like this moment, when I seem almost restored to the feasible. Then it goes, all goes, and I'm far again, with a far story again, I wait for me afar for my story to begin, to end, and again this voice cannot be mine. That's where I'd go, if I could go, that's who I'd be, if I could be.
>
> (Beckett, 1967, No 4)

Remaining positive and holding on to faith, such as I describe it in Chapter Seven, requires the production of a strong relationship and attachment, as the patient tries to stay with the painful reality of her situation and not revert back to servitude to a narcissistic object (internal or external).

In his *Essays on the Art of Theater*, Brecht stated:

> It is not enough to demand insight and informative images of reality from the theater. Our theater must stimulate a desire for understanding, a delight

in changing reality. Our audience must experience not only the ways to free Prometheus, but be schooled in the very desire to free him.

(Brecht, 1954)

The therapy, in which the echoist is beginning to liberate herself from her object (critical-voice) and to use her own-voice, faces a similar challenge to the one described by Brecht above. Her therapist, like the audience, is also engaged in the process of liberating her through understanding, changing her reality, and holding a desire for her to be free. Brecht goes on to say:

Theater must teach all the pleasures and joys of discovery, all the feelings of triumph associated with liber\ation.

(Ibid.)

There are many aspects of joy, and, indeed, triumph, in the echoist's emancipation from such a destructive object, and these can be seen in developing relationships in the patient's life as well as in her therapy. This liberation, however, is often marked more by pain than joy for the echoist, who, rather than feeling free, can experience the weight of taking responsibility to be unbearable, because she has not, as an infant, learned to take it gradually. It can feel overwhelming and burdening, and the therapist must be willing to take the lion's share of the load to help the echoist continue on the journey of growth.

Liberation from an object that has to some degree protected the echoist from her exposure to aspects of the human condition, however, requires her suddenly to face the ontological anxieties of being for-herself, which I call "Life Anxiety". This involves an ontological guilt, such as that described above by Holzhey-Kunz, in which the echoistic patient who risks taking space in the room and in the world, must face the consequences of this and be willing to bear the anxiety in doing so. This anxiety manifests in many ways, as her relationship to using and taking space evolves in the treatment.

The changing relationship to space

Space has many different functions in working with echoists, and we cannot assume it holds or represents the same meaning for each individual. We can, however, make some meaningful distinctions between some of these, and consider their uses conceptually and clinically. As I have discussed at length, the creation of triangular space (Britton, 1989, p. 86) is required to enable observation and reflection on relationship dynamics in the therapeutic couple and in the echoist's internal world. Once she has been able to introject a relationship in which she is an observer as well as a participant, the echoist can use this newly formed object relationship to have more insight into her external relationships, and to have more awareness of the impact upon her when she is with a narcissistic other. Because being part of the ENC (Chapter Eight) feels so natural, and to some degree essential to the echoist's survival, the ability to recognise the impact on her while it is happening has the effect that Brecht (1936) called the *verfremdung-seffekt* – the making strange of the everyday. In theatre the *verfremdungseffekt* functions as an interruption to what is felt to be real and concrete, alerting the audience member to the constructedness of reality and generating in him a feeling that reality is always fluid, unfolding, and being created and that he can intervene and act to effect change.

This seems to operate in a very similar way to what Bion described as waking up from the numbing feeling of reality, requiring both therapist and patient to notice and feel incited to intervene and to act. When the echoistic patient is able to start to notice that she plays a role in the unfolding reality, she can start to acknowledge some responsibility for it and act with her own agency as she begins to develop a stronger sense of a self.

Some echoist's will feel the therapeutic space to be under threat of siege from either an internal or an external object. For a patient who has grown up with a narcissistic parent who has intruded on her own internal world and into her thoughts for her whole life, a sacred therapeutic space can feel like the very opposite of safe. Such a patient may express conscious fears of the space being violated and a phantasy of her narcissistic partner or parent finding out where she is and breaking through the door to get her. More often it will be expressed through dreams and daydreams of terrorist attacks or in transferential feelings that the therapist is trying to get inside the patient's mind. The patient may become remote or close off as a way of avoiding this pain, or she may, as I have said above, attempt to pull the therapist into the space to protect her from its threat. Guilt is also prominent in the echoist and at the heart of her plight is an ontological guilt for existing at all. This can be experienced as another defence against the painful feelings evoked in taking space. It is clear that the therapist needs to understand and be incredibly patient in enabling the creation of a psychic space that such a patient may eventually be able to use. The following vignette illustrates a recovering echoist's awareness of her specific relationship to space and her ability to share this with the therapist, as the establishment of a safe space was slowly evolving.

Vignette 18: Michaela

Michaela, a twenty-five-year-old mother of three small girls, had been in twice-weekly face-to-face therapy for two years. After a period of what she came to call "fire-fighting", which involved managing a constant onslaught of attacks from an external narcissistic parent from whom she had estranged herself, she had begun to use the space to discover more about her own internal state, and the threat of siege she experienced from within. She had begun to notice, in sessions, an internal narcissistic object, whose voice – which resembled the parent's voice – attacked her every time she allowed herself to believe she had something for herself. She had not, however, realised that this included the very essential element, *life*.

The following session gives an account of ontological guilt, which is at the very heart of the echoist's state. In the last break, she had ordered a candle as part of her weekly shopping delivery. This candle had been the same brand and fragrance as the candle that the therapist usually had burning during Michaela's sessions. The patient had believed she had ordered it by accident and whenever she lit it during the break she was surprised to be reminded of the familiarity of the therapy room. She had found herself lighting it as a way of calming her mind when she felt anxious. She mentioned this, she said, because the therapist had had a different candle on the week of her return.

The patient arrived one day, wanting to check dates of the next break. The session unfolded as follows:

Michaela: Can we just check the dates that you are going to be away and the day and time you have agreed you are going to see me, on the week where I am on holiday during our usual Tuesday session.
[The therapist goes through the dates and times again with the patient and remains curious as to why she is checking them after agreeing them and writing them down just the week before. The patient looks at the candle for a moment and seems emotional and then looks down, quietly]
[Long silence]
[After about ten minutes the therapist catches the patient's eye and looks curiously at Michaela ... the patient looks startled as if she has just remembered she is in the room]

Therapist: You seem startled.

Michaela: Sorry. I was miles away.

Therapist: I wonder where you were.

Michaela: Nowhere really, just in a white space. I don't have much space to myself. It was quite peaceful really.

Therapist: So, you feel I have interrupted that quiet space ...

Michaela: No. I don't mind at all that you did. I think it was more that you noticed me.
[Silence]
[The patient becomes a little tearful]

Michaela: I'm just thinking about how I got into it now, that space. It feels silly to say, but just before I disappeared I had a thought about your candle. But I then thought "What a stupid thought it is" ... So I shut it down. I'm not sure what went on.

Therapist: You had a thought about my candle ... that got shut down before it could be spoken ... I wonder if we listen to the thought together we might be able to think about why it might have had to be shut down.

Michaela: Well you know I said I bought the same candle as your normal candle in the break accidentally, and that since we came back you have had the other candle, but I noticed that you've got this usual one back, the one I said I liked. [She is tearful]

Therapist: Yes

Michaela: Well I had the thought that maybe you have got this candle again that I like … but then I thought that's a stupid thought because I'd be pointing out something you already know, and anyway it might have nothing to do with me, the reason that you bought it ... sorry I'm not making sense …

Therapist: I think you felt that I had bought that candle because I had heard you say that you liked it. I think you felt that I had thought about you outside the sessions when I was buying my shopping. That you exist outside this room in my mind. And that your voice has been heard here.
[The patient sobs and sobs]

Michaela: That would then mean that you had done it because I like it and maybe you prefer the other one. What if your other patients don't like it, and they have to suffer it because of me?

Therapist: You describe what feels like a guilt for existing at all, for having an impact on the world.

Michaela: Yes. I've just realised if I say what I want then I'm really worried about how it affects other people.
[The patient is quietly reflective]

Michaela: I've just been thinking how amazing it is to me, what comes up here. Now that I'm not having to deal with all the events happening outside and we have this space, it is shocking to think what is going on much of the time inside me, and it feels so real. I think that my critical-voice shut me down before I even had a chance to speak. And you help me to notice it here. But what if it's going on all the time outside and I'm not noticing it.
[Cries more]

Therapist: Just before you had the thought that you couldn't speak, we were discussing the next break. I think you were reminded of how you had used the candle in the last break. I wonder whether it was a concrete symbol of something you feel you have here with me that you feel the object cannot take from you – the space we have here to think about the object and try to understand its intentions and its constant criticism of you.

Michaela: Yes, the candle does symbolise something real. The object can't take that candle away and I can light it at home whenever I want and watch the flame and smell the fragrance that reminds me of here. It can try to take away my good feelings but it can't take away the candle.

Therapist: So, it is a concrete thing that you can hold on to in the break that enables you to know that this relationship is real. And, therefore, it has so much meaning for you. The object very nearly robbed you of telling me how important it is for you, by taking away the space to think about it with me in this session.

Michaela: I've just realised that the white space, that I called peaceful, was peaceful because the object leaves me alone in that space. It's more like being dead really, or not existing at all, but *knowing* you don't.

Therapist: I think it is a state the object likes to have you in. Keeping you away from communicating your likes and wishes, or being able to receive anything from anyone else.

Michaela: Yes. That's probably why I don't go out to see people. The critical-voice is there all the time judging everything I say. I never say what I want to do even if it's where to eat or which film to watch in case someone else wants to do something else.

Therapist: If you speak you feel such guilt for existing at all that you are often content to stay in that white space, because it is peaceful. All the feelings you have about imminent threat or break-ins are provoked as soon as you exist in a visible way. You risk attack from absolutely anywhere ...

Michaela: Yes, it's dreadful. It's better not to let anyone know you exist sometimes...

[Thoughtful silence]

Michaela: But here when I do feel real and that I can be myself it's amazing to know I exist. I think that's why I like the idea that you might write about me. It is as if I can have my voice heard as evidence that I exist. I feel validated somehow. That you think my voice is worth hearing ... I met with an old friend of my parents' last week who has also cut off contact with them. She was surprised by all the toys in my house. She said when she used to come to visit my parents when I was a child, there were no toys anywhere, and no evidence that children even existed in our house.

Therapist: You had no concrete evidence of your existence.

Michaela: I've just realised the importance of the candle. I think my own existence feels so precarious most of the time, and that the candle is concrete evidence of a relationship with you in which I exist.

[She cries a little and then smiles as the session comes to an end]

Analysis

The echoistic patient is subjected to the most dreadful guilt for existing at all. The session above makes the distinction between the guilt one feels for defying an object or an authority figure – in this case the patient's narcissistic internal object and mother – and the type of guilt that is allowed to emerge in a space in which one has, to some degree, become emancipated from the object's assertions. She is then exposed to life-anxiety without the strength normally established in those who have had a more supportive development. This leaves her open to feeling that existing is, itself, an audacious act, because the echoist's natural state is to exist for, or through, another rather than for herself.

The vignette allows a distinction to be made between the concrete and the abstract, and further demonstrates how the ontological reveals itself through the ontic. For Michaela, her existence is symbolised through a concrete object (the candle), which she associates with a relationship in which she exists and can take space, even when her therapist is away. She is able to use this object to authorise her to take space in the world, and while the vignette itself reveals great degrees of anxiety resulting from this action, it also demonstrates the slow process of growth and emancipation from enslavement to both her external and internal narcissistic objects.

Conclusion

We can see from the examples in the book, and the summaries above, how the echoist can be helped in therapy through the therapist holding back, working with openness, flexibility, and patience and of the requirement upon her to exercise reflexivity during and after sessions and particularly in relation to her own countertransference. This chapter argues for a shift from existing paradigms of narcissistic relating towards an acknowledgment of an echoistic-narcissistic complex. I have also made a very clear case for the requirement for echoism to be considered as a clinical presentation and a theoretical concept in its own right, with further clinical material required and an on-going dialogue concerning a developing approach to working with this group of patients.

Future directions for echoism

This final section is an invitation to fellow practitioners and theorists of other disciplines to consider ways in which the concept might be developed further. This includes consideration of echoism beyond the enclave of therapy and analysis and within wider social and cultural contexts.

Implications for specialist training on working with echoists are made evident when we consider the highly complex set of events at the end of Chapter Nine. In addition to learning about the echoist as a clinical entity the chapter asserts the need for in-depth understanding of echoism. It demonstrates the requirement for therapists to be aware of their own, often unconscious, echoistic traits, and to have worked on these in their own therapy, analysis, and/or supervision, so as not to further damage the echoist.

I have begun to observe links between echoism and masochism,[2] which I have not taken up in this book, but which require further investigation, and which Pederson (2015) has made a contribution. Sartre's theories in *Being and Nothingness*

---

2 In Chapter One I discuss how Echo's love in the myth grows stronger with the pain of rejection. The evidence of this in the echoist, her clinical counterpart, is undeniable, and further study of how masochism manifests in echoistic narcissistic dynamics is essential.

might have much to contribute to this area of study. I have also begun to observe some interesting patterns in terms of how the echoist operates as a sexual entity in relationships – another area that requires further investigation.

In a world where narcissism has become a dominant force that can be observed in the behaviour of political figures and world leaders, it is also important to study further the role of echoists in boardroom politics, governmental campaigns, ideological and theocratic dictatorships, and in regimes of terror. An awareness of the presentation of vulnerable echoistic individuals who can be acted-through, might be further developed as a way of countering and preventing some of the powerful and destructive acts that are carried out under the orders of powerful leaders and tyrannical individuals.

Finally, there are important cultural implications for the acknowledgement of echoism. Not least amongst these is the recognition of Echo as both a literal and metaphorical symbol for all the marginalised or silenced voices, and for those who are overlooked and missed in therapy, in literature, and in the world.

It is necessary here to mention the debt owed to critical and literary theories, a detailed study of which cannot be taken up in this book. Their interrogation of different literatures, and studies of marginalised voices, hegemonic processes, gender prejudice, and dominant ideological power structures, has provided an invaluable perspective in helping me to discover why this concept has been largely ignored and to consider some of the invisible processes for which cultural determinism must take some responsibility. Lacanians, feminists, cultural historians, and other theorists will, I am sure, have much specialist knowledge to bring to bear on this subject, and it is hoped that this book will act as a catalyst to further such studies and encourage others to take up the mantle from here.

The imbalance of the paradigm, in which the echoist was rendered and kept invisible through the dominant lens of narcissism, needs to be redressed. Beckett reminds us of the terrible state of absence and isolation experienced by the echoist, and the pain in not being able to have her own voice:

> That's how he speaks, this evening, how he has me speak, how he speaks to himself, how I speak, there is only me, this evening, here, on earth, and a voice that makes no sound because it goes towards none, and a head strewn with arms laid down and corpses fighting fresh, and a body, I nearly forgot.
>
> (Beckett, 1967)

It is my intention, therefore, that *Echoism: The Silenced Response to Narcissism*, is the first word on a comprehensive theory of echoism and an evolving approach to working with it clinically.

References

Anderson, R. (Ed.) (1992). *Clinical Lectures on Klein and Bion*. London: Routledge.

Beckett, S. (1967). *Stories and Texts for Nothing*. New York: Grove Press. (*Nouvelles et textes pour rien*. Paris: Les Editions de Minuit, 1958.)

Beckett, S. (2014). *Echo's Bones* (Ed. M. Nixon). London: Faber & Faber.

Bion, W. R. (1946). The leaderless group project. *The Bulletin of the Menninger Clinic, 10*: 77–81. In: C. Mawson (Ed.), *The Complete Works of W. R. Bion*, Volume IV, p. 31. London: Karnac, 2014.

Bion, W. R. (1957). Differentiation of the psychotic from the non-psychotic personalities. *International Journal of Psycho-Analysis, 38*: 266–275. In: *Second Thoughts*. London: Karnac, 1967. And in: C. Mawson (Ed.), *The Complete Works of W. R. Bion*, Volume VI. London: Karnac, 2014.

Bion, W. R. (1959). Attacks on linking. *International Journal of Psycho-Analysis, 40*: 308–315. In: *Second Thoughts*. London: Karnac, 1967. And in: C. Mawson (Ed.), *The Complete Works of W. R. Bion*, Volume VI. London: Karnac, 2014.

Bion, W. R. (1961). *Experiences in Groups and Other Papers*. London: Karnac.

Bion, W. R. (1962). *Learning from Experience*. London: Karnac.

Bion, W. R. (1963). *Elements of Psycho-Analysis*. London: Karnac.

Bion, W. R. (1965). *Transformations: Change from Learning to Growth*. London: Karnac.

Bion, W. R. (1965b). *Memory and Desire*. In: C. Mawson (Ed.), *The Complete Works of W. R. Bion*, Vol VI. London: Karnac, 2014.

Bion, W. R. (1967). *Second Thoughts: Selected Papers on Psycho-Analysis*. London: William Heinemann Medical Books. Reprinted London: Karnac, 1984. And in: C. Mawson (Ed.), *The Complete Works of W. R. Bion*, Volume VI. London: Karnac, 2014.

Bion, W. R. (1970). *Attention and Interpretation: A Scientific Approach to Insight in Psychoanalysis and Groups*. London: Karnac.

Bion, W. R. (1992). *Cogitations* (Ed. F. Bion). London: Karnac.

Bion Talamo, P. (1981). Ps⇌D. *Rivista di Psicoanalisi, 27*: 626–628.

Brecht, B. (1954) *Essays on the Art of Theater*. In: J. Willett (Ed. and Trans.), *Brecht on Theatre*. New York: Hill & Wang, 1964.

Britton, R. (1986). The effects of serious parental psychological disturbance as seen in analysis. Unpublished paper read to the British Psychoanalytical Society.

Britton, R. (1989). *The Missing Link: Parental Sexuality in the Oedipus Complex*. In: R. Britton, M. Feldman & E. O'Shaughnessy (Eds.), *The Oedipus Complex Today: Clinical Implications* (pp. 83–101). London: Karnac.

Britton, R. (1998). *Belief and Imagination*. London: Routledge.

Britton, R. (2003). *Sex, Death, and the Superego: Experiences in Psychoanalysis*. London: Karnac.

Britton, R. (2004). Narcissistic disorders in clinical practice. *Journal of Analytical Psychology, 49*: 477–490.

Britton, R. (2015). *Between Mind and Brain: Models of the Mind and Models in the Mind*. London: Karnac.

Britton, R., & Steiner, J. (1994). Interpretation: Selected fact or overvalued idea? *International Journal of Psycho-Analysis, 75*: 1069–1078.

Byron, G. G. (Lord) (1816). *Prometheus*. In: J. Mc Gann (Ed). *Lord Byron - The Major Works* (p. 264). Oxford: OUP.

Davis, D. (2005). Echo in the darkness. *Psychoanalytic Review, 92*: 137–151.

Danto, A. C. (1975). *John Paul Sartre*. New York: Viking.

Deutsch, H. (1942). *Some forms of emotional disturbance and their relationship to schizophrenia. Psychoanalytic Quarterly, 11*: 301–321.

Deurzen, E. van (2010). *Everyday Mysteries: A Handbook of Existential Psychotherapy*. Hove: Routledge.

Eliot, T. S. (1959). *Four Quartets*. London: Faber & Faber.

Emslie, B. (2012). *Narrative and Truth: An Ethical and Dynamic Paradigm for the Humanities*. New York: Palgrave Macmillan.

Esslin, M. (1991). *The Theatre of the Absurd*. London: Penguin

Feldman, M. (2003). *Doubt, Conviction and the Analytic Process: Selected Papers of Michael Feldman* (Ed. B. Joseph). London: Routledge.

Ferry, L. (2014). *The Wisdom of the Myths*. New York: Harper Collins. 2014

Freud, A. (1949). Report on the Sixteenth International Psycho-Analytical Congress. *Bulletin of the International Psycho-Analytical Association, 30*: 178–208.

Freud, S. (with Breuer, J.) (1893d). *Studies on Hysteria. S. E., 2*. London: Hogarth.

Freud, S. (1905d). *Three Essays on the Theory of Sexuality* (1905). *S. E., 7*. London: Hogarth.

Freud, S. (1910c). *Leonardo Da Vinci and a Memory of his Childhood. S. E., 11*: 57–138. London: Hogarth.

Freud, S. (1912e). Recommendations to physicians practising psycho-analysis. *S. E., 12*: 109–120. London: Hogarth.

Freud, S. (1915c). Instincts and their vicissitudes. *S. E., 14*: 109–140. London: Hogarth.

Freud, S. (1919h). The uncanny. *S. E., 17*: 217–256. London: Hogarth.

Freud, S. (1920g). *Beyond the Pleasure Principle. S. E., 18*: 1–64. London: Hogarth.

Freud, S. (1950a). *Project for a Scientific Psychology. S. E., 1*: 281–391. London: Hogarth.

Gadamer, H.-G. (1960). *Truth and Method*. New York: Sheed & Ward.

Hegel, G. W. F. (1970). *Philosphische Propädeutik*. Werke, Vol. 4. Nürnberger und Heidelberger Schriften 1808–17. Frankfurt am Main: Suhrkamp.

Heidegger, M. (1962). *Being and Time* (Trans. J. Macquarrie & E. Robinson). Oxford: Blackwell Publishing. (Orig. 1927 (Ger.).)

Heimann, P. (1950). On counter-transference. *International Journal of Psycho-Analysis, 31*: 81–84.

Holzhey-Kunz, A. (2014). *Daseinsanalysis* (Trans. S. Leighton). London: Free Association.

Holzhey-Kunz, A. (2016). Why the distinction between ontic and ontological trauma matters for existential therapists. *Journal of Existential Analysis, 27*. (Presented at World Congress for Existential Therapy. London, 14–17 May, 2015.)

Holzhey-Kunz, A. (2017). Personal communication.

Ionesco, E. (1958). A reply to Kenneth Tynan: The playwright's role. *The Observer*, 29 June.

Joseph, B. (1982). Addiction to near-death. *International Journal of Psychoanalysis, 63*: 449–456.

Joseph, B. (1989). *Psychic Equilibrium and Psychic Change: Selected Papers of Betty Joseph* (Ed. M. Feldman & E. Bott Spillius). London: Routledge.

Kierkegaard, S. (as Johannes de Silentio) (1843). *Fear and Trembling* (Trans. W. Lowrie Ed. Dragan Nikolic. USA: Dragan Nikolic, 2012.

Klein, M. (1932). *The Psycho-Analysis of Children*. London: Hogarth.

Klein, M. (1946). Notes on some schizoid mechanisms. *International Journal of Psycho-Analysis, 27*: 99–110.

Klein, M. (1952). The origins of transference. *International Journal of Psycho-Analysis, 33*: 433–438.

Klein, M. (1955). On identification. In: *Envy and Gratitude and Other Works* (pp. 141–175). London: Hogarth, 1975.

Klein, M. (1957). Envy and gratitude. In: *Envy and Gratitude and Other Works* (pp. 176–235). The International Psycho-Analytical Library, 104:1–346. London: Hogarth and the Institute of Psycho-Analysis, 1975.

Klein, M. (1958). On the development of mental functioning. In: *Envy and Gratitude and Other Works*. The International Psycho-Analytical Library, 104:1–346. London: Hogarth Press and the Institute of Psycho-Analysis, 1975.

Levy, K. N., Ellison, W. D., & Reynoso, J. S. (2011). A historical review of narcissism and narcissistic personality. In: W. K. Campbell & J. D. (Eds.), *The Handbook of Narcissism and Narcissistic Personality Disorder* (Ch. 1). Hoboken, NJ: John Wiley.

Malkin, C. (2015). *Rethinking Narcissism: The Bad – and Surprising Good – About Feeling Special*. New York: Harper Collins.

Mauriac, C. (1958). *La Littérature Contemporaine*. Paris: Albin Michel.

Mawson, C. (2004). Pseudo-free association: The sophisticated analytic patient and 'as-if' relating. *British Journal of Psychotherapy, 18*: 509–522.

Nietzsche, F. (1997): *Daybreak: Thoughts on the Prejudices of Morality* (Ed. M. Clarke & B. Leiter, Trans. R. J. Hollingdale). Cambridge: CUP.

Orwell, G. (1949). *1984*. London: Penguin, 2004.

Ovid (2004). *Metamorphoses: A New Verse Translation* (Trans. D. Raeburn). London: Penguin.

Pederson, T. C. (2015). *The Economics of Libido: Psychic Bisexuality, The Superego, and the Centrality of the Oedipus Complex*. London: Karnac.

Pirandello, L. (1968), *Six Characters in Search of an Author* (Trans. F. May). London: Heinemann.

Rodman, F. R. (Ed.) (1987). *The Spontaneous Gesture: Selected Letters of D. W. Winnicott*. Cambridge, MA: Harvard University Press.

Rosenfeld, H. (1952). Notes on the psycho-analysis of the super-ego conflict of an acute schizophrenic patient. *International Journal of Psycho-Analysis, 33*: 111–131.

Rosenfeld, H. R. (1964). On the Psychopathology of Narcissism. In: *Psychotic States: A Psycho-Analytical Approach* (pp. 169–179). New York: International Universities Press, 1965.

Rosenfeld, H. R. (1970). On projective identification. Paper presented to the British Psychoanalytical Society. *Bulletin of the British Psychoanalytical Society.* And: International Colloquium on Psychosis, Montreal, November 1969, as: Contribution to the psychopathology of psychotic states: the importance of projective identification in the ego structure and the object relations of the psychotic patient.

Rosenfeld, H. R. (1971). A clinical approach to the psychoanalytic theory of the life and death instincts: an investigation into the aggressive aspects of narcissism. *International Journal of Psycho-Analysis, 52*: 169–178. Reproduced in J. Steiner (Ed.), *Rosenfeld in Retrospect: Essays on His Clinical Influence.* Routledge, 2008.

Rosenfeld, H. R. (1987). *Impasse and Interpretation*. London: Routledge.

Sabbadini, A. (2014). *Boundaries and Bridges: Perspectives on Time and Space in Psychoanalysis*. London: Karnac.

Sartre, J. P. (1943). *Being and Nothingness* (Trans. H. E. Barnes). London: Routledge, 2013.

Sartre, J. P. (1944). *Huis Clos* (Ed. K. Gore). London: Taylor & Francis, 2016.

Sartre, J. P. (1965). *Nausea.* London: Penguin. (*La nausée* (1938). Paris: Gallimard.)

Savery D. C. (2013). *The Challenges of Meaninglessness and Absurdity Addressed through Myth and Role Play*. Chapter 7 In: Van Deurzen, E. & Iacovou, S. et al, *Existential Perspectives in Relationship Therapy.* Palgrave Macmillan.

Segal, H. (1957). *Notes on Symbol Formation. International Journal of Psycho-Analysis, 38*: 391–397

Segal, H. (1977). Counter-transference. *International Journal of Psychoanalytic Psychotherapy, 6*: 31–37. Reprinted in: *The Work of Hanna Segal*, (pp. 81–87). New York: Jason Aronson, 1981.

Segal, H. (1997). *Psychoanalysis, Literature and War: Papers 1972–1995* (Ed. J. Steiner). London: Routledge.

Segal, H., & Bell, D. (2012). The Theory of Narcissism in the Work of Freud and Klein. In: P. Fonagy, E. S. Person & J. Sandler (Eds.), *Freud's "On Narcissism: An Introduction"* (pp. 150–175). London: Karnac.

Shakespeare, W. (1609). Sonnet 62. In: R. G. White (Ed.), *The Complete Works of William Shakespeare.* New York: Sully & Kleinteich.

Spillius, E. (1992). Clinical Experiences of projective identification. In: R. Anderson (Ed.), *Clinical Lectures on Klein and Bion* (pp. 59–73). London: New Library of Psychoanalysis Series. Routledge Press. Published in Association with the Institute of Psychoanalysis, London, 1991.

Spinelli, E. (2007). *Practising Existential Psychotherapy.* London: Sage.

Steiner, J. (1993). *Psychic Retreats*. London: New Library of Psychoanalysis Series. Routledge Press. Published in Association with the Institute of Psychoanalysis, London.

Steiner, J. (Ed.) (2008). *Rosenfeld in Retrospect: Essays on His Clinical Influence.* London: Routledge.

Stewart, J., & Nun, K. (Eds.) (2010). *Kierkegaard and the Greek World: Volume 2, Tome II – Aristotle and Other Greek Authors.* Farnham: Ashgate.

Strachey, J. (1934). The nature of the therapeutic action of psycho-analysis. *International Journal of Psycho-Analysis, 15*: 127–159. (Based on a paper read at a meeting of the British Psycho-Analytical Society on June 13, 1933.)

Wälder, R. (1925). The psychoses: Their mechanisms and accessibility to influence. *International Journal of Psycho-Analysis, 6*: 259–281.

Williams, M. H. (2007). *Your Teenager: Thinking About Your Child During the Secondary School Years.* London: Karnac.

Woolf, V. (1931). *The Waves*. London: Hogarth.

Index

Abraham, biblical story of 8, 34, 110, 112, 115, 117, 119
absence of being, state of 68, 154
Aegisthus 114
Agamemnon, myth of 8, 111–115
alien object(s) 37–40; concept of, definition 37
alpha-elements 11, 19, 20, 33, 103, 156
alpha-function 11, 20, 33
Anderson, R. 35
angst 53, 63, 82, 106, 143; ontological 45, 66; *see also* anxiety(ies)
annihilation anxiety 82, 107
anxiety(ies): annihilation 82, 107; defensive echoist's, defences against 72–74; life 76, 156, 162, 166; myth, as container for 19; ontological, see ontological anxiety(ies); and silence, connection between 137; social 116
Aristotle 3, 21, 114
Artaud, A. 3
Artemis 112, 113
art therapy(ies) 135, 160
as-if patient 68; Vignette 4: Dr L 69–70
as-if personality(ies) 61, 62, 67–71, 103, 145; as narcissistic disorder 68
autistic spectrum 5

bad-faith (*mauvaise-foi*) 42–46, 49, 63, 128; replacing responsibility 56
Barnes, H. 44
basic assumption(s) 125; dependency 129; fight-flight 129; pairing 129–130
Beckett, S. 3, 75, 143, 152, 153, 161, 168
Being: concept of 44; and echoism 52; existential phenomenological approach to 41–57; existential sense of 7; modes of 7, 29, 52, 63; and narcissism, Vignette 2: Mrs J 50; ontological

categories of 43; responsibility for 57; Sartre's modes of 7; theory of, Sartre's 44
being-for-itself (*être-pour-soi*) 45–47, 49, 56
being-for-oneself, defences against 49
being-for-others (*être-pour-autrui*) 46, 51, 52, 54, 56, 61, 63–67, 87; ontological state of 41
being-in-itself (*être-en-soi*) 45, 46, 48, 51
being-in-the-world 7; concept of 42, 47, 49, 52, 63, 65, 66, 73
being-through-others 41, 52, 56–57, 75, 87–90, 127; psychic defence of echoist 87
being-with vs knowing 22
Bell, D. 36
Bentham, J. 47n2
beta-elements 11, 19, 21, 33, 156
Bion, W. R. 7, 72, 79, 120, 128, 163; alpha-elements 19; alpha-function 11, 20, 33, 103, 156; basic assumptions 125, 129; beta-elements 11, 19, 21, 33, 156; container-contained 11, 19, 27, 32–35, 40, 102, 103, 125, 130; countertransference, experience of 37; ego-destructive superego 27, 38, 119; free association to myth 84; ideal-ego 33; K, domain of 106; leaderless group 137; nameless dread 19, 38, 83, 156; negative capability 29, 55, 83, 93; questioning use of myth of Narcissus 153–154; selected fact 28; withholding memory and desire 55, 95, 121
Bion Talamo, P. 28n4
borderline patients 30, 62, 68, 103, 104, 145
Brecht, B. 3, 161–163
Brentano, F. 44